D1459545

Stewart Lee

Content Provider

Selected Short Prose Pieces

2011–2016

WITHDRAWN FROM STOCK

ff

FABER & FABER

First published in 2016
by Faber & Faber Limited
Bloomsbury House
74–77 Great Russell Street
London WC1B 3DA

Typeset by Ian Bahrami
Printed and bound in the UK by CPI Group (UK) Ltd, Croydon, CR0 4YY

All rights reserved
© Stewart Lee, 2016

The right of Stewart Lee to be identified as author of this work
has been asserted in accordance with Section 77 of the Copyright,
Designs and Patents Act 1988

Those pieces first published in the *Guardian* and *Observer* reproduced
with kind permission

A CIP record for this book
is available from the British Library

ISBN 978-0-571-32902-1

10 9 8 7 6 5 4 3 2

To Barry Hogan and Deborah Kee-Higgins of All Tomorrow's Parties, who gave me the weekend of my life, in Prestatyn, North Wales, in April 2016.

Introduction

I started doing stand-up in the late '80s and got my first paid gig in September 1989, at the Bedford Pub in Balham, south London. Do look for it. It is still there. But everyone that drank in Balham back then – Goblin Dave, Welsh Pete, the one they called "Maestro", and the piano-playing woman with the plastic head – has been priced out. Only Arthur Smith, the Redondan king of SW12, remains, hiding out across the road in an art deco block of flats the local legends say Hitler personally spared from blitzkrieg.

I was twenty-one and a half years old when I became a semi-professional stand-up. The first time I got asked to write funny columns was, undeservedly, for a short-lived comedy magazine, *Deadpan*, in 1994, off the back of being a radio comedian.

I dug out my juvenile efforts recently. They were adequate. Gratifyingly, the me in the stories wasn't really me. He was a character, a kind of would-be bohemian columnist version of me, eager to impress, pleased with his own cleverness, fabricating meetings with Kurt Cobain and imagining shared-stage-fright ferry flights across the English Channel with Stephen Fry.

At least, I assume it was a character of sorts, one that I consciously created to provoke myself into the generation of copy, but I can't be sure. Who was I then? What was I thinking? I may be reverse-engineering a truth I wish existed. Sadly, looking at the magazine pages, I appear to have allowed myself to be photographed for my byline picture in a south London greasy spoon, young and gaunt and smoking a cigarette, which suggests a blurring of the boundaries. Maybe I was in deep cover. Maybe I still am. I don't know. Whatever, I wish I was still 12 stone and sickly and could smoke a pack of cigarettes before breakfast without throwing up.

Deadpan folded after a year and I don't remember any of the funny columns I got asked to write by any other outlet being much good at all for the next decade or so. That doesn't necessarily mean they weren't. I can't remember much about the decade of the '90s. I was drunk for a lot of it, and then depressed towards the end, I think, in retrospect. It's all a haze of London comedy-club cellars viewed from the stage through a jazz photograph pre-smoking-ban fug; motorway service stations in Doppler effect from the transit van windows on loss-making tours with the Lee & Herring double act, where big theatre gigs with our big promoter made me less than my usual solo slots on pub-cellar mixed bills paid me alone; and people arguing in hotel bars and Little Chefs; and intrigue in the toilets at the Comedy Café in pre-hipster Old Street, its upstairs room the London circuit's unofficial social club in those fondly remembered long, late Saturday nights of the early '90s, Roger Mann on his hands and knees, pulling faces from behind a sofa; and all of us getting drunk in Indian restaurants in tiny towns recently fucked by Thatcher; and me going deaf at rock and roll gigs in Camden and Harlesden and Islington and Manette Street and Charing Cross Road. Polvo! Yo La Tengo!! The Fall!!!

What a decade it was. I went to Canada and Australia. There was unconsummated American network interest in my stand-up act and sit-com and movie scripts. My weight went up and down, and so did my bloodstained pants, from toilet seat to toilet seat, all across the world. I made money on TV and doing my stand-up on the club circuit, and lost it all on Edinburgh fringe solo shows and our double-act tour debts. I grew up into grunge, and for a brief time my natural dress sense overlapped with fashion, and popular music sounded like what I had once imagined it might do, if all the things I already knew about and loved cross-fertilised and bred.

I was engaged to a Britpop tastemaker, and then disengaged. I ruined a few lives, I expect. I wasted other people's time, and my own. I performed much of the work I was offered with a sense of dazed detachment, as if I was better than it, yet I seemed unable to commit to any coherent alternative. I ate curries and toasted cheese and tuna sandwiches and little else, and it is no surprise I was unwell. I owned, and wore, leather trousers, with a sense of entitlement. I failed to grasp a succession of nettles, and nailed nothing to any sticking plates worth speaking of.

I was busy all the time, night after night, yet I emerged blinking into the new century with little to show for all those hours on stage, except a small flat, over a shop in a then liminal north-east London borough that was subsequently deemed upmarket, the sale of which made me more money than any job I have ever done, buying me, and others of my generation in similar situations, an unearned second chance, even as the door of opportunity slammed permanently shut in the face of those of similar social backgrounds unfortunate enough to have been born a decade later.

I can't find any of the occasional filler columns I wrote for the *Guardian Guide* in those years. I am glad. I was a prick for most of the '90s, and I think my supposedly funny writings of the period probably went the same wandering way as my stand-up. I had lost track of whatever was essentially me, caught up in zeitgeisty '90s cynicism; enacting misguided projectile vomiting at soon to be discarded, and now nostalgically remembered, liberal orthodoxies; trying to write and perform what I imagined was expected of the young educated men of the period.

Sometime around the end of the decade I lost the ability, financially and creatively, to perform live (as detailed in my first book, *How I Escaped My Certain Fate*), and anything I wrote for newspapers over the next few years was either serious music criticism, which kept the wolf-man from the door and got me free CDs during an extremely lean half-decade, or whiny think-pieces about the injustices of showbiz – "failure justified", as the comedian Simon Munnery witheringly dismisses all autobiographical writing.

When I returned to stand-up in the mid-noughties, it was as someone with nothing to lose, broke, disillusioned and defeated by legal wrangles around a supposed theatrical smash hit I had worked on. I might as well do what I wanted as a stand-up comedian, as nothing else had worked out anyway, and I had no dependants and no real needs. But, like Morgan Freeman's jaded jailbird in *The Shawshank Redemption*, the capricious parole board of Fate decided to free me at exactly the point where I had no options left, and my 2004 live stand-up "comeback" show was a critical hit.

When newspapers, excited by the possibility of the passing web traffic my new-found acclaim might generate, started asking me for funny columns again, I found myself writing in the same devil-may-care spirit. This new approach began when the *Guardian* requested a piece on the 2011 royal wedding.

The clown theorist Gaulier had once told my friend, the theatre-maker Rob Thirtle, that one should perform comedy as if the next action would result in your death. I decided to write like I was trying to get myself sacked. (I have tried to perform my TV stand-up shows in this vein too, and reaction to the recently broadcast fourth series suggests I may at last have succeeded.) I gave the *Guardian* a stream-of-consciousness screed, scrawled out as if by a man trying to score points, name-dropping obscure occult practitioners and half-remembered historical facts, grasping towards some unified theory of meaning known only to the addled and insecure author.

I wasn't trying to write only as someone trying to be funny, but also as if I were someone desperate to impress. Clearly it worked. *"I've got an English Degree and I'm gonna use it – reminds me of a passage in Frank Skinner's book, when, after he graduated, he became impossibly pretentious pseud, until someone knocked the shit out of him in a pub (sadly this has never happened to Lee),"* wrote a reader called Whiteyed, of my royal wedding column.

I found it helpful to write partly as the sort of person the hate-filled teenage me imagined would be asked to write for a stuck-up broadsheet newspaper like my left-wing, middle-class girlfriends' mothers read in the '80s. A pompous twat, no less. And then the *Observer* asked me to do it again, every time that David Mitchell was away, which, luckily for me, was often, as he now had new and time-consuming husbandly duties to tear him away from the gadfly whirlwind of London high society he had previously been enslaved by, his byline picture a Dorian Gray-style portrait masking his true decline. Victoria Coren's gain was my gain also.

I knew my way around stand-up. I knew that if I chose to reject certain supposed genre rules, I was doing so from a position of knowledge. But I didn't know about being a columnist. I loved Mark Steel's columns in the now tragically defunct *Independent* newspaper, where the burning passion and cold logic of his beliefs dovetail beautifully into perfectly constructed jokes; I loved Suzanne Moore, who wears her heart on her sleeve and makes little personal stories have massive political resonance; and Richard Herring, with whom I had written and performed a double act, mainly in the mid-'90s, had done daily blogs for the best part of a decade that laid his life embarrassingly and amusingly bare.

But none of these were how I wanted to write, and I find the modern mania for total, moment-by-moment honesty in a columnist's work personally problematic. My mere presence at a social or cultural event does not mean I have consented to become a character in the ongoing online or print media part-work of someone else's autobiography. Something I said to you in a queue for a show in Edinburgh was conversation, Andrew, and not a press statement for Internet publication.

We now live in an age of full disclosure, via blogs and memoirs and chat-show appearances. I realised I wanted to walk away from the expectation that the columnist should write a kind of continuing soap opera of their own life. Though rooted in fact, I changed most of the personal details in the supposedly true stories herein, fabricated others entirely and randomly altered, for example, the location of my home and the age, number and gender of my children from week to week. I was not interested in being a "personality", and yet had accepted a writing job that normally requires the author to be one. And I attempted to defeat this expectation with lies.

One thing that has changed since I first wrote supposedly funny columns for newspapers is the proliferation of Internet access, meaning one can now look online and see what the public think of your work. Reading comments below YouTube clips of my stand-up in the late noughties encouraged me to make the act even more like the sort of act the people who hated it would hate; and likewise, reading the *Guardian*'s "Comment Is Free" contributors' opinions and verdicts helped create my columnist "character" in opposition, like a slow-motion, week-by-week interaction with a real audience, similar to a stand-up's live experience, but at four frames per minute.

It requires a strong will for writers to process all the online hatred directed at them, especially when the worst of it is systematically generated by someone you know, operating under a multitude of translucent pseudonyms, often referencing each other's comments as if they were real. But I started to feel, as the months passed, that I was engaged in a weirdly symbiotic relationship with people who despised me, trying to confirm their prejudices and inspire in them ever more creative splurges of contempt.

One might argue then, to be generous, that the columns are the work of many hands, that the voice they came to be written in was itself shaped by the hostility directed towards it, becoming more obtuse, self-satisfied and pretentious as a direct response to the extent to which those very qualities annoyed its detractors. One might argue that. But if this book covers its cost, I will nevertheless be keeping all the money, and the people whose comments have been included can go fuck themselves in the ass.

This isn't a complete collection of all my published writing since my mini-epiphany, when I covered that 2011 royal wedding. Indeed, in compiling this selection of exactly five years' worth of columns, the editor Andy Miller and I have left out some pieces on the grounds that they were too serious to be included here and were not intended as principally funny exercises, therefore breaking the tone of the book as a whole. And we have also declined to include pieces that one or both of us thought were shit, of which there were too many to mention individually.

The writing included here may be bad, as many critics of it have said, but it is the writing that this character would have produced at this time, of that there can be no doubt. And I know this, because I am this implausible columnist-comedian character, to an extent, and I have decided that these are the things, good or bad, that he would have written at that point in time, had he been real, which he sort of is.

So, what you have in your hand is a magic-carpet ride through five years of topical and ephemeral broadsheet liberal-newspaper comedy-opinion journalism, which was meant merely to be smiled at and then used to line a cat's litter tray, and never to be collected in such a prestigious form by the renowned distributors of quality literature, Faber and fucking Faber. Hang on to your hats and look out for that first step. It's a doozy!

Content Provider

Stewart Lee's insider's take on William and Kate

Guardian, 27 April 2011

The selection of Kate Middleton, a lowly commoner drawn from the very dregs of society, as Prince William's bride has been the subject of great speculation, much of it thinly veiled snobbery. But Britain is broken. Social mobility is at a historic low, state education and public healthcare are in crisis, and our own prime minister has blamed the truculent immigrant and his concealed wife for our lack of national cohesion.

Once upon a time, royal marriages were political acts that forged links between different nations. Instead, William and Kate's wedding will bind this nation to itself, and in marrying so very far beneath himself, I believe the young prince has made a heroic and deliberate sacrifice to achieve this end.

Pause for a moment. Imagine being Prince William. Imagine knowing that the best justification most rational people could come up with for your heavily subsidised existence was that you were a symbolic figure. And symbolic of what, the boy must wonder. History? The land? The nation itself? A notion of refined nobility? Grace under pressure? Or perhaps some abstract idea of temporal continuity? Unable to escape being a symbolic figure, the prince's recent activities suggest he has chosen instead to embrace the role in the most profound way imaginable. And, I believe, this is why the wedding of Prince William and Kate Middleton itself seems symbolic on an admirable and unprecedented level.

Jessie L. Weston's 1920 study of Holy Grail mythology, *From Ritual to Romance*, pictures Britain as a wasteland, an image appropriated by T. S. Eliot to describe the aftermath of the First World

War. The Fisher King must search the devastated terrain for the Holy Grail, and drink from it to heal the land. Broken Britain is that wasted land. William is that Fisher King. Kate Middleton is that lovely grail, full not of the blood of the crucified Christ, but of the blood of the Middletons, who run a children's partyware business in Berkshire. And Kate's wedding to wise William is a ritual that may help to fix what David Cameron's vision of the Big Society so far has not. For in choosing Kate, a simple girl from a school near Swindon, as his bride, William is in fact taking each and every British subject – man, woman, old, young, black, white, Christian and Muslim – into his royal bed, and binding us all to each other in the white heat of his princely passion.

Kate was educated at Marlborough College in Wiltshire. It is a private school, yes, but it is no Eton, and its most famous alumni are little more than flannelled fools: the comedian Jack Whitehall, the children's author Lauren Child, and the pop musician Chris de Burgh, whose 1976 Christmas hit "A Spaceman Came Travelling" describes an alien being's disappointment in the shortcomings of human society – disappointments it appears William shares, and is trying to address in his own esoteric way. But his motives for plucking a bride from such an inauspicious establishment are, I believe, twofold, and we must admire and accept the occult reasoning behind his selfless choice.

First of all, Marlborough College, where Kate Middleton flushed into womanhood, is set in a magical landscape that has been declared a world heritage site, being only five miles from the exact centre of the Avebury stone circle. Perhaps Kate's growing body absorbed the magical energies of the region. Perhaps it did not. It does not matter. She is from, and she is of, the ancient wetland. The arrangement of the 6,000-year-old circle, and the stone rows, burial chambers and mounds that surround it, is explicitly symbolic, explicitly sexual and explicitly ritualistic, and as such it shares the same transformative agenda as Friday's royal wedding.

In Avebury, the West Kennet Avenue, a long row of erotically paired stones, uncoils snake-like from the circle, as if to penetrate nearby Silbury Hill, a fecund thirty-seven-metre-high female belly, which rises from the marsh to meet it. The prince has taken his lowly bride from within this charged landscape, where our ancestors celebrated the union of man and woman in stone and earth, and began the communal processes that forged a nation from their descendants, the broken nation that William the Fisher King must now heal. Our shaman prince could not have chosen a better receptacle for his magical purposes than Kate Middleton, a peasant-spawned serf-girl, sodden with the primordial mire of the Swindon-shadowed swamplands.

Secondly, in choosing a commoner for his bride, William gives hope to millions of socially disenfranchised Britons. Only two Tory generations ago, the prime minister Margaret Thatcher was proud to proclaim herself "a grocer's daughter". A mere twenty years since she passed power on to John Major, a garden-gnome salesman with six O-levels, it is impossible to imagine either in government today, composed, as it is, principally of former members of the elite Oxford vomiting society the Bullingdon Club. The state-schools system is stretched to the limit; the withdrawal of further education grants deters poorer students; and government contributions to the Bookstart scheme, which gives books to children who might otherwise have none, have been halved. It is not possible to imagine a Thatcher ever getting out of Lincolnshire today, let alone becoming prime minister.

But in snatching Kate from the gutter, William stooped even lower than he would have done had he chosen Margaret Thatcher for his bride. Kate's parents aren't even grocers. They sell novelty hats and paper plates. It's no coincidence that as genuine social mobility in broken Britain is eroded, so commoners turn to the National Lottery, *The X Factor* and *Britain's Got Talent*. Winning them represents the only chance real people have to change their circumstances significantly. It could be you. And, like some giant illuminated penis flying over the rooftops of suburban homes and frothing at random passing women, William has pointed himself at Kate Middleton, the Susan Boyle of social mobility. In declaring her his princess, he brings hope of real change to millions of people denied a decent education and the means to better themselves, to millions of tiny babies denied even books, that one day they too could be randomly rewarded with untold wealth and privilege.

The wedding of my wife and I was a small affair, with forty or so guests. We were not required to arrange our day along magical or symbolic lines, though admittedly some aspects of the Catholic wedding ceremony confused me, and my wife is yet to explain the tradition whereby I have been obliged ever since to sleep alone each night on the toilet. But as a symbolic figure, poor Prince William's wedding is hostage to political expediency. Consider the faces he will see as he and Kate make their solemn vows.

From the world of government, the prime minister and Mrs David Cameron, and the deputy prime minister and Ms Miriam González Durántez, holding whichever suit the prime minister has chosen not to wear; from the faith communities, the Reverend Gregorius, Anil Bhanot, Malcolm Deeboo of the Zoroastrians, the Venerable Bogoda Seelawimala Nayaka Thera, Obi-Wan Kenobi, Optimus Prime, Yog-Sothoth, Captain Marvel and Cardinal Cormac Murphy-O'Connor; and from the twin spheres of entertainment and sport, Mr Ben Fogle, Mr David Beckham and Mrs David Beckham, Mr Madonna Louise Ciccone, and Sir Elton Hercules John and Mr Sir Elton Hercules John. Candles in the wind all.

But as he gazes at this golden shower of dignitaries, it is William who will have the last guffaw. He knows that this was not so much a wedding as a psychic rescue operation, a healing ritual for broken Britain, a pantomime of hope for the terminally hopeless. In taking Kate Middleton as his bride, Prince William, more than anyone in any position of power in Britain today, has tried at least to do something to help. I hope sincerely that both of them are very happy.

My perfect pub

ShortList, 12 May 2011

ShortList is a beard-trimming-device review magazine, given away free to stupid wealthy young men on the London Underground. Asked to write one of their weekly "My Perfect Pub" columns, and emboldened by my Guardian *experience of the previous month, I decided to write the piece not as me, but as a delusional alcoholic who lives on bar snacks and washes in pub toilets, and who was using the column as a cry for help, accidentally revealing the miserably small compass of his experience, ending the piece on a deliberately inconclusive hanging cadence. I expected* ShortList *to reject it, but they ran it as written. I wondered what, if anything, the Patrick Bateman-esque young City professionals, glimpsing at it on their morning commutes, must have made of it.*

Once, on a country walk with my father's sister's family, I rudely called my uncle an idiot for letting his unpredictable Alsatian off the lead in a sheep field near Watersmeet, North Devon. Our lunch destination was The Ship Inn, Porlock Weir, where, as a punishment, I was made to sit outside in the rain under a corrugated iron sheet eating steak-and-kidney pie while everyone else went inside. I was twenty-eight years old.

My ideal pub would have no music, no TVs and no sport. No one would talk to me. There would be draft bitters from small brewers and pork scratchings in see-through plastic bags on which there's no manufacturer information.

You have to go to quiet places where the old guys drink. The Waverley in Edinburgh, for example, which opens and closes on the owner's whim. The Defoe on Stoke Newington Church Street, London, is good too. Nobody bothers you. There is always good bitter there, such as Tribute from Cornwall.

There are some great bars in Scotland and the islands that are quiet and unspoiled. Long, thin slits of places. But on Lewis they don't even have women's toilets in the bars, which is a bit much.

The Ship Inn in Porlock Weir, Somerset, does nice steak-and-kidney pies, and there is a corrugated-iron thing you can sit under outside if it's raining. There are bowls of water for dogs too.

One of the few nice things about touring is trying to get in a nice pub somewhere before last orders, especially in the more rural places, and drink some bitter you've never heard of. I wish someone would name a bitter after me.

I love pubs. If I didn't have kids or a job or a wife, I would just sit in nice pubs all day, reading and drinking. You could eat scratchings and crisps so you wouldn't have to cook when you got home. And there are usually toilets where you can wash yourself.

The National Trust doesn't even trust us to have our own thoughts

Observer, 5 June 2011

The National Trust has concealed recordings of eight celebrities inside benches. Undoubtedly, listening to Claudia Winkleman while contemplating Quarry Bank Mill might help to sensualise the horrors of Industrial Revolution working conditions. And we will one day wonder how we managed to enjoy the 520 acres of Felbrigg Hall without a bench upon which visitors have been invited to "rest their weary bottoms" by Stephen Fry.

To be fair, Winkleman and Fry are among the best television personalities available, turnips in a sea of turds. But, as a National Trust member, the speaking-celebrity-bench scheme causes me to contemplate the cliché of dumbing down. (As does the Trust's website for Felbrigg Hall, inviting visitors to "look in the library, the 'internet' of the 18th century". Were books only unevolved websites? Why is "internet" in inverted commas? And unless Felbrigg Hall library is full of pornography, hundreds of unattributed Tim Vine one-liners, and thousands of anonymous comedy-forum posters saying that I am a "smug ****ing ****", it is not at all like the "internet".)

I joined the National Trust in a spirit of class hatred, and keep my membership card on a shelf next to my CD reissues of the first four Crass albums. I used to be breathless with pleasure at the thought that these massive country piles no longer belonged fully to the bucktoothed scum who inherited them, living in poverty in one wing while *Daily Mail* readers stamped dog muck and Shippam's paste into their carpets. The professional posh man Julian Fellowes last week identified such prejudice as the last acceptable hatred. The hostility he and his oyster-guzzling friends experience would be unacceptable if directed towards the poor. But making jokes at Fellowes's expense is quite different to mocking the disenfranchised.

Fellowes is privileged and well connected. Apparently, he has the ear of the Queen, the hand of Princess Michael's lady-in-waiting, and something unsavoury that once belonged to the Duke of Edinburgh in a pooper-scooper in the glove compartment of his Nissan. Indeed, it is muttered privately in royal circles that Fellowes's obsession with the monarchy has gone too far. I have nothing against Fellowes. I met him when I appeared on his BBC4 grammar quiz show, *Never Mind the Full Stops*, for money. Like all posh people, he was utterly delightful and entirely incapable of deliberate malice. Why, one could listen to them for hours, going on about what they imagine life is like.

I have mellowed over the years, and now part of what lures me to National Trust properties is not hatred of the posh, but the sadness of these places and their stories, their quiet and dignified tragedy. Fellowes says he believes that the quest for social equality is a pointless folly. Certainly, the cultural and political achievements of the denizens of the Trust's inherited homes, understood through the artefacts they left behind, would seem to reveal them as our natural betters, if only because they had the resources to pursue finer things for their own sake. But who were they really? It seems we can no longer trust the National Trust.

I forget which house I was in when I first saw through the matrix. I was looking at the bookshelves in the lady of the house's recreated 1920s reading room. Their contents seemed, surprisingly, weighted towards decadent authors, and included a number of first editions of Ronald Firbank, a rather louche figure to find in such surroundings. I asked the guide in the room what sort of person this broad-minded reader had been. "Oh," he said, "those books are brought in from a central National Trust depository. It's used to furnish many of the properties. They may not be from this house originally. She may never have read those writers." I felt the whole world wobble. The room had been dressed, like a set. The character of the lady of the house had been implied and constructed by the set-dressers. What was I looking at exactly? What was real? What was imaginary?

I stumbled out to other rooms, to kitchens, into which it was now standard Trust procedure to pump the artificial smell of newly baked bread, to the laundry rooms, where the same is done with artificial odours of fresh washing. Of course, displaying a historic home requires a number of brutal creative decisions to be made – do you maintain the gardens in their seventeenth-, eighteenth- or nineteenth-century state, for example? – but I felt I no longer knew what kind of experience I was supposed to be having. I thought about my own home and wondered if I was real or whether some cosmic National Trust set-dresser had conjured my whole being from a cryptic arrangement of compact discs and comic books.

I was shaken. Although I still visit National Trust properties, I now prefer the country houses where, somehow, the aristocracy have managed to cling on without capitulating, lacking the cynicism to fictionalise their own living spaces. At an ancient abbey on a North Devon peninsula, the perfectly preserved lady of the house passed us in tennis shorts and stopped to chat about the shrubbery, a glorious rare bird, still queen of its own protected woodland. At a great house in Cornwall, ringed by rhododendrons and an ancient hill fort, a volunteer guide showed us the family's collection of golliwog children's books and offered, guilelessly, that they "don't hold with that political correctness down here". The experiences were entirely unmediated. All smells were real, though, admittedly, I remained the source of most of them.

Meanwhile, at the National Trust property, where a woman may or may not have read Ronald Firbank, the smell of soiled undergarments was not recreated in the cupboard below stairs, where the lord had forced himself upon the serving wench. Nor was there blood spattered across the stable wall from where he split fatally the skull of a slovenly groom. I had to imagine that. The National Trust was subliminally directing the way I responded, emotionally, to the raw material of the property, constructing a narrative that it wanted me to follow, to the exclusion of my own interpretation. What was the National Trust? The very name seemed suddenly sinister, the sort of newspeak name you would give an organisation that was neither national nor trustworthy. It seemed like the sort of organisation that would give a bench the voice of Stephen Fry, not trusting its foolish patrons to have their own thoughts while contemplating the hills, the clouds, the future, the past, thinking of things near, and thinking of things far.

If Damon Albarn is serious about the occult, shouldn't we call him Damien?

Observer, 10 July 2011

The seventeenth-century witchfinder general, Mary Hopkin, roamed Essex on top of a horse, burning witches and stuffing her bearded face with purloined olden-days tavern fayre – crusty bread rolls, steak-and-ale pies and banana splits. And yet, crawling from Colchester in a crackling cloud of dark energie, it appears the spawn of at least one of the satanic miscreants Hopkin once hounded haunts the cultural landscape of Britain even now. Its name? Damon Albarn.

Speaking to the *Observer*'s little sister paper, the *Guardian*, last week, the former singer of The Blur confessed: "Magic and the occult are part of my life. I've got to come out of the closet," like some kind of Enochian Duncan Norvelle. The Britpop man even claimed to have contacted the spirit of Elizabethan mage John Dee, about whom he has written a pop musical, but the crepe-necked kabbalist was, apparently, unwilling to communicate.

So, is D. Albarn – whose initial sounds the same as John Dee's surname – as sincere in his insane devotion to the occult as his former band-mate, the tall one with the farm, seems to be in his desire to create cheeses for his Tory neighbours' dinner tables? Or is D's deranged enslavement to evil just one of the survival strategies all mainstream celebrities employ in search of South Bank Centre Meltdown-curating gigs and garbled Alan Yentob hagiographies? To satisfy your gnat-like attention spans, the arts survivor must "evolve", less like an artist and more like a primordial glob.

For example, if viewed as an "artist", David Bowie makes no sense at all. He seems to be little more than a perpetually spooked moth in slip-ons, sputtering, in a series of self-shaming leaps towards imagined relevance, from one swiftly guttering fad to another – grunge metal, drum and bass and having a skellington face. But imagine Bowie instead as a cunning lichen, an adaptive tuber or a semi-sentient mould, endlessly reshaping himself in search of the moisture of acclaim, and it is easy to understand him. D. Albarn, however, has played a better game than the talcum-faced pierrot and now no massive publicly and privately funded multimedia arts project is too small for him to accept.

"It is not for me to draw parallels between my own life and that of Christ," runs the opening line of Irish writer Fiachra MacFiach's new autobiography, *The Autobiography of Ireland's Greatest Living Genius*. Likewise, it is not for me to draw parallels between my own life and that of D. Albarn, and yet I recognise his moves. I was part of the short-lived early-'90s idea that "comedy was the new rock'n'roll", around the same time D was part of the Britpop movement.

Both of us have survived by exploiting the goodwill of one-time teenage fans who have grown up to be journalists and regional culture tsars, and who can now give us glowing reviews and valuable commissions in order to post-rationalise their adolescent crushes. But even in a culture where it is fashionable for newspaper columnists and salaried blabbers to defy the supposed atheist orthodoxy with cautious credulousness, D. Albarn has gone one further than famously faith-ridden celebrities such as Ian Hislop, and that woman with the energy-draining face in *Episodes*, would ever dare. He has embraced the occult.

I was ready to dismiss D's devilish conversion as a Bowie-like toadstool gambit, but a quick glance at the Blurs' career reveals a series of events that only make sense if you view them as part of a magical working of the upmost seriousness. Consider.

During the early '90s, satirist-thinkers David Baddiel and James "*Loaded*" Brown were among a group of dedicated activists

working hard to repopularise the forgotten activity of men masturbating their penises over pictures of naked women. This
ancient practice had all but disappeared during the '80s, if the
results of contemporary questionnaires in Talulah Gosh fanzines
and *Living Marxism* were to be believed. Then, in 1995, D. Albarn
appeared alongside some sex models in the music video for his
song "Country House". But D was not trying to ride a wave of
then fashionable pornographic revisionism. By consorting with
fallen women he was, I believe, trying to position himself as the
Gnostic Christ of Ordo Templi Orientis lore.

When the album *The Great Escape* was beaten in sales by Oasis's
(What's the Story) Morning Glory? it seemed to be the final humiliation in the so-called Battle of Britpop, a dispute not dissimilar
to the magikal wars that see followers of rival sects, such as the
Temple of Set and Anton LaVey's Church of Satan, fling curses
at each other across the astral plane. But nearly two decades later,
could the mere existence of the Beady Eye album be seen as evidence of the warlock D's ultimate victory? And was it the evil
influence of some malignant magic spell of D's that made his
rival Liam Gallagher fidget so on The Chatty Man's show last
week? "Worms of the Earth, your burrows forgotten / Wriggle
instead in Liam's bottom," D and his milk-carton homunculus
sing to the smoking cauldron, I expect, or something like it.

And, let us not forget, on the main stage of Glastonbury, the
sacred site, D appeared twice in succession. Once in his old form,
as the singer of Blurs, and then again, reborn as the musical
director of The Gorillas, a magus holding a crowd of thousands
spellbound as he conjured dances and songs from the shuffling
corpses of the undead – Lou Reed, Mark E. Smith and Shaun
Ryder.

Predictably, the last few weeks have seen many of D's Britpop
contemporaries announce their own occult projects. The Echo-
bellies are to reform, not as a band, but as a druidical sex cult,

and Louise Weeners of The Sleeper is planning a light-hearted chick-lit novel about Ithell Colquhoun and her magic goose. In a reversal of these new norms, Northamptonshire magician Alan Moore is to perform a one-man dance piece about the rise and fall of Menswe@r.

I don't doubt for a moment that D. Albarn is anything but utterly sincere in his enthusiasm for the occult. But let the seeker tread carefully, for stronger men than he have been swallowed by the dark side. Mickey Mouse thought that he would be able to use the occult to clean his floor more quickly than was reasonable, but he soon became the terrified victim of loads of singing brooms. D. Albarn might master the darkness, but it may be more likely that the darkness will master him.

"We await your sneering article on Islam with bated breath."
Angel the Interceptor

"Little thing: the Witchfinder General was called Matthew Hopkins and not Mary Hopkin. At the very least either Lee or his editor should have been alerted to the fact that Mary Hopkin is the name of a woman and, as such, unlikely to be given authority to burn anyone." Pegasus Rose 2011

What a tragic wasted opportunity to present a true portrait of the Iron Lady

Observer, 15 January 2012

I have been too busy to see *The Iron Lady* (which I assumed was a distaff spin-off from Marvel's *Iron Man*), but nonetheless I am now about to use it as a lead-in to discussing the critical rehabilitation of Margaret Thatcher. I did, however, find time to watch *Troll Hunter* last week, an enormous metaphor for Norwegian national identity, which engaged more critically with Norway's mythologised past than *The Iron Lady* does with ours. I expect. I haven't seen *The Iron Lady*, as I said.

Phyllida Lloyd's Thatcher biopic includes some daring sight gags employing the literal snatching of milk, but softens the controversial prime minister's legacy. The sympathetic figure of the ageing Maggie is played, by all accounts brilliantly, by the always excellent Glenn Close, her micro-managed Hollywood features magically transformed by hours of painstaking make-up into those of a normal-looking British woman. The old Thatcher remembers her career and divisive and unpalatable riots and strikes and wars acquire an inevitable multiplex gloss.

I have two similarly market-skewed biopics in production, both featuring Oscar-coveting actresses in disfiguring prosthetics, both factually tweaked to avoid punter alienation. In *The Meat Man*, the elderly Jesus (Meryl Streep) sits in heaven remembering when lovely wise kings gave the young Jesus (Glenn Close) presents, his outrageous egalitarian teachings forgotten. In *Der Fleischmensch*, the elderly Hitler (Meryl Streep) sits in his Berlin bunker, recalling his struggles to be taken seriously as a young landscape artist (Glenn Close), the problematic Nazi years now merely light comic relief.

Conveniently, the appearance in the National Archives this month of secret Thatcher-era documents, revealing some surprising moments of sensitivity, has come at a good time for improving perceptions of the Iron Lady and the current Conservative Party, both of which, despite undeniably strong performances from their charismatic leads, have suffered at the hands of critics, and are unlikely to spawn long-running franchises.

In the light of these documents, Thatcher has been praised for not agreeing to the "managed decline" of Liverpool proposed by her '80s colleagues. Here, we see the soft heart of Margaret the Woman, the tear-stained blouse of Maggie the Mum. I believe countries should be run like small businesses, and just as one would close down a loss-making shop or sack a sickly employee, so unprofitable towns and their unproductive citizens should be let go also. But Thatcher the maternal metal mother chose to view the feckless Liverpudlians somehow as legitimate stakeholders in their nation, deserving of the support of their own government, and she would not cast them out into the Wirral, to smelt stolen road signs, spit and form heroically self-regarding and influential neo-psychedelic groups.

There are many revelations in the released documents that appear with hindsight to show Thatcher implementing unambiguously brilliant and pragmatic strategies. Much has been made of how, despite the terrifying reality of their threats to her, she nevertheless "opened the back door for negotiations with the IRA" and initiated the peace process that Tony Blair took credit for. I went to the Public Record Office to scour the documents.

Oddly, the idea of opening the back door for negotiations with the IRA never appears in the body of any of the Cabinet transcripts themselves, but only in the margins of Thatcher's personal parliamentary briefings. Here, the phrase "open the back door for negotiations with the IRA" is written in Thatcher's own hand, often underlined, or followed by mass exclamation marks, as if to remind the femme ferrous that she must follow up the idea later. And yet there never seems to be any obvious relationship between the idea of opening the back door for negotiations with the IRA and the content of the printed texts the handwritten recommendations append.

I checked the dates. Thatcher writes "open the back door for negotiations with the IRA" on documents dated 31 March 1982, 2 May 1982, 9 February 1985, 3 March 1985, 19 July 1987, 24 May 1988, and every 10 May, or the Friday nearest to it, throughout. On the first six dates, respectively, terrorist Nelson Mandela was moved out of sight to Pollsmoor prison; the Argentinian warship the *General Belgrano* was torpedoed outside the Falklands exclusion zone with the loss of 323 lives; Russ Abbott's haunting pop single "Atmosphere" peaked at number 7 in the UK chart; the miners' strike ended; Nick Faldo claimed victory in the Open; and the anti-gay Section 28 legislation was passed. All these events would have been causes for celebration either for Margaret Thatcher herself (Russ Abbott fan), for her husband Denis (left-handed golfer) or for both Thatchers (known right-wingers).

The significance of 10 May was more confusing, until good old Wikipedia revealed it to be the date of Denis Thatcher's birthday. Despite the attempts of oxymoronic contemporary Tory feminists to appropriate her, Margaret Thatcher was a traditionally dutiful and obedient wife. Was "opening the back door for negotiations with the IRA" a code for some kind of treat for Denis, who attended a nonconformist public school, or did it really refer to clandestine attempts to lubricate republican relations? And did it explain Thatcher's intermittently unusual walk, which her biographer, Charles Moore, famously described as a "dignified scuttle"?

The implication that these "back-door negotiations with the IRA" occurred on days of celebration for the two happy Thatchers humanises Maggie in a way that Glenn Close's, admittedly uncannily accurate, impersonation of the woman simply does not. Lloyd draws a discreet sheet over Thatcher's back-door negotiations and concentrates instead on visual puns about milk. Sadly, in hindsight, Lloyd must realise that *The Iron Lady* would surely have earned more than its usual two- or three-star reviews if only she and Glenn Close had shown the courage to bring Thatcher's back-door negotiations to the silver screen in detail, perhaps in 3D. But in preserving untarnished the cast-iron enigma of Margaret Thatcher, this stainless-steel sister, this un-fatigued metal maiden, Lloyd ensures the legend of this particular Iron Lady will never rust.

"When writing an article, please get the smallest of facts straight. That is not Glenn Close portraying Margaret Thatcher, but the wonderful, Meryl Streep." Lady Jaine

Shame on you, Alex Salmond, for selling us out to the Bullingdon Club

Observer, 5 February 2012

As the Scottish independence campaign rolled forward it struck me that there were all sorts of English newspaper commentators, on both sides of the argument, who felt they had special licence to pontificate about the issue due to some tenuous ancestral link to Scotland. I attempted to make fun of this. The piece was largely misinterpreted and I subsequently found that the stage-door staff at various theatres had dozens of handwritten hate letters waiting for me, from angry Scots who thought I was serious. In fairness, the level of discussion of the subject nationally was so inane they could be forgiven for mistaking the piece below as genuine, and it generated over 1,200 mainly negative below-the-line comments. (If I wrote for some shit clickbait-driven paper like the Telegraph *I'd have been made editor.)*

Britons from Scotland are the butt of many jokes. They are, apparently, financially cautious, fond of liquor and mistrustful of fruit. They delight in sexualised invertebrate torment and underestimate in their provision for female public toilets. And they overindulge in recreational drug abuse. In fact, one of the few insults witty enough to be forgivable is Samuel Johnson's playful 1755 dictionary definition of the drug ketamine as "A tranquilliser, which in England is generally given to horses, but in Scotland appears to support the people". But I don't think jokes such as this have spurred Scotland to sever England's apron strings.

Before I go any further, let me explain that, like all English broadsheet columnists, I absolutely love Scotland. I spent most of my thirties thinking I was Scottish, before realising I had misread my adoption papers. But would I have been Scottish had I been made of Scottish sperms but raised as English? Or is national identity the result of cultural conditioning? Wee Jimmy Krankie, winner of the Most Scottish Person in the World 2003, aside, who is Scottish anyway?

Curiously, as a teenager I enjoyed all the Scottish indie bands – The Cateran, The Primevals and del Amitri (first album only); in my twenties, I was inspired by quintessentially Scottish writers – Neil M. Gunn, George Mackay Brown and Ossian the bard; cheap Scottish shortbread sustained me in the lean years of my thirties; and, more recently, it was that treacly Scottish heroin that finally freed my imagination to make me the important artist I am today. I even spent my honeymoon, admittedly in error, in Shetland in December 2006. And when I first crossed the border, to the Edinburgh fringe in 1987, I felt I was coming home.

Realising I wasn't Scottish left me bereft. I no longer had any genetic claims to the heathery Highlands or the literary high grounds. Alex Salmond's self-satisfaction with imminent Scottish independence is understandable, but he reminds me of the mayor of a small provincial town, who has got ideas above his station, because his brother-in-law has a cow that defecates ice cream; the sort of cocky provincial mayor who then topples off a stepladder while unveiling a statue of the cow, which has made the town rich, and falls into a trough of its frozen anal produce. I would love to put the case for non-independence to Alex Salmond but I doubt he would speak to me again.

I first met Alex Salmond at a reception for young English play-wrights at the new Scottish Parliament during the Edinburgh fringe festival in 2004. The event celebrated a scheme whereby we collaborated with Scottish translators to make our work saleable north of the border, a process that involved the painstaking inser-tion into our texts of thousands of swearwords, such as "cunt" and "fuck". I attended the event with Mark Ravenhill, whose 1996 play, *Shopping*, had been retitled *Shopping and Fucking* for its hit 1997 Edinburgh run. This Scottish On Stage Swearing Initiative had led to the massive popularity with Edinburgh fringe theatre audiences of a newly sworn-up version of Richard Thomas's *Jerry Springer: The Opera*, to which I had helped contribute a further 6,000 new obscenities specifically for the Scottish market.

At the event, Alex Salmond and I were standing next to a buffet overflowing with Scottish produce – venison, Baxters soup, Highland Toffee, shortbread, heroin and salmon. "I'm sorry," I said, "I didn't catch your name." "Alex Salmond," Alex Salmond said, but because we were standing near the salmon at the time, and because he had a Scottish accent, I assumed Alex Salmond had said: "I like salmon." So I said: "Yes. I like salmon too, but what is your name?" Again, he said: "Alex Salmond." And I said: "Yes. I like salmon too, as I said, I like all the Scottish foods. What did you say your name was?" After a further fifteen minutes of this, and in a prophesy of future national relations, I Like Salmon walked quietly away with his financial backer, Brian Souter, the bus magnate accused of homophobia whose fleet of vehicles may yet ship undesirables south.

As someone who once thought he was Scottish, I understand more than anyone Scotland's anger at the English. Directives from Westminster seem more irrelevant to we Scots than ever, now that the Cabinet is essentially an elitist cabal run by former members of the exclusive, window-smashing dining society, the Bullingdon Club. And none of them is Scottish either, apart from the bad-news patsy Danny Alexander and the eel-faced Trot fantasist and yacht fancier Michael Gove, who is adopted anyway, and could have ended up being raised anywhere in the UK, and so cannot make any especial claims for being anything but an orphan with a grudge.

But what the Scots must understand is that the Bullingdon Club Cabinet has as little in common with the average English person as it does with the average Scot. If 5.5 million largely non-Conservative-voting Scots sever their links with us, there are 5.5 million fewer of us to say no to Bullingdon Club rule.

Mel Gibson's 1995 film *Braveheart*, while an admittedly appalling and historically inaccurate confection of gay-hating fascist propaganda, did inspire the desire for Scottish independence at grass roots. But the abysmal film is not without a certain nobility. Its closing reel takes place at the Battle of Bannockburn, the Garden of Eden of modern Scotland's Genesis myth. Robert the Bruce, who betrayed Braveheart at Falkirk and is now a puppet king loyal to the English, turns on his masters, liberating the Scottish people. At its simplest, this scene is about the Scots defeating the English. But it is also about doing the right thing, about a powerful figure going to the aid of those in need.

In turning his back on us, the English, in our hour of need against the common enemy of the Bullingdon Club government, Alex Salmon is not the Robert the Bruce of the Battle of Bannockburn, noble and brave. He is the Robert the Bruce of the Battle of Falkirk, a self-interested turncoat, piercing the heart of the everyman Wallace with the lance of his own vanity and pride and leaving the body, like the body politic of the nation of England, to be castrated by David Cameron and have its once erect British penis flung into the air to be snatched by pigeons and ducks. In short, Salmon is something no son of Wallace would ever want to be: a coward, fleeing the good fight, and leaving those who fight on to suffer their fates alone. I never thought I'd say it, but today Alex Salmon makes me glad I am not Scottish after all.

"I have to say I am rather disgusted with this article, not only is it homophobic it is also fueled with racism of the kind I know is unacceptable in this day and age. In your article you say you love Scotland but it is obvious you don't like the people who live in Scotland. It is over educated small minded people like yourself who think they know everything and have the right to

laugh about it, when in fact you wouldn't last a day in the shoes
of the everyday people who live and work here to make sure
the tax man gets his dues. Who are you to pass judgement? You
have shown its people like you with a heritage of being able
to afford university education (then blow it all on trying to be
funny LOL!) and land a cushy job as a 'columnist' who think
they have the right to pass judgement on those who get by and
live there lives as best they can. Scotland doesn't need negative
people with such a wasteful high education and such low intelligence. I am glad you are not Scottish. If cultural conditioning
is not needed and unnatural to you then it is clear you are not
Scottish. You are in fact lost. You are in fact a victim of your
own culture, learnt from a sheltered book and bank of mom
n dad and not a natural culture bestowed upon you from life
experience and self worth . . . I pity you. I guess that's why you
thought trying to be a comedian was the best option for you, as
you are a bad joke. And as for the elite cabinet I am sorry please
don't make me laugh!! Westminster is so corrupt with its elite
corporations, underhanded shananigins bailing out the banks,
cutting public sector jobs, then funding wars that are criminal!
Devolution is about bringing politics home for everybody. I am
not highly educated but I do believe I could write a more intel-
ligent piece without sensationalizing my thoughts for attention.
You are like a cheap version of an early Madonna wannabe. I
am actually shocked the *Guardian* employs you, however from
what I have gathered in recent news no media corporation is
without there criminal activity being brought to court. I guess
they thought if we cant hack then lets just make things up!
Inevitably you know that without Scotland Britain will fall
into a trough of its own frozen anal produce. I am sorry but if
you think being a comedian makes this article acceptable then
please go back and try some funny jokes that make people laugh
because you are no politician." Greensdelight

I was getting on so well with Gillian Welch. Then David Cameron butts in

Observer, 12 February 2012

Last week, I was reading *Word*, the culture primer for time-poor ageing hipsters, a midlife crisis in magazine form. Apparently, in December, the Tory feminist MP Louise Mensch (whose ill-judged jokes about Occupy protesters on a recent *Have I Got News for You* sank slowly and silently like quern stones dropping down a deep Cotswold well) took David Cameron to see Gillian Welch, the alternative-country pioneer. But should horrible people be allowed to go to cool stuff and ruin it for nice people?

I loved Gillian Welch. Once. "I Dream a Highway", from 2001's *Time (The Revelator)*, occupies a hazy space where mountain music dissolves into visionary minimalism, while "No One Knows My Name" explores brilliantly the social weightlessness of adoptees. But now David Cameron has tapped his Tory toe to it. Roy Chubby Brown recently spoke movingly to the *Morning Star* about trying to discourage the English Defence League members in his audience, who had missed the irony in his "I Am Asylum Seeker" song, and Kurt Cobain killed himself when he realised his followers included sports fans. But Gillian Welch, who now plays to politicians, has neither attempted to police her crowd, nor had the decency to remove herself by violent force, as an ongoing concern, from the marketplace.

And so now I have to throw all my Gillian Welch CDs away. And her partner's solo album. And the great album they made backing Robyn Hitchcock. Scratch them and smash the cases and shred the sleeves and throw them in the bin with all the dirty nappies and the soiled underwear and the dressings full of blood and pus. And it's a shame. Because I loved them. (I'll keep the rare bootlegs, obviously, and illegally download the albums proper if I miss them. Gillian Welch, David Cameron's performing pig, no longer deserves payment.)

Why was Cameron there anyway? Welch's music is not the music of library closures and the stoppage of disabled babies' free nappies. Great art ought to be incomprehensible to the dead-hearted politician. But then Ken Clarke comes along, with his brilliant Radio 4 *Jazz Greats*. Were his real parents bereted beatniks who abandoned him as a baby in a golf-club toilet to be raised by Tories?

What soulmates can jazz-loving Ken Clarke possibly find at Tory conferences? I imagine him, sitting alone in the hotel bar, nibbling a grey pie at night, his suede shoes fading, with Art Pepper solos spinning inside his lonely Tory head. I'll be your friend, Jazz Ken. Perhaps Ken's happy to be part of the party of penury, hoping decades of decay will inspire a generation of black kids to hard-bop their way out of the ghetto, generating more jazz to enthuse about on Radio 4.

It is inappropriate of Ken Clarke to love jazz, and cruel of David Cameron to attend a Gillian Welch show, or indeed any live event except sport, which is of no value. It must be obvious to him that the majority of fans of anything good would despise him and that knowing he was in the room would foul their experience. But the fact that David Cameron selfishly chooses to attend anything ever shows how little he appreciates the financial sacrifices ordinary people make to go out and reveals the abject contempt in which he holds the electorate.

For David Cameron to attend a Gillian Welch show is the equivalent of him standing in front of another great American icon, say Edward Hopper's *Nighthawks*, and daubing it with his own faeces. "No One Knows My Name", especially, occupied a special room in the house of my heart, and now David Cameron has blundered all around that house in his Bullingdon Club blazer, drunk on champagne, with dog muck on his spats, smearing it on everything I hold dear, and telling me to "calm down" while I plead with him to stop.

The first time I personally was confronted with the moral dilemma now known as Welch's Hot Potato was after a performance I directed at the National Theatre, when I suddenly found my hand being shaken warmly by Michael Portillo. At first, I assumed it was the Cuprinol wood goblin, but then I realised I had touched a Tory and so I ran to the kitchens and plunged my hand into a pan of boiling water, before cutting it off and throwing it into the Thames. Dead fish floated upwards and the river foamed with much blood. But I have since met the charming Michael, and his painfully shy wife, Diane Abbott, on BBC TV's *This Week*, where he apologised for my stump and asked me to accompany him to the Greco-Roman wrestling at this year's Olympics. (I also worked with Ann Widdecombe once, who sadly was a lout. But then you should never meet your heroes.)

My second experience of Welch's Potato was in 2004, when I had co-written the libretto of an opera, and it's detailed in my second book, *Hypocrisy Excused* (Faber £7.99). Our PR woman announced Cherie Blair was coming to see the piece and that we would all stay and meet her. (These days, I doubt PRs would want the toxic Blairs coming near their brand. It would be like boasting that your premiere had been attended by the Moors murderers.)

Blair's Iraq war was in full swing and I told the PR I wouldn't glad-hand a warmonger's wife. "If it makes any difference," the disappointed woman said, "Cherie will be accompanying her friend, the head of Scope." I accepted the idea that the warmonger's wife being with a charity worker equalled a kind of moral carbon trading, where wheelchair provision balanced out child-bombing, but I did not want to meet Cherie Blair.

But then, did not Jesus sup with the tax gatherers and prostitutes? And so as Jesus supped, should I not sup also with the woman from Scope, and Cherie Blair, even though when she supped, Cherie Blair's weird flat lips were bound to look extra creepy? No. On this occasion, Jesus was wrong. Cherie Blair could go sup herself. But to avoid making a fuss, I just quietly went home early without telling anyone, Welch's Potato discreetly dropped.

Did the hot potato of David Cameron's attendance burn the palm of Gillian Welch? Did she care that the Bullingdon Bruiser bopped to that bluegrass beat? Whatever, it's over for me and Gillian Welch now. Goodbye, my country girl, and thanks for all the memories. Let the dead bury their own dead, drive the plough over their bones, and let's pretend it never happened. Scorch the earth and never look back. And I've a new three inches on my overcrowded shelves.

"What a load of bollocks." Robert M. Jones

How I was busted by the O—— Advertisement Enforcement Office

Observer, 22 July 2012

"Visiting athletes enjoying their first taste of an East End curry have just discovered a new purpose for their Olympic Rings!" That was the tweet that started it all. Fans of me and my comedy work will know I am an inescapable presence on the Twitter social networking site and have more than 900,000 followers. It's not an ego thing. Drip-feeding a few gags every twenty minutes helps me to maintain my customer base and the discipline of being humorous in 140 characters or fewer forces me to develop different kinds of comedy from the multi-award-winning, long-form, idea-driven monologues I am best known for. When you've won two British Comedy awards, a BAFTA and a Chortle award all in the same year, it's easy to rest on your laurels, and I find that grappling with Twitter's stylistic limitations helps me keep my wits sharp and my comedy muscle match-fit.

The throwaway Olympic Ring gag isn't among my best work, admittedly, drawing as it does a simple and direct comedic comparison between the Olympic Rings themselves and the perhaps inflamed anuses of visiting Olympians who might perhaps have gone out for a curry in the East End of London, maybe around Brick Lane, and who might then perhaps have ordered a dish that was somewhat hotter than advisable, perhaps leading to soreness later when defecating. I'm not saying this did happen or ever will happen. It probably didn't and probably never will. What I am saying is that if it did happen, and if the information that it had happened were somehow to leak out into the public domain, then there would be more than ample opportunity for we satirists to use the word "ring" in both its Olympic and its rectal sense.

Anyway, the gag, which I made on the Twitter network three days ago, wasn't intended to be analysed to death. It was just supposed to be a bit of spur-of-the-moment fun, something to keep my fans in the loop and my follower numbers up until the next pithy bon mot, although I noticed David Baddiel had re-tweeted it to Jonathan Ross, who in turn had re-tweeted it to United Nations secretary general Ban Ki-moon, who in turn had re-tweeted it to Ricky Gervais, who had then sent it to all his followers, without clear attribution, sadly. But what I could not have anticipated was the Olympic ring of fire that the gag would cause to surround me over the next forty-eight hours.

I wasn't aware of the extent to which unauthorised use of key Olympic phrases is being policed during the Games this year. Nearly 300 "Advertisement Enforcement Officers" are on hand to ensure that only the Olympics' official sponsors get sole commercial use of a list of Olympics-associated phrases so extensive it even includes "summer", "bronze" and "London".

Astonishingly, an independent butcher, Dennis Spurr of Weymouth, has already been told to remove a sign showing his bespoke sausages in the shape of Olympic Rings. Had I known this, I perhaps wouldn't have been so surprised when, on Friday at 5 a.m., a team of a dozen Olympic Advertisement Enforcement Officers dressed in matching McDonald's- and Coca-Cola-branded NBC suits battered down my door and pinned me up against a bookcase, while my wife and children looked on in horror.

Once the hoo-ha had died down and I had tweeted my near-million followers to tell them I was OK, we all sat around the conservatory table with a pot of tea. While the Olympic Advertisement Enforcement Officers regretted their heavy-handed entrance, it transpired that the problem was that there was already a precedent for action against an Olympic Rings/anus comparison.

Last week, a cheeky chemist in Truro, Paul Deakley, put up a humorous handmade sign, written in marker pen, saying: "This summer, why not soothe your Olympic Rings with Anusol." Even though the haemorrhoid-ointment manufacturers had not asked Deakley to advertise their product in any manner at all, let alone such a controversial one, it was decided that Deakley's business, which is not an official Olympic sponsor, was profiting by association with the Olympics. (Obviously I hadn't known this Deakley guy had already done an Olympic Rings/anus gag, and if I had, I wouldn't have done mine, but it is difficult for professional comics to stay ahead of the pack now that any amateur clown has access to Twitter, online blogs, cardboard and marker pens.) But either way, Deakley's Olympic Ring joke counts as "ambush marketing", and it's just the sort of thing the Olympic Advertisement Enforcement Officers are cracking down on.

"But hang on," I said. "My Olympic Rings tweet was just a joke. It had no commercial application." "Well, we would argue that it did," offered the lead Olympic Advertisement Enforcement Officer, Leslie Macintosh, and asked me what I thought the point of my Twitter feed was.

Without thinking it through, I answered: "Well, to flex my comedy muscle and to maintain links with the people who come and see me live and buy all my DVDs."

"Exactly," she said. "So in other words your appropriation of the Olympic symbol served the purpose of furthering your own business interests. We're not monsters. We can't, and wouldn't, stop an ordinary member of the public using the phrase 'Olympic Rings' to another member of the public, even if they were using it as a euphemism for anuses, but the fact that you can generate increased income by using the phrase means you are in contravention of our sponsors' agreements."

I packed a bag and said goodbye to my children. Leslie had explained the official questioning process might take some days.

"I don't understand," said my son through his tears. "Am I allowed to say 'Olympics' or not?"

"Yes," I told him. "I think you are allowed to say 'Olympics'. But I'm not sure that I'm allowed to quote you saying the word 'Olympics' in a piece I might write for money. It's all very confusing."

I spent the next forty-eight hours waiting to be processed, sitting on a stone bench in a damp cell in Newham. By the end of the ordeal I had Olympic Ring problems of my own but realised it wouldn't be appropriate to tell my million-plus Twitter followers anything about that!

Movements afoot to return Tony Blair to Labour's seat of power?

Observer, 12 August 2012

Tony Blair's appearances, over the summer of 2012, on platforms with Ed Miliband, only served to dent the then Labour leader's credibility. It seemed, reading between the lines, that Labour advisers privately hoped Blair would just go away and stop hanging around and reminding Labour voters how he had betrayed them.

In my shabby north London arts/media ghetto, one is never more than six feet from a rat or six degrees of separation from a New Labour politician. Only last month, I saw shadow chancellor Ed Balls fingering a homity pie at the farmers' market. Some friends are even acquaintances of opposition bigwigs. And some of them can't keep secrets.

Because my wife is a feminist (though typically unable to return my CDs to the correct genre, chronological and alphabetical position on the shelves when she brings them in from the car), I do some of the childcare. Being the only dad at Messy Play, a spy in the cab of gender, I realise men's conversations are status-securing exchanges of valuable facts, whereas women's are a two-way ebb and flow of non-assertive opinion, emotional support and bitchy gossip.

"June's friend's friend, the New Labour guy, is having terrible trouble with his plumbing." "Erectile dysfunction?" "No," said Pauline, "a problem with his actual plumbing. They had to get a man last month because for about five days there was a number two that just wouldn't flush away. It wasn't especially big but what was weird was it looked like Tony Blair." The mums shrieked with laughter. "What do you mean, it looked like Tony Blair?" I asked, smelling a story. "Did it look like the whole of him, with arms and legs, or just his face?" "Just his face, I think," said Pauline. "I don't really know. I'm not supposed to say anything. Apparently the spin guys are really worried about the story getting out."

The next day, I myself had to call a plumber. I had accidentally put cat-litter crystals into the dishwasher salt compartment and they needed to be sucked out by a professional. I don't know anything about sport, so I volunteered: "Hey. Apparently there's a New Labour politician round here and last month he had to call a plumber because there was a turd with the face of Tony Blair that he couldn't flush away." "Walls have ears," the plumber laughed, adjusting his turban. "That was one of my call-outs. It was really like Tony Blair too." "In what way?" I asked. "That's the funny thing," the plumber said. "It didn't really look like him, but it just was really like him. It was obviously him. It seemed evil. And it was smiling. And no one in the family could remember having done it."

For a few minutes, the plumber sat in silence, staring, fondling his tools, puzzled by the memory, at £80 an hour plus call-out. "Whoever told you got one thing wrong, though," he said, snapping out of it. "It wasn't last month. It was yesterday. And it wasn't a he. It was a woman politician. And she told me not to tell anyone about it. So if you wouldn't mind . . . that'll be £400 please."

Either Pauline was mistaken, and had mixed up the gender of the politicians, or there were two different north London New Labour politicians plagued by persistent voting floaters. And how could Pauline have told me a story last week that the plumber said only happened yesterday? Maybe there were two "Tonys"? Or maybe only one, but it was using the sewer system as a kind of personal transport network between the toilets of former minions. Or the whole thing was nonsense.

After lunch, I saw Diane Abbott, our local New Labour MP, with whom I am on nodding terms having been on Andrew

Neil's BBC2 politics show with her three times, in the post office. Intrigued by the toilet tale, I decided to chance my arm. "Have you heard about this poo that looks like Blair?" I laughed. She gripped me tightly by the wrist and dragged me away.

Sitting out of sight, spy style, on a bench in the park, which has recently been beautifully refurbished, Abbott was fearful and nervous, but masked it with a bristling anger. "Who told you about this? The damn thing only appeared this morning. My cleaner is at home spraying it with Febreze and hitting it with the toilet brush but it keeps resurfacing. You'd better not tell anyone. This is a bloody PR disaster waiting to happen. I suppose you bloody know about all the others too? You know about Ed's problem?"

"Ed Balls?" I offered, having assumed the Blair poo Pauline had mentioned at Messy Play was plaguing the toilet of the shadow chancellor, who lives locally. "No. Balls's problem is small-time. Ed Miliband." I could see Diane Abbott was torn. On the one hand, she knew she shouldn't be telling me, a stand-up comedian with an occasional *Observer* column, about Ed Miliband's plumbing problems, but she was clearly desperate to unburden herself.

"Ed Miliband's personal House of Commons toilet has been home to a persistent floater with the face of Tony Blair for six weeks now." "Can't they just flush it away?" I asked. "That's the problem. Ed flushes it away, dozens of times a day, and it just keeps coming back. In the end, he got John Prescott to go in and do a big massive fast wee on it, smashing it all to bits, and they flushed the fragments away, but then they just seemed to re-form and it came back, looking even more like Tony Blair than before."

"Don't worry, Diane. It will be all right," I said. "No. It won't be all right," she shouted. "The toilets of dozens of senior New Labour MPs all over the country are being regularly infested by a poo with the face of Tony Blair that just won't flush away. What's going on? And if this gets out . . . it's a gift to the Tories. It's like a joke, a bad joke, some heavy-handed routine about Blair coming back, smiling and . . . don't you dare write this up in one of your columns."

"You don't have to worry, Diane," I assured her. "I hardly think the *Observer* would stoop so low as to run a full-page column on some poo with the face of Tony Blair. People would assume the story wasn't true and just think it was the most pathetic, puerile, pointless piece of so-called satire ever run in a British broadsheet newspaper." Then her phone rang. "Pavlika. No, Pavlika. Hit it. Hit the bloody thing with a broom. Smash it to fucking pieces."

"I'm disappointed to see facile scatological rubbish like this in the *Guardian*, and surprised that nearly all the comments are favourable. I can only imagine Mr. Lee wrote this as a bet with Diane to see how childish and unfunny an article could be published. Clearly the limbo bar has yet to be lowered." Uxbridgecandidate

This truly was an event that regenerated a community, but what of its legacy?

Observer, 19 August 2012

I'm not into sport. The Olympics in London passed me by. We were in Edinburgh, and my brother-in-law lived in our house and went to see everything. I feel really bad about this now. It was a major event and I should have taken the kids to see at least some of it. Their own kids will ask them why I didn't. I don't read the sports news, but when all the hagiographic post-Olympic appraisals, vast tracts of which are essentially copied and pasted below, were run I began to feel marginalised. I didn't understand how seriously people took the London Olympics until after this piece was published and perfectly nice parents at my kids' Hackney school who had volunteered for stewarding looked at me like I was evil.

It has been just over a week now since the dead cat on the pavement outside the house was finally taken away, with no little ceremony, by Hackney Council Environmental Health, and already talk in the coffee shops on Stoke Newington Church Street has turned from the emotional highs and lows of its daily decomposition to the likely benefits of its legacy. Though some maggots are still visible, crawling in the gutter near where the dead cat lay, it is too early to say if they will hatch out into flies and what kind of flies these flies, if indeed they be flies at all, will grow up to be. The brown, dead-cat-shaped stain on the pavement, however, is expected to remain partially visible for decades, providing inspiration for generations to come and transforming the economic fortunes of the entire district.

When the dead cat first appeared on the pavement outside the house just over three weeks ago, I admit I was one of those who was sceptical about its long-term value to the borough. After all, there had been dead rats, a dead pigeon and even an inexplicable dead fish in the street before, and they had had very little positive impact on the area. "A dead cat on the pavement in Hackney?" I scoffed. "It will be a disaster. The lady who teaches t'ai chi will probably steal it to make a hat. The infrastructure will not be able to cope. And Hackney is not even on the Underground so the transport links will be horrendous. And the nature of the dead cat's sponsors is so clearly in opposition to the ideals of putrefaction the dead cat itself embodies that the whole idea has already been undermined, surely."

How wrong I was. After some teething troubles, the 393 bus soon rose to the challenge, delivering crowds of morbid gawpers from all over north London to view the rotting pet via specially marked-out Dead Cat lanes; and no one could have predicted what a great sponsor the taxidermist on Essex Road turned out to be, despite the fact that the shop is dedicated to the unnatural preservation of dead animals, while the dead cat itself visibly and robustly espoused the natural laws of decomposition ever more profoundly with each passing day.

Like many locals initially unconvinced by the idea of a dead cat, I soon became obsessed with it despite myself, running out into the road every few minutes to check the progress of its slow physical erosion. Everyone in the family had their own favourite aspect of the process. I became fascinated with the gradual recedence of its beautiful green eyes into its collapsing brown face, the children enjoyed the slow stiffening of the furry limbs, while my husband and his mates from the pub, typically, loved the bit when "its arse fell into the drain", an event disproportionately well attended by the sponsors and their clients!

There was something for everyone in the gradual decomposition of the dead cat and one could sense the sometimes divided community of east London – black, white, Muslim, Jew, Turk, Kurd, young, old, men, women, children, pensioners, lesbian, gay and transgender – being brought together by their shared bleak fascination with the inescapable fecundity of death, from whose icy clutches no mortal can ever wriggle free.

The variety of life forms contained within the rotting cat, in competition for the resources its bloated corpse offered, yet co-operating together as one, was a wonder to behold. Flies from many lands crawled over it, laying their eggs in fertile patches of damp flesh, and soon the carcass was alive with wriggling larvae. These tiny parasites' sportsmanlike efforts to eradicate the host body caused, apparently, questions to be asked at the Football Association as to why Premier League footballers could not behave more like these maggots, which had so inspired lawless young people watching the putrefaction of the cat carcass.

In our house, the cheese fly maggot, *Piophila casei*, has become something of a hero, despite being cruelly mocked by TV comedian Frankie Boyle on his Twitter account, for looking "like that midget c*** Hervé Villechaize from *Fantasy f***ing Island* with two tea strainers sellotaped over his f***ing face". Though only eight millimetres long, *Piophila* regularly hopped fifteen centimetres around the cat's body, a feat that made Boyle's cruel and ill-judged jibes look to everyone sitting on our garden wall like a definite case of sour grapes.

The decomposing cat's spectacular opening ceremony turned out to be a vital strategy in winning over the doubters and the tolerance of the schoolkids who usually sit on the wall by where it was, selling small parcels of crack for pocket-money prices. Unrehearsed gaggles of infants dressed as Swedish detective Wallander sang a Blakean eulogy to the now abandoned Bookstart scheme, while veteran ska band Bad Manners, who had met at Woodberry Down school, performed their 1980 pro-hard-liquor hit "Special Brew". Then Lady P, the Hackney grandmother who swore at rioters last August, jumped from a nearby window using a Happy Shopper bag as a parachute, the climax of an ill-disciplined but exuberant event that avoided all the usual opening-ceremony clichés in favour of opaque nostalgia and endearing have-a-go theatrics.

The closing ceremony was no less impressive, featuring, as it did, TV comedian Russell Brand, who used to buy drugs in the area. "I got all me smack round here," he chirped, "and now look. A dead cat. This place has gone up in the world and no bleedin' mistake, your lordships. *Citius, altius, fortius* and such like!"

Who can forget the hilarious song that Brand then improvised himself on the spot? "Dead catty-watty. Catty-watty woo. Catty-wat, Wittgenstein, big stinky poo!" After Brand's wilderness years in America, and the whole Sachsgate scandal, we all realised finally that he was a national treasure, and forgave him as one. Indeed, the very public rehabilitation of Russell Brand may yet prove to be the most enduring and valuable legacy of the whole decomposing cat.

But now the cat is gone and the spontaneous street party that has been raging in the road this month has abated. One of the students five doors down stumbled out the morning after the final night of celebration, in a dirty nightie emblazoned with an image of the decomposing cat. "Jesus!" she shouted, to no one in particular. "The decomposing cat is gone. But everything's still broken, all the butterflies are dead, I'll never own my own home and they just closed the library. Bastards."

"You see, when a supposedly respected, famous 'comedian' such as yourself resorts to writing about a dead animal on the pavement, pretending it has amused and fascinated a community, I can only feel extremely sorry for you. Clearly, the cat should have been removed and not left on the pavement. If you find all this amusing, you're a very poor specimen of a human being.

You're not big. You're not clever. You're just pathetic. You could decide at some point to grow up. I wish you luck with that."
Clare London

Brooks and Cameron's texts? They're pure Shakespeare

Observer, 11 November 2012

There has been much inappropriate, salacious and opportunistic speculation about the exact nature of the withheld communications between the former News International redhead Rebekah Brooks and the current Conservative Party brownhead David Cameron, much of it in extremely dubious taste. I doubt, for example, whether the self-styled grand inquisitor, Tom Watson MP, would be pleased were someone to make public all his private business messages to the gravy girls at his local branch of the Gourmet Meat Pie Emporium! But unlike Watson, my main interest in the Brooks–Cameron messages is not political, or prurient, but linguistic and literary.

Admittedly, it is possible that, were the full texts of the pair's missives to be brought to light, public confidence in Cameron would be destroyed for ever and the government would collapse, leaving a gaping power vacuum into which Ed Miliband might find himself tumbling, with all the undeniable historical impact of a damp sock falling into a deep trench latrine. But for me, what posterity will choose to preserve from the dialogues is Brooks's response to Cameron's 2009 Conservative Party conference pep talk: "Brilliant speech. I cried twice. Will love 'working together'." The pellucid message fascinates, dazzling in its mystery, possessed of a bluntly opaque poetry, and will continue to resonate long after the star-cross'd pair themselves have completed their fearful passage, and death lies upon them like an untimely frost. Consider.

Brooks's unusual use of apostrophes, rather than quotation marks, around the words "working together" appears to suggest that Brooks's idea of her and Cameron 'working together' has some entirely different and privately understood meaning from the normal idea of "working together". Would italics have helped? Could Brooks and Cameron have been planning to be '*working* together'? Or were they going to be 'working *together*'? Or, worse still, '*working together*'?

Perhaps the much-quoted phrase from the duo's original communiqué cache, "country supper" – as in "I do understand the issue with the *Times*. Let's discuss over a country supper soon" – should also have had apostrophes around it, or have been in italics? Would "Let's discuss over a '*country supper*' soon" have done more, or less, to inflame the suspicions of Watson's puritanical left-wing cabal? Its presumably deliberate echoes of Hamlet's lecherous pursuit of "country matters" would certainly not be lost on the Eton-educated Cameron. Rhythmically and dramatically, the substitution is almost too perfect.

> Hamlet: Lady, shall I lie in your lap?
> Ophelia: No, my lord.
> Hamlet: I mean my head upon your lap.
> Ophelia: Aye, my lord.
> Hamlet: Or did you think I meant country suppers?
>   (*Hamlet*, Act III, Scene ii)

Elsewhere in the message's nine words, Brooks brilliantly and economically evokes the idea of the uncontrolled emotion Cameron's egalitarian political vision inspires in her: "I cried twice."

Twice! Brooks cried twice. The weeping did not begin and then eventually subside, like the snotty bawling of a young foolish girl attending a Russell Brand gig or officiating the back-garden shoebox funeral of a beloved hamster. No. The weeping began, was contained by sheer force of will, and then the undeniable power of Cameron's crazy utopian dream of Privilege for All overcame Brooks a second time, like an enormous yes.

Make no mistake, Brooks seems to say, this was not some easily won epiphany, like the gut animal reaction to cheap music or cheap perfume, but the unwanted outcome of a struggle for self-control that failed, against Brooks's will, and then failed again. It was a *Fifty Shades of Grey*-style tussle with unbidden idealistic desires that nonetheless found their way to the heroine's unwilling and wounded heart. If I might be so bold, the sentiment could only have been more dramatic had Brooks expressed it thus: "I cried. Twice." But journalists are trained to write in sentences.

Cameron knows this. And so does Brooks. And for Brooks to break so boldly a fixed professional and grammatical law would perhaps have betrayed the pair far more convincingly than any amount of clanking innuendo about the riding of disobedient horses.

Time passes. We drive our carts and our ploughs over the bones of the dead. Leveson recedes into the memory fog. Now Savile looms aloft like Whitby Dracula newly transported in Transylvanian coffin dust, and other figures take shape in the mist, drawing the eye, dead-cat style, from country suppers. The air changes to soundless damage. Cameron will leave no legacy, and Brooks will be a stain upon the saddle of time's swift stallion, no more. But choice phrases often linger long after the names of those who uttered them are forgotten: "It's black over Bill's mother's"; "Oh! Oh! Mr Peevly! Mr Peevly!"; "That's you that is"; and the immortal "I cried twice". Brooks's words will ring down the ages, divorced from the speaker and her addressee, but emblazoned as the new gold standard of emotional veracity. The *News of the World* is gone and the coalition will collapse. What will survive of us is love.

What does the insect community make of ITV's celebrity freak show?

Observer, 25 November 2012

Periodically, I am changed into a monstrous verminous bug. My wife recognises the signs, locks me in the cellar and slides saucers of milk and slivers of lard under the door to sustain me. We do not know why this transformation occurs. We suspect it may relate to some form of deep-seated shame or self-loathing, perhaps rooted in a childhood experience, or brought on by watching too many ITV celebrity reality shows, which we know are wrong, and yet are drawn to despite knowing better. But the vile metamorphoses are soon over. I become an insect for little more than a month, at most, each time, so we continue with our lives as normal, my poor wife making increasingly feeble excuses as to why she must attend all the cheese evenings, ceilidhs and tombolas alone.

My second life as a bug is not without its consolations. Crawling around our cellar, I was easily able to identify the source of a persistent damp patch in the scullery above, a task that a visiting specialist would have stung us heavily for. And in many ways I find the society of insects preferable to that of humans. Currently, they hide in cracks in cavity walls, and I hide with them, looking over your shoulders as you watch *I'm a Celebrity . . . Get Me Out of Here!*. The insect community's response to the degrading ITV1 hit is extremely illuminating.

Earlier this week, I lay in a brickwork fissure on my armour-hard back with Franzi, an ant, and Josef, a cockroach, and discussed the new series of Ant and Dec's jungle-based exploitation freak show. Franzi, the ant, is infuriated by it. She is not against humans per se, and indeed considers me a friend. But she has been angered in the past by what she calls our "boiling water thing", admits that our use of ants as an off-the-peg simile for something that is easy to crush irks her, and is saddened by the gradual global failure of communism, which she saw as the only chance humanity had of organising itself into a sustainable social structure. But even Franzi despairs of *I'm a Celebrity . . . Get Me Out of Here!*.

Josef the cockroach explained the insect world's hostility to the show. "It's not so long ago you seemed to seek to understand us. You were watching *The World about Us* and *Life on Earth*, sympathetic portrayals of the natural world, produced by your brilliant BBC, surely the pinnacle of human achievement. David Attenborough avoided clumsy anthropomorphism or the tendency to attribute morality or consciousness to creatures such as Franzi and I, who are essentially automatons driven by need and instinct. But even all those sentimental computer-animated films where a succession of Jewish American stand-up comedians make various innocent insect species into unwilling vehicles for their own urban sexual neuroses seem like *War and Peace* compared with *I'm a Celebrity . . .* It represents humanity at its worst."

Franzi elaborates. "Take this Eric Bristow of yours that you have now, for example. Once he threw his mighty stings with terrible accuracy, like a deadly Japanese wasp. Now what is he? In our nests, when a male ant has outlived his sexual usefulness, he is flung out into the cold to die. It is the kindest thing. Look at your Bristow, hanging around the fringes of human society, sniping at the young females and the homosexual, angered by his own impotence. We would let him grow flimsy wings and fly away to a dignified death, not make an entertainment of his decay." But Franzi the ant is not angry. Instead she seems to pity us.

"Your David Haye that you also have now is no better," continues Josef the cockroach. "He is supposed to be a fighter. But when they locked him in the box of our insects he pretended to be so bored he asked to be let out, as if it were somehow beneath him to remain, leaving your old women and your young girls shaking, alone and afraid. He is a liar and a coward. Would this David Haye be brave enough to climb up and nibble the crust of a scab on the arm of a sleeping British tourist, many thousands of times his size? No. In the cockroach kingdom this David Haye would be shunned and left to die. We would have no use for him and his lies."

"Bees would recognise the plight of your Nadine that you have now," explains Franzi, "the overwintered queen, her fertility diminished, due for replacement. But bees give their old expendable sovereigns the option of living out their last days in peace. Her pitiless subjects merely expelled her. You are beneath contempt. And the core of the problem is this: in your *I'm a Celebrity . . . Get Me Out of Here!* you use us insects as a source of entertainment, a fear resource, to be showered in clusters onto the burned faces of your famous citizens as if all we were good for was to amuse you with our supposed repulsiveness . . ."

And then Josef interrupts, "But it is you who are repulsive. You view the natural world as a mere sideshow to entertain your indolent masses. Your starving birds fly away. Your poisoned trees die. Your filthy rivers choke. Your pathetic harvests fail. Your miserable cities flood. All because of your selfishness and laziness. You know what will outlast the entire collapse of your species?" he asks rhetorically. "Cockroaches!"

"And Paxo stuffing," I offer. "The sell-by dates on the Paxo stuffing in the cupboard upstairs are two or three hundred years away. I only noticed recently. It's amazing." Franzi and Josef ignore my attempt to lighten the mood.

"Rosemary the Large is the only human in the show who would earn the respect of insects," suggests the ant, after an awkward pause. "She thinks of the collective good of the group. She is without ego. That is why, when she lay down and slept amid the crawling creatures, they left her unscathed. They recognised her nobility. She is a queen among humans. The rest of you . . . you're like boys poking an ants' nest with a stick. You make me sick."

"One other thing," pipes up the cockroach, "your Ashley Roberts that you have now looks much better with her hair down. Like a different person. Amazing."

Upstairs I can hear my wife calling. Weeks have passed. She wonders if I am in a fit state to return. But up there in the light, everyone is talking about *I'm a Celebrity . . . Get Me Out of Here!*. I tighten my thorax and refuse to shed my skin. It is better down here in the dark.

"Reminiscent of Kafka's *Metamorphosis*." Odysseynumber5

Interlude: *ShortList*, Censorship and the *New Statesman*

In December 2012, as part of my promotional duties for a new DVD, my publicist suggested I write a funny piece for ShortList, *the aforementioned stupid men's lifestyle magazine which is given away free on public transport. The magazine asked for a rundown of the worst things about my year, which I duly provided. It turned out they enjoyed it so much they asked for it to be extended by a further 200 words. Alarm bells rang and I asked my publicist to check if they actually intended to cut some sections, which were integral to the build and purpose of the piece, and replace them with new material, but weren't keen on admitting this. Here is the magazine's response.*

> *Sorry I wasn't clear. We were actually hoping for two replacement entries as a couple of the subjects Stewart has tackled will be problematic for us to get into the mag. We've got commercial business planned with both Paddy Power and Dyson so these are the two we'd be looking to replace with a few of Stewart's initial suggestions below to take it back up to 1200 words. Also, given that he was on our cover a few weeks ago, is there another name we can use other than Jack Whitehall?*

I withdrew the piece. As you will see, it wouldn't work with the removal of those sections, as I tried to write it as a parody of a punchy male lifestyle magazine's trivial idea of comedy annoyances, which then works round to a conclusion of massive existential despair.

The piece as written is below. And it is followed by a piece I wrote the following week: a Christmas ghost story for the New Statesman's *then guest editor, the comedian Robin Ince. After a long struggle, I finally ended up using, and making sense of, my rather bruising experience with* ShortList.

Lowlights of 2012

Piece for ShortList *magazine, intended for 1 December 2012, but withdrawn at the writer's request*

I appreciate that there have been many genuinely terrible events this year, but those that have sickened me the most haven't involved massive loss of life or the destruction of entire nations, but have been instead smaller, less obviously catastrophic incidents, which nonetheless seem to suggest that we, as a species, have no heart and soul, and deserve to be destroyed by global warming as soon as is practically possible. Here's my top ten!

1) Irish bookies Paddy Power add a promotional jockey figure to the back of the 3,000-year-old English chalk hill figure, the White Horse of Uffington. The horse may have been a tribal emblem, or have been of religious significance. To me it's a beautiful place of pilgrimage after a contemplative walk along the Ridgeway, one of the most edifying long-distance paths in the world. To Paddy Power it was a publicity opportunity, that's all, and it saddens me whenever I think of the desecration they inflicted on the horse's graceful lines. Bookies operate a tax on desperation. I hope everyone who works for Paddy Power, or thought this was funny, is fucked to death by a giant white horse, the cold-hearted sport morons.

2) Poachers cut off thousands of rhinos' horns, which have no medicinal value, for the Vietnamese homeopathy market. Pretty soon there won't be any more rhinos, but Vietnamese people who've drunk powdered rhino horn will still be dying painfully of cancer, which is some consolation, I suppose.

3) Jimmy Carr dodges tax. 99 per cent of the highly paid work Carr does is a futile waste of time which degrades the human spirit. But at least, we assumed, he was paying tax on the massive

fees he received for it, and putting something back into schools, hospitals, etc. Except that he wasn't. John Bishop said, "Jimmy Carr's tax arrangements are like his jokes. Every comedian in the country wishes they'd thought of them." You could say that. Or you could say, "Jimmy Carr's tax arrangements are like his jokes. Easy to admire from a technical point of view but lacking in any essential moral core." And Carr's only punishment? To be briefly satirised by Jon Richardson on *8 Out of 10 Cats*, and then shouted at by some builders. Hopefully this will at least sabotage Carr's shark-eyed attempts to work the Liberal Satire Market on shit like Channel 4's *11 O'Clock Live*. He writes good gags, though, and once offered to lend me money. But it's not enough.

4) Chris Moyles dodges tax. Same as Jimmy Carr, except marketing himself as "ordinary bloke", while stealing your ninety-year-old gran's licence money rather than the dirty cash of the alcopop companies that sponsor all Channel 4 shows. Worse than Jimmy Carr, then. And he tried to cover it up. Imagine taking money for *The Gospel According to Chris Moyles*, admitting in your own Introduction that you knew it was a bit of a shit book, and then not even paying the tax on the fee. How can he live with himself?

5) From beyond the grave, Jimmy Savile's secret glam-rock Dracula reign of terror allowed the Right and media big business to kick the apparently self-loathing BBC to death. And you tolerated it. Remember that, when all TV is *I'm a Celebrity . . . Get Me Out of Here!* and all TV news is Adam Boulton licking gravy out of George Osborne's gusset. Remember that you stood by and did nothing.

6) Danny Boyle's *Isles of Wonder* is temporarily viewed by people who have never been to the theatre in their lives as somehow subversive, but is in fact the last gasp of publicly funded art. Boyle thought he was slyly mocking the government with his millions of dancing NHS nurses, but the assembled dignitaries just stood

back and smiled through gritted teeth because they knew they were about to destroy for ever all the regional theatre operations that nurtured this smug liberal hipster, once they'd milked him and all his gullible volunteer friends dry for the grand opening ceremony of their sterile corporate egg-and-spoon festival.

7) James Dyson, who invented a kind of wanker's Hoover, described the whole idea of teenagers being interested in arts and culture as "going off to study French lesbian poetry", a dismissal that manages to be racist, sexist, homophobic and anti-intellectual all at once. Good French lesbian poetry renders Dyson's Hoover irrelevant anyway. It doesn't matter how dirty your flat is if you have a book of French lesbian poetry to transport you. Here's hoping Dyson's billionaire penis will be torn off in the suck-pipe of one of his own Hoovers, a fate that would never befall a French lesbian poet.

8) Young rich people living in shared Hackney houses. Imagine Jack Whitehall. Now imagine loads of Jack Whitehalls, some of whom are women, all living in a shared house, the front yard piled high for years with rotting pizza boxes, because they're just passing through, temporarily, raping east London for dirty-realist experiences, until their parents buy them all luxury flats way off west. They're the only kind of young people that can afford this city now, and that's why it's dying. Imagine them, with their double-barrelled names and braying laughs, having noisy all-night parties, the decks operated by a man in a deep-sea diving helmet, inflicting ironic '80s Human League records on the lovely little old lady two doors down whose husband fell at Dunkirk, and for what? For these Jack Whitehall-faced cunts?

9) Drug dealers do business outside my door from 11 p.m. to 4 a.m. most nights, which I don't mind in and of itself, but they allow their menacing weapon-dogs to foul the footpath incessantly and with nonchalant impudence. What can you expect? They have already abandoned the social contract. But should my

two-year-old have to stamp her wellies into excrement which could blind her just so shared Hackney houses full of Jack Whitehalls can stay up all night talking about how hilarious Rufus Hound is on that thing?

10) Last week, I woke up at three in the morning and looked out of my window to see a hooded man leaning on my gate and pissing through it, for two or three minutes, onto my path. There are many bushes and walls within a few seconds' walk from my gate. At the end he took a tissue out of his pocket and wiped the excess urine from his penis, though not from my gate, before heading off, avoiding all the excrement left by the drug dealers' dogs. My kids potter about in the four-foot-square space we laughably call the front garden. I had to get up early and go out and throw Dettol over everything, being careful to wipe any frozen piss off the ironwork gate itself. What's going on? Contempt? A collective inability to see the bigger picture? It begins with Paddy Power shitting on the Uffington horse and ends with a man pissing on my gate. I have hated 2012. I expect next year will be worse.

"A View from a Hill": A Christmas Ghost Story

New Statesman, December 2012

Earlier today I arrested Stewart Lee as an accessory to multiple charges of arson, assault and grievous bodily harm. And I have just received confirmation that he will spend the festive season in the cells, with no possibility of bail. Mr Lee used his one phone call to contact his wife, who, he said, was furious that he was now unlikely to make it to his brother-in-law's by the evening of the 24th. Amusingly, he claimed this was the only good thing to come out of the whole affair, but I understand he is a comedian, so I am less impressed by his ability to make light of the situation, and feel that what seemed a special moment between us was, for Mr Lee, just business as usual. Nonetheless, Mr Lee maintains, with some degree of certainty, that this is, on balance, his worst Christmas to date.

Detective Inspector M. R. James, 24/12/12.

My best Christmas was 1988, though it wasn't strictly Christmas. It was the 21st of December, the Winter Solstice. But as my companion that evening, Julian Fullsome-Swathe, explained, the 21st had always been the date of Christmas until someone moved the calendar by four days. He couldn't remember who exactly, but it was three in the morning and we were some distance into our second thermos flask of magic mushroom tea, which made all notions of the measurement of time seem rather slippery. Julian and I were undergraduates in our final year at Oxford. He was top public-school stock and stiff-uppered military background, going back centuries, and I a lower-middle-class forelock-tugger. But I liked Julian, and was genetically and socially predestined to serve him.

In recent months, Julian had become intent on pursuing various experiences which, he explained darkly, he would never be able to enjoy subsequently due to the secretive career path upon which he had chosen to embark after graduation. This was Oxford in the 1980s, our elderly English professor was romantically rumoured to be a talent scout for the intelligence services, and Julian was perfect James Bond material. And now, in the final months before the black cloud of unknowing he was entering finally and fully enveloped him, I was leading him along a snowy Wiltshire Ridgeway by starlight, aglow on the psilocybins I'd purchased from the old didgeridoo player who lived in the converted ambulance in the public car park on Port Meadow.

High above the Ock Valley, we scrabbled through the Iron Age undulations of the White Horse hill fort, until we beheld the elegant flanks of the prehistoric hill figure itself, four hundred feet of chalk, flourished outlines hugging the graceful curves of the upland, a view as close to a holy vision as a confirmed agnostic like myself might ever achieve, and one of the few sights that still stirs in me troubling twinges of the scoundrel patriotism.

Then, as now, I fancied myself a keen folklorist. I explained, breathlessly, to Julian that the horse might commemorate King Alfred's AD 871 victory over the Danes at the Battle of Ashdown; or date back 3,000 years at most to the later Bronze Age; or have been formed when the ground was stained by the very blood of the dragon St George was said to have slain. The state of mind we were in, all three explanations seemed equally probable. "They say that if England is threatened, the horse will rise up from the hill and take revenge," I said. Julian, who had come prepared, was now cranking out his favourite childhood song, Jackie Lee's theme from the 1965 Yugoslavian children's TV series *The White Horses*, from a scratched seven-inch single on a vintage portable Dansette. "The White Horse is rising, Stewart," he said. "Can't you see it?"

Even before my arrest, Christmas 2012 wasn't going well. I'm a stand-up comedian for a living. I cope reasonably well with the job itself. It's the promotional duties I find taxing. I have a new stand-up DVD available for purchase, entitled *Carpet Remnant World*, which has sat as a non-mover at number 12 in the Amazon charts for two months now. Viewed as a niche art-comedy turn, I can't afford to supply my product to supermarkets at a cheap enough price per unit to make them stock it; panel-show promotional opportunities don't work for an act as lugubrious as mine; and whenever I am interviewed I usually manage to say something ill-considered, which, when decontextualised by Jan Moir, makes for a minor *Daily Mail* horror story, to the understandable embarrassment of friends and relations.

To show willing to my financial backers, I usually spend the months surrounding the release dates of my work writing supposedly amusing think-pieces, appended with DVD details, for liberal broadsheet newspapers. Their readerships comprise, for better or worse, my key audience, and I attempt assiduously to maintain their loyalty, and their respect, by flattering their intelligence, while simultaneously insulting their core moral and political values.

This year my publicist had been uncharacteristically keen that I write a piece for a magazine called *ShortList*, which is given away free on the street to passers-by and offers expert advice on style and fitness, the latest in films, gaming, culture and technology to time-poor young professionals in search of an off-the-peg identity they haven't earned. I doubted that anyone who liked my work would read it, and tried to wriggle out of her request, but our financial backers were keen for me to ensnare the lucrative male grooming market, and it was agreed that I would submit to *ShortList* an amusing thousand-word end-of-year round-up of ten things I hated about 2012.

I arrogantly imagined I could complete this assignment in such a way as to satisfy *ShortList*'s editors while also maintaining the trademark subversion of expected media tropes my customer base has come to expect from me. The deadline was Thursday 13 December, and I was due to file this *New Statesman* Christmas story you are reading now four days later. Despite being chiefly responsible for our two small children due to my wife's current professional ambitions, I imagined I could easily complete both in time. The *ShortList* piece would take me five or six minutes, the *New Statesman* story a week at least.

That evening, Monday 10 December, my stepfather rang me from the Worcestershire village where he lives, telling me he thought he had seen my old university friend, Julian, sitting on the pavement outside the second-hand bookshop in Malvern, crying. I believed him. I had seen Julian sat in the same place, in the same state, eight or nine years ago, the haunted look I had first seen on his face that night at the White Horse more pronounced than ever.

Things had not gone well for Julian. He couldn't say why. Though I avoided trying to guess what had happened, many different possibilities suggested themselves nevertheless. The SAS had originally been garrisoned at nearby Malvern Wells, GCHQ employed thousands of spooks down the road at Cheltenham, and in the '50s and '60s Powick Hospital, not far away en route to Worcester, dosed thousands of unwitting patients with LSD. Local pub backroom folklore regularly tied these strands together, leading to the assumption that any wild-eyed vagrant drifting through the region was some former intelligence services insider whose brain had been wiped out of political necessity by ruthless government scientists. Was it melodramatic to assume that Julian himself had perhaps done something in the service of the Crown that was now deemed best forgotten?

Sadly, it would pain me too much to detail Julian's paranoid ramblings in full. I'm sorry to say the White Horse, and especially its vengeful coming to life, loomed large in all of them. The fact that I must have felt a degree of responsibility for this is borne out by my taking him immediately to the cash point and giving him everything I had in my account – in those pre-DVD-deal days, a sorry £260. Heartbreakingly, Julian then dragged me to a large puddle near the former Winter Gardens, insisted it was Malvern spring water, bubbling up out of the earth, and demanded that I join him in lapping it up. I drank as much of the muddy mixture as I could stand, but Julian no longer inspired in me the loyalty he once did, and I left him there licking alone.

The *ShortList* piece proved more difficult to pull off than I had patronisingly imagined. I had hoped to pastiche punchy lad-mag style and twist it to my own ends, but there's a head-butt economy about gadget porn that's actually hard to approximate, and one learns a grudging respect for it when trying to parody it. My idea was to list ten things that had disappointed me in 2012, avoiding the usual celebrity- and automobile-based value judgements a typical *ShortList* contributor might usually finger, and to use instead specific incidents from the year to establish, point by point, a portrait of general existential despair that would subversively stun *ShortList* readers stumbling across it by accident. And I almost got away with it.

I began writing the *ShortList* anti-review of the year on the morning of the 13th by complaining about the Irish bookmakers Paddy Power. In March, the gambling business had, without permission from the National Trust, who manage the site, mounted a massive picture of a jockey overnight on the back of the White Horse of Uffington, driving pegs into its prehistoric surface, in order to promote their betting outlets at the Cheltenham Festival race meeting. Paddy Power desecrated what is either a religious site, a work of art, or both, in the name of grubby commerce, and then treated anyone who objected as if they were a humourless curmudgeon. "I hope everyone who works for Paddy Power, or thought this was funny, is fucked to death by a giant white horse, the cold-hearted sport morons," I concluded, lads'-mag style.

Then I took aim at James Dyson, whom I called the inventor of "the wanker's Hoover" for describing teenagers interested in arts and culture as fools "going off to study French lesbian poetry", and I wrote that I hoped "Dyson's billionaire penis will be torn off in the suck-pipe of one of his own Hoovers, a fate that would never befall a French lesbian poet". But a call from my daughter's nursery reporting sickness and loose bowels meant I had to collect her early, and I spent the rest of the day caring for her. My son returned from school in a similar state, and I was unable to resume writing until both had fallen finally and fitfully asleep at around 11 p.m.

From the initial two examples of crass, philistine attitudes – Paddy Power and Dyson – I then worked through various others, including the shared houses in my Hackney street with filthy front gardens piled with rubbish, all full of young middle-class trustafarians holidaying in other people's lives, each with the face "of Jack Whitehall"; to a more specific disgust at the drug dealers who let their feral weapon-dogs defecate outside my gate every night; and at the young man I watched urinating, at some length, into my doorway late one Saturday evening, when there are much more convenient walls and hedges all around; all of which seemed to me to part of the same general contempt for basic human decency.

"It begins with Paddy Power shitting on the Uffington horse and ends with a man pissing on my gate," I concluded. "I have hated 2012. I expect next year will be worse." I finally filed the piece twelve hours late, at 4 a.m., my work delayed by the stomach bugs my children had doubtless picked up from the human and animal urine and excrement smeared around the front door of their home. I bet my publicist a nominal wager the piece would be rejected by *ShortList*.

The next morning, having got the children to school and nursery, I went back to bed until 11, intending to then begin on the *New*

Statesman Christmas story you are now reading. But my amused publicist woke me with a call to tell me that, *au contraire, ShortList* liked the piece so much they wanted an extra 200 words, comprising a further two entries, making a top twelve of things I'd hated in 2012. I set to work, not a little bemused, if inconvenienced, and then alarm bells based on years of working with lying media scum rang. Presumably, *ShortList* could see the piece worked as a whole, and couldn't just be filleted into fragments, with one section substituted for another, couldn't they? Or were they perhaps covertly trying to cut sections, and get me to write replacements, without telling me? My publicist asked them directly, and the predictably disheartening reply arrived.

> Sorry I wasn't clear. We were actually hoping for two replacement entries as a couple of the subjects Stewart has tackled will be problematic for us to get into the mag. We've got commercial business planned with both Paddy Power and Dyson so these are the two we'd be looking to replace with a few of Stewart's initial suggestions below to take it back up to 1200 words. Also, given that he was on our cover a few weeks ago, is there another name we can use other than Jack Whitehall?

But that night on the White Horse with Julian a quarter of a century ago had meant a lot to me. It had been an epiphany of sorts, and I genuinely believed the hill figure to be an expression of the triumph of the human spirit and imagination. So I said I wouldn't be able to submit anything to *ShortList* after all. I was not prepared to be held hostage by Dyson, Paddy Power and Jack Whitehall. But my writing time for this *New Statesman* story that you are now reading had been seriously eaten into by the *ShortList* business; there was the not inconsiderable matter of two outstanding sets of infants' excrement- and vomit-stained sheets needing to be washed; and I had promised my stepfather I would go to Worcestershire that weekend to help him move an antique sundial.

It was late on the night of Friday 14 December when I finally began work on the *New Statesman* Christmas story, abandoning it only at 3 a.m., after a misguided and drunken attempt to retell the Nativity from the point of view of a sceptical shepherd, from which we only have this extract: *"Cows moo, sheep baa, baby, virgin, carpenter. A political manifesto in the form of a tableau. I know my Isaiah, that suffering servant shtick, and so does whoever went and stage-managed this."* It was going nowhere, and I needed the *New Statesman* gig to plug my DVD.

The next morning I bundled the sickly and protesting children into their car seats and set off for Worcestershire. A few miles short of my stepfather's I stopped at the Caffè Nero in Malvern for a coffee. The three of us were sitting around a window table, mainlining caffeine and fruit smoothies, when across the road in the graveyard of the eleventh-century priory I suddenly saw Julian, a decade more worn and ragged, but Julian nonetheless. And he saw me. I beckoned him to join us and negotiated him into accepting a hot tomato-and-pasta-based dish.

Julian and I made awkward small talk while the children plastered stickers of Peppa Pig into Peppa Pig-shaped spaces in Peppa Pig comics. He told me about the Malvern Hills, the Herefordshire Beacon and the Iron Age hill fort, the Wyche Cutting rich in salt, the winter sun over the frost, the view out towards Wales, and Clutter's Cave, where you could shelter and drink spring water from the cliff face. I told him about my promotional obligations for the DVD, and *ShortList* and Paddy Power, Dyson and Jack Whitehall. I remember that I said to him, "Every single story connected to the White Horse is about fables of national identity in one way or another. Imagine if we went over to Ireland and painted a picture of Oliver Cromwell onto the front of the Newgrange Burial Chamber and then tried to make out it was a bit of fun." In the light of what was to happen, this idiotic imperialist joke was a flippant comment that I bitterly regret. Who knows where Julian had been serving, and what part of our now politically awkward British imperial history his actions may have been written out of. Did I trigger something?

My stepfather's sundial could wait. Over a second festive gingerbread-flavoured caffè latte, Julian and I laughed about how our lives couldn't have been more different. He said he appreciated how, when we last met, I had given him everything I had, and said he'd repay the favour one day. Even utterly destitute, he still gave off that refined sense of minor-aristocratic decency, as if I was in his debt, as if he were the high-status figure. My almost two-year-old daughter registered Julian's innate superiority immediately and stared at him intently throughout our encounter, a little in love, and then watched him silently as he strode off back through the gravestones, his military bearing at odds with his dishevelled appearance.

As I drove on to my stepfather's, I remembered that night on White Horse Hill, twenty-four years ago. Julian had said the White Horse was rising. And slowly, the equine figure shook itself free of the turf, and stood, and stamped its feet. Then it turned, snorted and leapt through the snow and out into the stars. But I didn't see it. Only Julian did. And as he watched the White Horse canter across the face of the moon, he turned and gripped me tightly by the shoulder, suddenly and irrevocably changed: "If in the future, Stewart, you should ever need anyone eliminated, and without a paper trail that connects to you, come and find me. That's all I can say." Then he turned away. "Now watch that White Horse fly."

I finally filed the *New Statesman* Christmas story dreadfully late in the day on 17 December, having taken the venerable magazine's deadline to the wire. Pin-eyed from late-night cycles of coffee and wine, I took the afternoon of the 18th off, and then resolved to spend the next week planning for Christmas. And, three days later, the atrocities began.

Eighty-eight branches of Paddy Power were firebombed during the small hours of 21 December, and the business's chief executives Patrick Kennedy and Cormac McCarthy both woke to find the severed heads of white horses next to them in their beds; eighty-eight dead white horses, their genitals horribly mutilated, were left on the doorsteps of eighty-eight branches of Debenhams, whose chairman, Nigel Northridge, is also a non-executive director of Paddy Power; James Dyson awoke to find himself bound with the flex of a Dyson cleaner, his home surrounded by dozens of Dysons, somehow modified to broadcast, through the apertures of their distinctive suck-funnels, readings of the works of Renée Vivien and Natalie Barney: *"My brunette with the golden eyes, your ivory body, your amber / Has left bright reflections in the room / Above the garden. / The clear midnight sky, under my closed lids, / Still shines . . . I am drunk from so many roses / Redder than wine."* And passers-by, silenced by the beauty, cursed the cold-hearted inventor. And somewhere in Knightsbridge Jack Whitehall, newly crowned British Comedy Awards King of Comedy, opens his eyes to find his childhood pet hamster eviscerated and paper crowns smeared with dog excrement hung around the eaves of his penthouse apartment.

What I found difficult to understand, having checked Mr Lee's college records, was that the Julian he wrote about appears not to have existed at all, as if he fabricated the character in his *New Statesman* Christmas story for some reason to which only he was privy. Other than that, our investigations show that every other part of Mr Lee's story is entirely accurate.

Detective Inspector M. R. James, 26/12/12

What's so bad about UKIP members being foster parents?

Observer, 2 December 2012

I wrote this piece partly because, as a fellow adoptee, I am fascinated by Michael Gove. I wonder if he, like me, is troubled by a sense of the sheer randomness of life, of how the privileges we both enjoy could equally well have been privations. I doubt it. My guilt, or alternatively my understanding of the capricious unfairness of life, has translated me into a socialist, if one of the much derided champagne variety. But Gove is, inexplicably, a Tory. Perhaps he genuinely believes conservatism is the best way to make a fairer society, and is not just in it for himself.

I first became aware of Gove in around 1990/1, when Richard Herring and I somehow became staff writers on a Channel 4 opinion/comedy show called Stab in the Dark. *We were supposed to help polish up think-pieces by the three presenters, David Baddiel (the comedian, who we knew), Tracey MacLeod (the critic, who became a kind friend and was the first person ever to give me a compact disc, Matthew Sweet's unsung classic* Girlfriend, *and who got a Long Ryders album signed for me on her radio show) and Michael Gove (then a journalist, who we didn't know, and who was actually quite funny in an Eeyore-ish kind of way). I doubt he remembers either of us. The show, which had quite an experimental style, seemed a bit rubbish at the time, but it was better than much of what has followed on Channel 4 in its wake. And we got to meet Arthur Scargill one week.*

While working in Gove's orbit I realised I knew his name from somewhere. Then I remembered. As teenagers, he and I had been published in the same vanity pressing chapbook of poetry by teenagers from independent schools, Independent Voices III. My own shit poem was about people being gay or something. Gove's, far more interestingly, was about a boy who resented all the posh rugby lads at his posh school for getting the girls, while more deserving specimens like him were passed over. I can remember the

burning sexual jealousy and rage of most of the key stanza here, in France,
as I write this in a Center Parcs cabin, without having to refer to a hard copy,
which I still have:

> *The vomit lies not on the floor now,*
> *They keep it stored up in their heads*
> *Blah blah blah blah blah blah parties*
> *On the way to acquiring more beds.*

Ever since I recalled his verse I have seen Gove's political career as, firstly, a
bid to get accepted by those same posh sporty cunts – Cameron, Boris, George
"Pencils" Osborne, etc. – and then, secondly, as an attempt perhaps to get
revenge on them somehow. Add to this the fact that we now know Gove is an
adopted misfit, worried that he is a cuckoo in the nest, and it is possible to
use wonky pop psychology to retrofit the poem into a terrible prophecy of his
political ambition.

Anyway, some UKIP supporters had been involved in an adoption row,
inevitably misrepresented by the right-wing press as far more black and
white an issue than it was. The below-the-line comments on my piece in the
Observer *were the usual litany of false victimhood:*

> *"You don't have to do much to incur the wrath of SL and the other*
> *guardian's of the new etiquette of the middle classes, namely 'PC'.*
> *Expressing any nationalist sentiments whatsoever and opposing on-going*
> *mass immigration will more than suffice. The unfairness and imbalance*
> *that the guardians insist on with their enforced privileges for their chosen*
> *minorities is clear to see. Likening the humble UKIP members to 'apes'*
> *is presented here as clever, satirical and amusing. Suggesting that certain*
> *other chosen privileged minorities are like 'monkeys' on the football pitch*
> *will land you in jail." David*

> *"So not being able to make the racist tag stick we have a crude connota-*
> *tion with UKip members and apes. Of course this is to be expected and*

no doubt we will see a lot more of this type of propaganda. The real question is, and it is a quite worrying one; is that if somebody wishes to leave the EU and wants to join or vote for a party dedicated to that they are somehow less than human. What this article actually amounts to is downright racism of the crudest kind. I thought the Guardian *was against that type of thing. This article is easily the worst I've ever read from this paper. It serves no purpose in informing, neither is it amusing in any way shape or form." Awkward Squad*

And the orphan Gove waded in.

I have been commissioned to write a libretto about Tarzan by an American minimalist composer who wishes to remain anonymous, and who, I suspect, will have little difficulty in doing so. My new patron initially thought the apeman story a worthy operatic subject, having noticed the inherent musicality of Tarzan's famous cry: "Ooh-ee-oh-ee-oh-ee-oh-ee-oh-ee-ooh." Our Tarzan must be a tenor who looks good in a loincloth and has the ability to sing and swing on a vine at the same time. In the world of opera, this significantly narrows the field. At first, I wondered if the raising of a human child by apes was an appropriate story for an opera, but as I began my research at the British Library this month, it suddenly seemed more relevant than ever.

Last weekend, Michael Gove maintained that UKIP members should be allowed to foster or adopt children, irrespective of their politics. Gove is ideally placed to comment as he is an adopted man and thus a huge asset for the Conservative Party. Unlike his colleagues, Gove wasn't born with a silver spoon in his mouth, and by the time his friends from the Bullingdon Club had offered him theirs to lick he had moved on to knives and forks anyway, which I have often witnessed him deploy with forensic accuracy and dispassionate precision upon any morsel of food foolish enough to fall into his dish.

But do the politics of an adoptee's parents, or of anyone's parents, affect their children? Gove's adoptive family were Labour voters. He is a Conservative. Were Gove's biological parents Conservatives, and if so, is conservatism something that is passed on genetically, like eczema? Was there nothing Gove's adoptive family could do to nurture his nature, just as Gregory Peck in *The Omen* could not change the fact that his adopted son Damien was the offspring of Satan and a goat? And is Gove's view on the UKIP parents an honest one, born of heartfelt personal experience, or is it, given UKIP's growing power, politically expedient to confirm to their supporters that they could make fit parents?

Deep in a British Library vault, I found a set of late-1880s letters exchanged between the then prime minister, Robert Gascoyne-Cecil, the 3rd Marquess of Salisbury, and the explorer Sir Henry Morton Stanley. Stanley is famous for his catchphrase "Dr Livingstone, I presume", which finally rang true after decades of irrelevance when, quite by chance, he encountered a physician of that name at Lake Tanganyika in 1871. The letters shed some light on both the possible inspiration for Edgar Rice Burroughs's classic 1912 novel, *Tarzan of the Apes*, and on the current UKIP fostering controversy.

Exploring the Belgian Congo in 1889, Stanley was made aware of the existence of an abandoned boy, whom he presumed four years old, being raised by presumably friendly apes. In a derelict treehouse, documents and personal effects led Stanley to presume the child a British aristocrat. Stanley presumed to write to the prime minister, himself an aristocrat, asking if he should presume to take the noble child from the ape family that were raising him, quite successfully, irrespective of their simian ways. I began to search the archives for Cecil's reply. In the meantime, I instant-messaged Michael Gove to ask him what he would have done had he been in Cecil's position.

I have known Michael Gove personally for over half my life. We first met in 1985 at the launch party for a prestigious book that compiled poetry by and about privileged teenagers, called *Independent Voices III*, in which we both featured. My poem, though of no value, was better than Gove's, which was a twisted and impotent declaration of moral superiority to the sort of bedpost-notching yahoo rugby boys whose interests he now serves. Seven years later, "Govey" remembered me and asked me to be a joke writer for the struggling comedy triple act he had formed with David Baddiel and the restaurant critic Tracey MacLeod. We still exchange Christmas cards.

"Hi. Nice 2 hear from U!" Gove texted back. "Glad the comedy is going well 4 U. In answer to your question, I think it would have been wrong in 1889, as it is now, to say that a child should be taken from a loving home when parents have been successfully looking after him or her for years, simply because they were apes and ate roots and grubs and lived in trees. Then, as now, we need less ideology when it comes to making sure children are in loving homes. Anyone who decided that being an ape, on what was by then a mainstream branch of the primate family tree, disbarred an individual from looking after children was sending a dreadful signal. C U @ Baddiel's @ NYEve! Lol! Govey."

Unlike Michael Gove's honest and straightforward reply, the then prime minister's response to Stanley's letters, when I finally uncovered it, was a familiar exercise in political pragmatism. In the three decades since the publication of Darwin's *On the Origin of Species*, many learned men had come to accept the shared ancestry of apes and humans, and the Women's Liberal Federation were uniting disparate suffrage organisations. Cecil's recommendations reflected match-fit political survival instincts that Darwinists would have recognised immediately.

"Should women get the vote," Cecil wrote to Stanley, "it seems inevitable to me that apes, who, if anything, seem to have more

70

in common with men than women do, will soon be able to vote too. I see no reason to offend millions of potential supporters in British colonies by categorising them as unfit parents at such an early stage in ape–human relations. Despite my declared and well-documented hostility to apes, the boy must remain where he is."

Thankfully, today's politicians are noble enough to ignore UKIP's potentially vital role in deciding the future of government and make pronouncements based only on what is best for children. Gove's distant precursor, Robert Gascoyne-Cecil, put politics before the welfare of the young. And yet, within a century, the great apes were all but extinct. Cecil's fear of primates wielding political influence turned out to be a delusion as ludicrous as the idea that the Liberal Democrats might one day do the same.

Oddly, interior scenes for the 1984 Tarzan film *Greystoke* were shot at Hatfield House, the historic family home to Robert Gascoyne-Cecil, on whose orders a little lord's life was betrayed, perhaps providing the raw material for Burroughs's Tarzan. Was the production's location finder, I wonder, self-indulgently abusing their professional position to enjoy a personal private joke that only they, and they alone, could appreciate?

"Presumably if Gove had been adopted by Conservatives (something which social workers wouldn't approve of in their ideal world) and ended up as a *Guardian* reading member of the SWP that would have been acceptable to you? You are the one with a fundamentally unimaginative and narrow mind." Lucy Hilt

New year raises the eternal question: is it possible to live a life without crisps?

Observer, 13 January 2013

For this piece, I took verbatim extracts from some typical New Year filler pieces about alcohol by various hack writers and just changed all the mentions of booze to crisps, feeding in a few of my own childhood memories and adult anxieties. But I hadn't realised that crisps were of such real concern to Observer *readers.*

Crisps. Those perfect golden wonders transform even the loneliest moments into treasured memories. Consumed with caution, crisps provide salty rewards for the dreary daily tasks of my paternal and professional duties.

As a child, every school holiday I would be left in the hot car outside a succession of Devon pubs with only a pint of Courage Best for company, while my father went inside to eat crisps. I associate crisps with freedom, maturity and independence. But, I wonder, would it be possible to live a life without crisps? For the crisps-eating broadsheet newspaper columnist, January is the perfect month to find out.

Little of significance happens in January. And yet we broadsheet newspaper columnists are still required to fill up space with our opinions. We are like dogs, involuntarily dry-retching up a wretched and unprofitable cocktail of acrid bile and foul gas, awaiting applause. Nonetheless, these columns won't write themselves, so earlier this week I began one of the standard New Year broadsheet newspaper columnist strategies: writing out a list of the names of famous people I imagined would be significant in 2013, based on information I have been sent in their press releases.

Then I realised that the list – youthful Irish rock band The

Strypes, female-friendly porn star James Deen, American gun lobbyist Alex Jones, nutshell King of Comedy Jack Whitehall and, representing women, celebrity diver and Sugababe Jade Ewen – was the same as one I had already filed for a rival Sunday newspaper, of people I imagined had been significant in 2012. As I lifted the first of the day's many crisps to my mouth, the solution hit me.

It was time to take the standard broadsheet newspaper columnist January fall-back position and file a light-hearted, semi-serious piece about New Year abstinence. Editors hope such pieces will reduce deaths among the last generation of readers still paying for newspapers. Perhaps they may even hold the gadfly attentions of today's young people, who have mistakenly picked up a Sunday supplement thinking it was some kind of inky cloak, like Lady Gaga might wear. But I love crisps. And it seems I am not alone.

Jamie Merritt, writing in the *Independent on Sunday* this month, confessed, "Like many of my friends I'm still worried about how many crisps I consume and how often I consume the crisps. We're a close-knit group of crisps-loving late-20s professionals, who all ate crisps reasonably heavily at university, and while none of us has ever ended up in A&E on a Saturday night, it's fair to say that we still eat crisps more than we should." Merritt wrote that he hoped for a "more sensible relationship with crisps for all of 2013", and concluded, with the unconvincing desperation of a man doomed to live his life under the yoke of crisps, "Why don't you join me?"

It would be beneath TV's Giles Coren to pen a standard festive "giving up crisps" piece, and so instead *The Times* commissioned his wife, Esther Walker, to write one about what it was like to be married to someone who was giving up crisps. Esther Walker is the heir to the Walker's crisps dynasty, and showbiz cynics have suggested, unfairly, that Coren only married her to get access to free crisps; but her admiration for her husband is obvious. "Two months ago, my husband Giles told me he wanted to stop eating crisps," Walker writes, with painful honesty. "Being an alcohol and pub reviewer, Giles comes across an awful lot of bags of crisps with his name on them, sometimes literally. He'd be back, sometimes after 8 p.m., missing his sock, his blanket, or his sandal, but with his pocket stuffed with loose crisps from a visit to a crisps shop he could not even remember."

Peter Osborne, writing in the *Sunday Telegraph*, sounded to me like an old-school Fleet Street crisps-muncher in denial. "I don't wake up yearning for crisps, like a man I knew twenty years ago," he honked. "He worked for the *Evening News* and used to bring a flask of ready-salted crisps, laced with plain crisps, with him into the office. In the end he turned into a giant crisp and blew away in the wind."

Osborne has the bullish machismo of the heavy crisps consumer, which I recognise from my own similarly transparent denials of crisps dependence. "Doctors (absurdly, in my view)", he continues, "advise that eating three to four bags of crisps a day – approximately half a large baked potato – is the maximum permissible for a man. Recently I'll do six or seven bags of crisps in an average day, which I don't regard as excessive. I only eat crisps at lunchtime if I go out drinking in a pub, which is not more than once or twice a day. I'll eat rather more crisps than this if I go out drinking at night with friends. But not that much more because I am one of those lucky crisps eaters who does not get violent or argumentative when I have had too many crisps to eat. I just get sleepy and want to go to bed."

Typically of *Telegraph* writers, Osborne even managed to put a right-wing libertarian spin on giving up crisps, pointing out that Hitler, from the Second World War's the Nazis, eschewed crisps, and describing all-round good egg David Cameron's well-documented weekend crisps-gobbling as "reassuring", before lapsing into another crisps-inspired reverie: "I like to arrive home around seven-ish," Osborne writes, "take off my crisp costume, put some empty crisps bags on my feet, lie down naked in the bathroom and pour a large bag of cheese crisps, mixed half and half with chicken crisps, onto the floor. Then I roll around in them, crushing them into tiny fragments, which I then lick up off the tiles. This is a very satisfying moment, when the cares of the day are lifted. Then I'll eat half a bag of crisps with dinner, before going to bed to think about crisps until I fall asleep on my pillow, which is a big multipack of crisps."

Sometimes, like my broadsheet newspaper columnist colleagues above, I think I, too, eat too many crisps. But in a moment of honesty, Peter Osborne imagines a life without crisps as something that "stretches ahead like a desert and fills me with gloom and terror". At least for me, at the moment, that gloomy and terrible crispsless terrain is varied by the opportunity, each January, to write a broadsheet newspaper column about the possibility of giving up crisps. But without crisps, I wouldn't even have that. At the risk of sounding Socratic, the crispsless life would not be worth living.

"Regarding life without crisps, i used to remove crisp from my grandson's lunch box and replace them with something else now he does not like crisp. The answer to cannot live without crisp remove them from your diet long enough and you will not want them good luck!" Daisy Devereux

"To think that this inane 'article' may have well paid the rent for January my heart really does not bleed for you, Mr. Lee. I feel offended by this cynicism." Niko2

"Who is this fathead, and why does he have the weirdest byline photo in the *Guardian*?" James Roberts

"Try cutting out potato flour products and rice from your diet . . . Try just cutting the bread out . . . Fact is humans are addicted to carbohydrates some more than others granted . . ." New Zealander

"I was on the Coroner's Jury for an inquest into the death by poison gas of a man delivering deadly chemicals to the Walker's Crisps factory in Beaumont Leys, Leicester. This may sound like a made-up event but IT'S ABSOLUTELY TRUE." Real Delia

"I can't believe the amount of comments. Set fire to a pringle and see just what you are doing to your body. Crisps are so unhealthy. Horrible." Terrence D

Fists full of sausage, Michael Gove declaims his vision of the future

Observer, 24 March 2013

During the years of writing my occasional columns, I find that certain real people become reliable quasi-fictional characters, just as they used to when I was in the outer orbit of the Spitting Image *writing team in the early 1990s. In March 2013 the fascinating Gove was in the news again, for pushing curriculum reform, and because it transpired that a provocative Twitter account, Tory Education News, was secretly helmed by some of his underlings. I'm not sure about this one, to be honest. It was a borderline case for inclusion. It gets a bit sickly at the end. Sorry.*

I first met the future education secretary Michael Gove in 1992. I was writing jokes for him when he was a satirist on the ground-breaking Channel 4 opinio-tainment show *A Stab in the Arras*. Last summer I attended the programme's twentieth-anniversary reunion, a sausage-on-a-stick event at M&M's World in Piccadilly Circus. Also partying were the show's other writer, known today as the frog-loathing novelist Tibor Fischer, and three of Gove's former co-presenters: the footballing comedian David Baddiel, the epicure Tracey MacLeod and Norman "Normski" Anderson, who was then, and remains, Britain's foremost Normski.

Despite remembering me, Michael Gove was unable to shake hands, as his two small fists were full of sausage meat that he had spat on and then squeezed into a pulp, but he was enthusiastic about the future. "There is a deeper philosophical question behind the forthcoming formulation of the new curriculum, Lee, and it is this, this, and this alone," Michael Gove proclaimed. "Namely, what is education for? Why test children at all? The answer, Lee, is this, and this only. It is in order to stratify society, to sift the wheat from the men, the sheep from the chaff, and the boys from the goats."

Pausing to compact his sausages, Michael Gove warmed to his theme. "There is an old saying in the Michael Gove family, Lee. 'Not every slave can be in the circus.' The facts children are taught are arbitrary. Of course, there is crude political capital to be gained from skewing their selection towards appeasing special interest groups – nostalgic patriots, frustrated nationalists, foaming Trotskyites, malleable religious factions, furious ethnic minorities and such like – but ultimately I'm looking for some way of judging one set of children against another. Which is why I have come up with one new, and revolutionary, subject that will be studied exclusively and by every child: Michael Goveathonics."

Michael Goveathonics intrigued me. But at that moment, Michael Gove was dragged away by a delighted Normski, who wanted to show him three statues of giant dancing M&M's that had captivated his imagination. "Look after Lee, we go way back," Michael Gove called to his attendant special adviser, Dominic de Zoot, who co-helmed the Twitter parody account Tory Education News. Soon Michael Gove was posing for photographers, his arm around Normski, his top button adrift, his tie suddenly askew, and wearing the rap singer's baseball cap at a coquettish angle. Zoot, carefree from sausage and coated chocolate as only a younger man can be, immediately forwarded me a first draft of a sample Michael Goveathonics exam paper from his app-pad.

Perusing the paper later, it dawned on me. All the questions in the Michael Goveathonics modules merely tested the pupil's ability to learn facts about Michael Gove. For example . . .

Question 3: Who, according to Michael Gove, "deserves, of all people, to come back from the dead and win a new following of thrill-starved souls in thrall to his dark magic"?
    a) Comedian Charlie Williams

b) Dennis Wheatley

c) Peter "Sleazy" Christopherson of Throbbing Gristle

d) Ali Bongo

Question 18: In Michael Gove's 1985 poem "Larking About", where do the sexually active teenage boys he both despises and envies store their vomit?

a) In sealed Tupperware boxes

b) In pint glasses

c) In their heads

d) In their souls

Question 27: What was Michael Gove describing when he said, "The cure might be worse than the disease"?

a) Going to bed wearing boxing gloves while a pupil at Robert Gordon's College, Aberdeen

b) Extra regulation of the press

c) Having his consistently bitten fingernails smeared with earwax by Matron.

d) Ed Balls

Question 104: The verb "gove" means . . .

a) To stare like a fool

b) To predict the future

c) To tame ferrets, shrews or weasels

d) To take plums from trees without consent

It was too perfect. Students completed the work online, allowing teachers to track their progress. Correct answers earned them points, which they could trade for images of spectacles or lips to make their own avatars further resemble Michael Gove. The answers to the Michael Goveathonics questions were undeniable and not open to debate, and should anyone question them, then Michael Gove himself would stand as the ultimate arbiter of right and wrong. Like some kind of god.

Although I'm not about to pretend that learning mathematical equations and proper grammar on a part-scholarship and a waifs' charity bung at a private boys' school was not an invaluable and unfair privilege, the incidents of my education that I remember being especially inspiring all occurred outside, or on the fringes of, the curriculum. At my infant school I learnt humility, having been kicked into the urinals amid hooting laughter and micturated upon at length. And that was just by the teachers! (I am no Pamela Stephenson Connolly, but I wonder if it was seeking to recreate this experience that drove me to become a stand-up comedian?)

At my junior school, our teacher blushed inwardly as she quietly stopped reading us Alan Garner's *The Owl Service*, having found it a little too fecund, thus sending me off to devour the book alone, sucked into a sphagnum bog of sexy druidical Celtoid mytho-poetics that were to leave unshiftable stains on the white underpant of my imagination.

In the second year of secondary school, an English teacher abandoned impulsively the proposed double spelling lesson to speed-declaim the entire second half of Albert Camus's *The Outsider*, turning vulnerable pre-teens into nascent existentialists.

And in the final week of sixth form the priest that taught me A-level religious studies stopped me in a corridor before lessons and advised me, apropos of nothing, that without doubt there could not be faith, setting me free, before hurrying away. This was a moment of lightning-strike educational clarity it would be difficult for even Michael Gove to quantify and replicate, and it had little to do with the ability to learn facts about Michael Gove by rote. And, in case you are wondering, the answers are b, c, b, a.

Farewell, BBC TV Centre. You were Britain's very own Disneyland

Observer, 31 March 2013

BBC TV Centre was sold off and there were a few half-hearted media trib-
utes. David Cameron had already said he would view the dismantling of the
BBC as "delicious", and I wrote this comically exaggerated piece as if the
vandalism of TV Centre was part of the Tories' overall anti-BBC philoso-
phy. Three years later John Whittingdale, the current culture secretary, makes
very little effort to conceal the fact that his supposed "reforms" are in fact a
political and commercial attempt to end the BBC, and the tone of this, then
exaggerated, piece, doesn't seem strong enough.

Last week, I attended the ceremonial destruction of BBC TV
Centre, which was enthusiastically blown to pieces in a controlled
nuclear explosion by a delighted David Cameron. With one
hand on the detonator and the other jiggling in his pocket, David
Cameron was flanked by representatives of the principal faith
groups, as well as leading commercial broadcasters, free-market
economists, wealthy pornographers and a child who had won a
hopping competition. The prime minister triumphantly flobbed
a final Green Ernie into the crater, before it was filled with a cele-
bratory cocktail of toxic waste, liquid concrete and dogs' messes.

A Red Arrows flypast drowned out the band of the Coldstream
Guards, playing a rousing rendition of Phyllis Dillon's "Don't
Touch Me Tomato", a personal favourite of the reggae-loving
prime minister and his family. The fading sun bounced one final
time off the smooth golden buttock of T. B. Huxley-Jones's naked
three-metre statue of the former head of entertainment, David
Liddiment. The media memories of an ungrateful nation sank
into a radioactive quagmire of history and animal faeces.

We can all remember where we were when BBC TV Centre was finally erased from the *tabula rasa* of human consciousness. I was being driven through a Paris underpass, watching a documentary about 9/11 on my iPad and wearing nothing but a rubber JFK mask. But can we remember where we were when we first became aware of TV Centre's existence? Former BBC director general George Entwistle, for example, claims the first he heard of the building was in a memo in November 2012, despite having already worked there daily for two months.

My own BBC TV Centre awareness began in 1981, during Roy Castle's BBC children's television show *Record Breakers*. The fact maven Norris McWhirter was, unusually, standing outside the studio in the distinctive concrete doughnut of TV Centre, acknowledging the applause of thousands of members of his centre-right pressure group the Freedom Association. The concerned libertarians were showing their opposition to sporting sanctions on apartheid-era South Africa by dressing up as Zulus and doing a mass hokey-cokey to Booker T and the MG's' "Soul Limbo", the theme for the BBC's cricket coverage. Norris McWhirter's record-breaking dream was to choreograph the largest centre-right dance that had ever been seen in the Shepherd's Bush area. And he realised it spectacularly.

But what stayed with me that day was not Norris McWhirter's freedom dance itself, but the fact that Norris McWhirter's non-partisan followers were cavorting in blackface through an identifiably existent environment, the actual BBC TV Centre itself. At that moment it struck me – the Dream Factory was a real place. And like many a light entertainer before and after me, I realised that one day I, too, had to go there and fashion a few dreams of my own.

It was almost twenty-five years later, in 1993, when I finally set my two feet firmly in BBC TV Centre for the first time. I was recording a television pilot of the youth-orientated Radio 4 comedy series I appeared in, *Doolally Delight*, and was to tape a further twelve individual *Doolally*s in TV Centre over the next five years, my contributions gradually deteriorating in commitment, focus and quality, to the embarrassment of my fellow performers, until the cup of suffering was at last taken forcibly from my lips. But TV Centre itself was every bit as exciting as I'd hoped it would be when I first saw Norris McWhirter's democratically provocative conga line weave through its concrete columns.

When I was a tiny child, my mother had begrudgingly made good on her promise to take me to Disneyland, even though it turned out my fatal brain illness had been misdiagnosed. Thrillingly, a Goofy had waved at me through the California haze as it emerged sniffing from a staff toilet cubicle. Goofys, it appeared, were real. But BBC TV Centre knocked Disneyland into a cocked hat in the physical avatar manifestation stakes.

Scurrying around the doughnut daily I soon saw, just going about their business like ordinary people, Alan Yentob, Sue Barker, Barbara Woodhouse and Rory McGrath, to name but four. These real, modern-day media Goofys were far more exciting than Disney's ill-defined dog–man hybrid, though Goofy's John Coltrane documentary was more insightful than Alan Yentob's. Sometimes I shared the super-Goofys' canteen, trying discreetly to sit as near as I could to Andrew Graham-Dixon, Lizo Mzimba, Rabbi Lionel Blue or Richard Stilgoe, in the hope of absorbing some of their mysterious powers.

When trying to record comedy shows in front of studio audiences at BBC TV Centre, the counter-intuitive genius that characterised the building soon became apparent. Three hundred or so disappointed people, who had actually applied for tickets to see Bruce Forsyth's *Play Your Cards Right* and had already been kept queuing for two hours in the rain with nowhere to get food or drink, were invited in weekly by the Ticket Unit throughout the '90s to sit on plastic pop-up chairs in an aesthetically hostile space and show their audible indifference to anything unfamiliar. It seems to me that TV comedy studio recordings favour dead-eyed, autocue-gobbling monologists, indifferent to the reality of the room, and penalise proper live performers, who are the best really. But the grand old duchess of Shepherd's Bush took me in her dying hand and gently fed me something I had previously never tasted. And that something was called Humility, my friends. And for that alone I will always love her.

It may seem absurd to you that such an instantly recognisable and effortlessly iconic building as BBC TV Centre should be obliterated, as if the optimistic post-war vision of educating, informing and entertaining that it embodied stands for nothing in the modern world. It would perhaps be most fitting if the charred remains of TV Centre were buried under the retail parks, tanning salons and luxury housing developments of the twenty-first century as quickly as possible. Last weekend, the BBC hosted a whole evening of dreary sentimentalists and weeping salary men crying about TV Centre's collapse, but as the deafening explosion signifying its destruction echoed around west London it spoke to me of a brave new tomorrow, where service providers compete to offer streamlined facilities to a broader range of production outlets, each triangulated towards specifically targeted demographics as outlined in the revised broadcasting remit documentation, at both national and regional level, within a very real virtual thinkspace.

I've seen Jesus and thanks to Iain Duncan Smith She's in a bad way

Observer, 7 April 2013

In April 2013 the Guardian *covered Iain Duncan Smith's ongoing attempts to reduce the number of people liable for disability benefits thus:*

> The government is increasingly using value-laden and pejorative language when discussing benefits and welfare, a Guardian *analysis has found, something poverty charities warn is likely to increase the stigmatisation of poor people. An examination of Department for Work and Pensions (DWP) speeches and press notices connected to benefits in the year to April 1 shows a significantly increased use of terms such as "dependency", "entrenched" and "addiction", when compared with the end of the Labour government. Fraud, which accounts for less than 1% of the overall benefits bill, was mentioned 85 times in the press releases, while it was not used at all in the final year of Labour.*

In March 2016 IDS himself was to quit the Conservative government in protest at George Osborne's proposed Budget, which he deemed too harsh on the disabled, even though the chancellor had already agreed to drop the welfare cuts by the time IDS actually resigned. Coincidentally, the former head of the department of work and pensions was part of the Brexit camp, aligned against the chancellor and the prime minister.

In imagining IDS subjecting would-be claimants to a super-collider-style veracity test, I pictured myself accompanied by various artists I admired, but who also seemed like the sort of figures the people's media monkey Danny Boyle would employ if he were asked to do something for the Establishment. I love Grayson Perry, whom I once met at a service station, and it turns out he is often in my audience; I like Martin Creed, with whom I was once on a bill at the Barbican; I knew A. L. Kennedy from her time as a more-or-less

incognito stand-up comedian, and she was always really nice; KT Tunstall
I met when she was working with my Americana hero Howe Gelb, of Giant
Sand, and I didn't know she was a famous pop star, she was so down to
earth; I have never met my fellow Faber author Mr Tumble; I hadn't met
Goldie at the time of writing, although, oddly, a few years later, he came up
to me on Tottenham Court Road, engaged me in conversation and was very
kind to me. Sometimes I think that when I write, I become a kind of god,
changing reality.

Over the Easter weekend I myself was deservedly one of a party of important contemporary artists invited by Danny Boyle to a research project buried beneath the Chipping Norton triangle. Our task was to use our visionary gifts to respond creatively to a government-initiated search not for the "God particle", but for God himself.

Donning a protective helmet, I entered the metal cage of a mine-shaft lift and descended with my fellow creatives – the artists Grayson Perry and Martin Creed, the novelist A. L. Kennedy, pop's KT Tunstall, the DJ Goldie and the children's funnyman Mr Tumble from CBeebies. Tumble, dressed as a clown, did an amusing mime indicating fear, Goldie pretended to bite at the bars of the lift with his metal mouth and Kennedy wrote something down in a Moleskine notebook, similar to one once owned by Ernest Hemingway. It was immediately clear that Boyle had chosen an inspired, if volatile, combination of personalities.

In a brightly lit subterranean chamber we were met by a crowd of boiler-suited bigwigs, including the secretary of state for work and pensions, Iain Duncan Smith, the minister for universities and science, David Willetts, and the minister for faith and communities, Baroness Warsi. Behind them, an ex-servicewoman with one leg who lived in a two-bedroom council flat in Leeds was being shot at high speed repeatedly and painfully through a sixteen-mile-long transparent tube, her unprotected head and limbs smashing endlessly into the curves of the structure. IDS explained the thinking behind the innovative project.

"All that stands between next week's significant shrinking of the welfare budget to a level that may be made to seem reasonable, and further shrinkage to levels that are definitely unreasonable, even to me, is the notion that to do so may in some way be fundamentally and morally wrong," he began. I looked around. Grayson Perry was already weaving a satirical tapestry and Tunstall was humming a sad melody into a Dictaphone. The battered benefits woman bounced off the cylinder walls.

"But many believe", IDS continued, "that notions of right and wrong are unimaginable without a notion of God." Baroness Warsi objected, conceding that secularists might possibly have their own morality too, but was drowned out by cries of "Calm down, dear!" and the screams of the test subject.

Willetts picked up the baton: "Iain charged my department with designing a long-term science- and welfare-based spectacle so cruel and gratuitous that it would surely draw any God worth his salt out into the open to use his magic to stop it. If the God does not appear, Iain feels it reasonable to press on with savings in the current welfare system without delay. And this, ladies and gentlemen, is that spectacle."

I and my fellow artists followed Willetts's pointing finger towards the apparatus, as the distressed amputee made another bruising circuit of the cylinder. I was astonished. Iain Duncan Smith and David Willetts had designed a God trap, with a hapless human as bait. Grayson Perry wove frantically in a furious rage, frightened of failing to document something significant, and Kennedy's notebook was ablaze, but Martin Creed had wandered into an empty corner of the space, where he was turning the lights on and off methodically and staring at a doorknob.

Warsi, who has been brushing up on her comparative religion since getting the faith and communities gig, objected to the pair's announcement. She said it was unreasonable to expect any God to manifest himself at Iain Duncan Smith's command. And that while Catholic belief in miracles clearly presupposed an interventionist deity, the former Episcopal Bishop of Edinburgh, Richard Holloway, for example, had defined the Protestant God as a kind of half-absent musical accompanist to human behaviour. Once more, the baroness was shouted down by her coalition fellows in mock Michael Winner voices and the crowd's attention was swiftly drawn back to the awkward impact squelches of the relentlessly bouncing dole scrounger.

I heard Iain Duncan Smith invoke Jeremy Bentham and John Stuart Mill's doctrine of utilitarianism – the notion that true morality was the achievement of the greatest possible good for the greatest possible number of people – and how this could be facilitated by the trickle-down effect of high spending by a wealthy minority whose capital needed to be encouraged to flow for the long-term good of everyone. But out of the corner of my eye, I noticed KT Tunstall and Mr Tumble crouched by a distant section of the tube, where it appeared, from Mr Tumble's helpful mime, that the test subject had finally run out of speed and slumped comatose to rest. My kids loved Mr Tumble but I realised that now was not the time to ask for an autograph.

"Look . . ." said Tunstall. I looked. It appeared, against my better judgement, that the bruised and unconscious one-legged female body behind the Perspex wall had somehow taken on the face of Christ, more Turin Shroud than Robert Powell, but Christ nonetheless. Duncan Smith and Willetts had noticed the transformation, too, and Warsi was already calming them.

"Do not worry," she said. "While Catholics believe this sort of manifestation possible, the Vatican paperwork needed to verify it will take years. Anglicans will regard such an appearance merely as symbolic, irrespective of whether it happened or not. The Muslim position is that the face of God should never be seen."

And at that she turned her back on the confusing scene and stared instead at the empty corner of the bunker, where Martin Creed's award-winning light-turning-on-and-off skills suddenly seemed more interesting to her than they had previously.

Kennedy and Tunstall decided that the Christ/benefits cheat hybrid needed help, but couldn't work out how to get to him/her through the walls of the cylinder. I tugged at Goldie's Edwardian cuffs and Mr Tumble mimed someone eating a massive sausage. Understanding immediately, Goldie knelt down and gnashed his way through the Perspex tube wall until he had made a fissure large enough for AL and KT to pull the work-shy deity through. "This entity has been harmed by being shot repeatedly around a sixteen-mile tube," declared Mr Tumble, suddenly and miraculously able to speak, "and will need help reapplying for her benefits on new terms and addressing the reductions in her weekly finances caused by the spare bedroom subsidy. This must be done online, on the phone in the case of emergencies, but never in person."

"Ho fucking ho – lets take the piss out of some poor amputee who gets blown to fuck then gets shits on royally by the lack of support they will receive for the rest of their life. Ho fucking ho. Middle class pseudo intellectual sham article." Hill View Star

Margaret Thatcher is dead. But someone has reinvented her life

Observer, 14 April 2013

Baroness Margaret Thatcher died on Monday. Or so they say. Whenever an important figure passes away, the usual marijuana-muddled conspiracy quacks are quick to suggest they faked their own death. But the demise of Baroness Margaret Thatcher has been accepted without question, even by friends of mine who love Nordic jazz fusion, live on houseboats, ride unicycles and eat only smoke. Can I, then, be alone in suspecting that, while she certainly did not fake her own death, perhaps someone faked Margaret Thatcher's life? Consider.

The reported death of Mrs Thatcher could deliver a serious blow to the Labour Party's gradual comeback. The Conservatives know they can consolidate this possibility by making themselves appear as the natural heirs to the late Lady Thatcher, but only if the perception of the baroness is micro-managed to appear unambiguously positive. By Wednesday the Thatcher years had been spun so enthusiastically that the proposed parliamentary celebration of her life that afternoon looked from the buttock-shaped space in my sofa like a man trap designed specifically to snap off Ed Miliband's testicles.

Cameron batted first, using his eulogy as an opportunity to reassert key Conservative ideals unchallenged, as if their efficacy were a matter of historical fact rather than critical interpretation, and knowing that any interruption from the Left would be perceived as disrespectful to the dead. This was a genius move, displaying previously absent degrees of cynicism and cunning that suggest Cameron might yet make a great modern politician. Lord Tebbit was even able, in a Shakespearean speech in the House of Lords later, to compare Mrs Thatcher not unfavourably with Christ (in their shared ability to differentiate ruminants), to only a few polite chuckles from astonished Church of England bishops.

The pro-Thatcher consensus had reached critical mass to the point that even suggesting something as innocuous as the baroness being "divisive" brought accusations of bias and bad taste. But I must have lived through a different 1980s, because I remember Lady Thatcher being actively despised. For whatever reasons, united in their hatred of the baroness were massive and vastly different sections of the population, and not just the imaginary Trotskyites Michael Gove is currently trying to resurrect from within their dusty donkey jacket winding sheets.

I wasn't on the miners' picket lines in the Thatcher years, nor was I blown up on the *Belgrano*, and neither was I battered at the Battle of the Beanfield. In the 1980s, I was, respectively, a middle-class charity-bung public schoolboy, a full-grant Oxbridge literature student, and finally a freelance plant taxonomy researcher and would-be stand-up. I could only imagine what hard work looked like, though I had seen an arts cinema screening of Alexander Dovzhenko's 1930 Soviet propaganda film *Earth*, about the hardships of Russian agricultural labourers, which gave me a fair idea.

Back then, I knew nothing about anything, admittedly. Maybe Margaret Thatcher was right to hasten the demise of an outdated mining industry, to sell off nationalised concerns to private investors, to enfranchise council-house occupants with the right to buy, to neutralise the National Front by appropriating some of its rhetoric, and to leave apartheid unopposed. I was a teenager. I don't know. At some point in the middle of the decade I discovered alcohol and I wasn't paying attention. I experienced and understood the world exclusively through the passive assimilation of culture. And culture, it appeared, hated Thatcher. Musicians hated Thatcher. Comedians hated Thatcher. Writers hated Thatcher. There were even aliens from the future in *2000AD* comic strips who hated Thatcher. And yet she still managed to get elected. Three times.

From my adolescent bunker the opposition seemed overwhelming. In 1982, 28,000 anarcho-punks had bought Crass's coruscating "How Does It Feel to Be the Mother of 1000 Dead?" seven-inch by the time Tim Eggar MP tried to ban it. Indeed, Eve Libertine's Thatcher impression on Crass's "Sheep Farming in the Falklands" single is so convincing that had Meryl Streep not been available for the recent hagiography, Libertine would have made an excellent replacement.

At the other end of the spectrum, in 1983 I remember a swinging Birmingham Odeon full of ordinary-looking couples, come to smooch to the newly pop-friendly UB40's chart-topping version of Neil Diamond's "Red Red Wine". Nonetheless, all were happy to sing along to the band's spectacular thirteen-minute Maggie-loathing dub workout "Madam Medusa", during which MC Astro advocated unequivocally, and to general approval, the assassination of the prime minister. The refrain "Madam Medusa. She can' offer anytin', gotta shoot her dead!" seems especially tasteless now, given Thatcher's targeting by the IRA, her fear of snakes and the problems she had with unmanageable hair. But these blood-baying punters weren't Class War bombers. They were normal brummies with babysitters on a bostin' night out.

One of the glib criticisms of '80s alternative comedy was that all Ben Elton had to do to make a mid-scale theatre full of Friday fun-seekers laugh was to diss the prime minister. Indeed, there was a genuinely terrible comic turn, whose name I forget, whose set consisted solely of working himself up into a berserker-like frenzy of incoherent fury while cursing Thatcher and the often overlooked Denis, in a scatological Jamaican patois, spiced with deeply personal and sexually and medically explicit imagery. In retrospect, his act was much better, and more genuine, than anything Ben Elton has ever done, but it is hard now to imagine what anyone saw in it.

I'm not saying these violent and rude responses to Thatcher's reign were valid, tasteful or justified, and I hope the *Daily Mail* message boards don't decontextualise this piece and say that I am. But they are tiny samples of a massive swathe of opinion so unrepresented by last week's media coverage, I began to wonder if I had imagined the entire '80s, and perhaps even Thatcher herself.

Was there really a time when a grocer's daughter could have afforded to go to Oxford University, and then find her way into the Bullingdon boys' club of the Conservative Party? All movements need their genesis myths, and Cameron's Conservatives are no exception. But even the staunchest Scottish nationalist will admit there's now no evidence for the existence of Ossian, the invented bard whose legacy stimulated the eighteenth-century Gaelic revival. The idea of a Thatcher is a very useful one, and she continues to be useful to the Conservatives, even in her artfully timed absence. But that footage of her in the gun turret of the tank . . . the flag that flaps across her face . . . slow it down. I swear it's unfolding in opposition to the direction of the wind. And that's just the start of it all.

Gobbling pâté allowed a nation to scoff at the legacy of Thatcherism

Observer, 20 April 2013

Margaret Thatcher died. Some people bought "Ding Dong! The Witch Is Dead", the song from The Wizard of Oz, *to try to get it to the top of the charts. Louise Mensch, a former Tory MP, suggested people follow* The Notsensibles' *advice to buy their 1979 novelty punk anthem "I'm in Love with Margaret Thatcher" as a counter-move. I'd always assumed the track was not a celebration of Thatcher, though The Notsensibles themselves would not clarify its actual intent. The Bishop of London remembered Thatcher criticising him for eating duck pâté. So I wrote this.*

During Margaret Thatcher's funeral on Wednesday, the Right Reverend Richard Chartres, the Bishop of London, boasted to all and sundry of how the late prime minister had once physically restrained him when he lunged at some pulverised ducks' breasts he had intended to cram into his mouth. Fatty duck pâté, it transpired, was a forbidden fruit of Thatcherism.

Like thousands of Thatcher refuseniks across the land, rendered impotent with irritation by biased media coverage and the insensitive splendour of her highly politicised funeral, I immediately rang up my local Waitrose and ordered a delivery of every punnet of duck pâté they had in stock. They could censor our views; they could rewrite the history books; but they could not prevent us pushing the very fatty pâté that Thatcher so despised up to the top of the weekly pâté charts. Or could they?

The *Daily Mail* saw the skyward sales of duck pâté as evidence of a "campaign organised by left-wing activists", but the truth is the anti-Thatcher pâté protest took off largely of its own accord. Nobody needed to be nudged. Even Morrissey, a staunch vegetarian, suspended his squeamishness and was pictured in the press the day following the bishop's indiscreet poultry-paste revelation licking his eleventh punnet of duck pâté clean, a beaming smile on his famously miserable face.

By Thursday evening duck pâté looked likely to be the week's top-selling pâté, and the BBC, cowed by the Conservatives as usual, moved into damage-limitation mode. Questions were asked. If, on Saturday, duck pâté was the nation's favourite pâté, would the hostess of BBC Radio 4's *Weekly Pâté Round-up*, Nigella Lawson, be gobbling it up as normal alongside the other forty-nine pâtés in the chart, or would a censorious exception be made? The controller of Radio 4, Gwyneth Williams, was grilled on air about pâté by the BBC's own Samira Ahmed.

"It is normal procedure, as you know," Williams explained, "for Nigella to eat a standard Waitrose punnet of each of the fifty chart pâtés live on air during the programme, while describing its taste to the listeners in a breathless eroticised voice. On Saturday, if the duck pâté is the people's most popular exotic paste as expected, she will instead sample only a teaspoonful of the protest pâté, after a brief chat with Nick Robinson and Heston Blumenthal aimed at contextualising the now politicised foodstuff for confused or vegan listeners."

Meanwhile, untroubled by the possible reduction in the licence fee should Cameron's Conservatives retain power indefinitely, Sky News was brazenly showing a loop of the channel's trophy comedy stars, Ruth Jones and Robert Lindsay, lapping up endless punnets of duck pâté at a sunlit seaside cafe. "A lot of my actor friends said they wouldn't appear on Sky TV eating loads of punnets of duck pâté," Lindsay said to Jones, over and over again, "but now they are saying they wish they had and that they have seen that they themselves are weak and that I am right and much better than them."

On Friday, when the duck pâté finally hit the number 1 slot, social-media-savvy Conservatives, led by the would-be personality Louise Mensch, staged a belated fightback. Mensch tweeted a picture of her husband, the Metallica manager Peter Mensch, allowing her his golden credit card to buy herself a pallet piled high with punnets of pâté de foie gras at an all-night New York deli. She encouraged her followers to do the same, hoping to "knock the miserable lefties' duck muck off the top spot".

Mensch's subversive idea spurted through the Twitterverse like a frozen spear of urine falling from an aircraft toilet, and soon pâté de foie gras was itself shooting up Nigella's pâté chart. Even David Cameron himself admitted to having bought some, which he planned to smear joyfully over other foodstuffs later that evening in the company of Helena Bonham Carter and her husband, Morbius the Living Vampire, both of whom, he was sure, would enjoy the chance to eat pâté de foie gras and celebrate the life of a woman who, whatever you thought of her politics, was simply remarkable and had saved us from the unions.

Overnight, duck pâté partisans noticed essential flaws in Mensch's campaign. Wasn't pâté de foie gras made from the livers of geese? And weren't geese, like ducks, both members of the Anatidae family? Was the goose sufficiently different from the duck for the purchase of its bloated liver to count as a protest against the purchase of the duck pâté? It was even rumoured that "foie gras" was the French for "fat liver". Wasn't it the fat content of the pulverised ducks' breasts that had led Thatcher to prevent the bishop from eating them? And yet here was Mensch urging her supporters to buy, as a tribute to the late fat-loathing prime minister, a pâté specifically named after its high fat content, and which contained even more fat than the pâté that had sickened the baroness when the Bishop of London tried to touch it. It was as if Louise Mensch was some kind of stupid, embarrassing, feckless idiot.

Sky News interviewed three diffident French pâté de foie gras farmers early on Saturday morning, who refused to be drawn on the fat content of the pâté de foie gras, the meaning of the phrase pâté de foie gras, or even the exact species of the bird from which pâté de foie gras was made. Giving nothing away, they were able to watch pâté de foie gras sales continue to grow, the pâté's naive Tory purchasers unaware of the irony of their actions.

Despite the best efforts of those aiming to register their displeasure, on Saturday afternoon Nigella Lawson revealed the duck pâté to have been displaced at the top of her pâté chart by a plantain pâté with Reggae Reggae sauce, made by the celebrity chef Levi Roots. She duly licked up little more than a sliver of the duck pâté and handed over to Nick Robinson, whose choice of language nonetheless toed the official BBC Tory establishment line.

The protesters, apparently, had "failed" to get the duck pâté to number 1. Perhaps, Nick, or maybe we had succeeded in getting it to number 2 against all odds, without the benefit of a marketing campaign, and with the might of Louise Mensch against us. Like so many aspects of the Thatcher legacy, it's a matter of perspective.

"Does anyone believe that about Morrissey? Seems unlikely, and there're are no other stories on the web to back it up."
Malamulele

The rich get richer, the poor get poorer and the coalition plays silly burgers

Observer, 30 June 2013

While preparing his Budget, George Osborne was photographed with a burger ordered from the high-class Byron outlet. A few months earlier a drunk TV researcher told me a stupid and clearly false rumour involving the young George Osborne, a dominatrix, some blindfolded gimps and some pencils. Ever since then I have tried to mention George Osborne and pencils in the same sentence as often as possible, while waiting for the knock at the door from the Government Death Squad. It has never come. So we must assume the story definitely was a lie, though at one point Google began to offer up the search option "george osborne pencil rumour".

George Osborne chewed his pencil nervously. It tasted funny. He worried where it had been. But his fellow Bullingdon boy Nat Rothschild had assured him he had burned all *those* pencils. Maybe this one had escaped the inferno.

It was Wednesday evening. Our conscience-stricken chancellor required sustenance. Lashed by the twin madames of ethics and economics, a weakened George Osborne had his servant call Byron Hamburgers, a deluxe tenderised-meat-patty outlet with branches all over west London. Soon a flattened circle of meat lay near the chancellor's left hand, the rich aroma inflaming both of his proud equine nostrils, and making one of his white legs tremble excitedly. George Osborne would need all the strength he could muster to sign off the punitive savings his heart told him the country deserved. And only an expensive meat parcel could supply that strength. George Osborne bit into the Byron burger. He felt the elasticated waistband of his underpant tighten, cutting the blood to his round buttocks, as he drove his pencil down hard upon the signature space of the spending review. There! The deed was done.

The scenario above is sheer satirical fantasy, of course, and it is lazy of the Left to make political capital out of the fact that the chancellor made welfare savings while eating a burger, even if it was a more expensive burger than any the average welfare claimant could ever afford. But it is hardly a state secret that Byron burgers are extremely popular with the right-wing politicos who dwell in the leafy paradise of west London. Byron is run by Tom Byng, a member of the same Old Etonian cabal as David Cameron himself and Boris Johnson. And the mass of juicy meat that top Tories ate in Byng's previous restaurant, Zucca, saw it described as the de facto works canteen of the Cameron set. Even Nicholas Clegg extols Byron's succulent flattened beef pads. The coalition has bonded over Byron burgers, and all its key players are proud to stand before their fellows and declare, "*Ich bin ein Byronburger.*"

But at what cost? The political class live in a west London playground no longer sullied by the unsightly poor, who have been ousted by housing-benefit cuts and rent hikes. But where have they gone? And can the Right's sudden and conspicuous consumption of Byron burgers be mere coincidence? Check Byron's progress on Google Maps and you'll see the shaped-meat retailer's eastern push follows the line of London's gentrification, and the enforced economic exodus of its underclass, in a microcosmic reflection of national trends towards the disappearance of the dispossessed. The crushed-beef chain's surge into once neglected areas like Hoxton and Tower Hamlets, while welcomed by venal estate agents looking for evidence that their patch is up and coming, is bad news for indigenous people. Chelsea types, in their pink trousers and yellow jumpers, are coming, displacing ordinary people, even as they themselves are ousted from the verdant pasture of their own west London homelands by the property power of Russian mafia and wealthy Arab Spring escapees. New Byron branches in Manchester and Liverpool reflect similar spurts of gentrification. The rich are eating at Byron in places where the poor once ate at Chicken Cottage, a name I will appropriate for my rural retreat when I too am finally displaced from the capital.

The food-press spin on the Old Etonian Tom Byng's company is that it represents a kind of credible indie alternative to the corporate McDonald's and Burger King chains. But earlier this month *The Times* reported that Jacob Rothschild, the father of Osborne's Bullingdon Club associate Nat Rothschild, is considering buying Byng's big burger business, though his plan to rename it as Bilder Burger has been seen as a potential PR disaster.

Crazed conspiracy theorists have placed the Rothschilds at the centre of bizarre and sinister speculations for centuries, but can their proposed annexation of Byron Hamburgers at this stage in Osborne's savings programme mean nothing? The Rothschild family's investments and intelligence are said to have determined the favourable outcome of the Battle of Waterloo, thus inflating the value of British currency. Why, in a time of austerity, has Osborne suddenly pledged millions to preserve the site of the battlefield? Is there a connection?

David Cameron's (now largely abandoned) appeals to the faith community to make his noble Big Society dream a reality seemed to exploit the possibility of eternal life as a reward for good works, hoping that the promise of heaven might incentivise the faithful into charitable actions, absolving the state of its financially unsustainable duty of care. But Cameron's doubtless sincere belief that the human spirit has a life, a value even, beyond the physical vessel that carries it is not one that is shared by Osborne's savings programme.

A pragmatic and bold realist, Osborne is, in essence, trying to balance the books in regard to the cost of the physical presence, in Britain, of each individual citizen. Does an individual earn the nation more, in the long term, than it costs the nation to keep them alive? And if not, how can the costs they generate be offset? We must continue our progress away from intensive care and out onto an abandoned trolley in a lonely hospital corridor. Is there some way of, to coin a current coalition buzzword, monetising the actual physical presence of the individual citizen?

Byron's standard 6 oz classic burger retails at £6.75. The average British person weighs 12 st. There are 224 ounces in a stone. $224 \times 12 = 2{,}688$. 2,688 divided by $6 = 448$. $448 \times £6.75 = £3{,}024$. In partnership with Byron, as the chain plays its part in the ongoing displacement and disappearance of the poor, Osborne is theoretically able to offer a return of up to £3,024 on potential meat provision units which, if left to deteriorate at their current level, may be nothing but a lifelong drain on the national balance.

Osborne knows this partnership offers a drastic solution which may prove unpopular with the electorate, even one primed to view benefit claimants as the enemy. Revealing the full extent of the programme's current operating levels will require caution. In the meantime, Clegg, Osborne, Cameron and their friends continue to eat Byron burgers with gusto. It is almost as if they are trying to dispose of the evidence.

The end of the world is nigh . . . anyone out there interested?

Observer, 6 October 2013

A peer-reviewed scientific paper assuring us of our imminent destruction by climate change had been published. As usual, it wasn't front-page news, except in the Independent, *and even that has gone now. Future generations will wonder how we sleep-walked to our collective doom, except that they won't exist. Never mind, I did my bit. I wrote a funny column, channelling old Jack Kirby Galactus comics.*

Last Monday the International Panel on Planet-Threatening Demi-Gods presented the most peer-reviewed scientific paper in all human history, giving unarguable evidence that Earth will be destroyed by a malevolent super-being called Malignos at tea-time (GMT) next Tuesday. I was on tour, sitting in Belfast airport departure lounge, when I read about it in the *Guardian*. It seemed like an important story, but I noticed other passengers skipping it in their papers in favour, for example, of a charming *Daily Mail* centre-spread of Photoshopped pictures of tiny people in a world made of massive vegetables. There was some giant broccoli that a bike had crashed into, and a little white man was standing next to it looking at the buckled wheel, scratching his head in astonishment. He simply couldn't believe it. He had driven his bike straight into some giant broccoli!

Malignos the Titan, according to the scientists' report, was four times the size of the Earth and wore pink Speedos, purple motorcycle boots and a lilac headdress, similar to Princess Beatrice's royal wedding hat, but almost infinitely larger. Apparently, the hungry space god has been drifting towards the Earth since the early '70s, in full view of astronomers, while shouting: "Resistance is useless. I will drain your planet of all air, water and minerals in an instant. Then everything will die." Scientists and politicians admit that they had some initial difficulty in comprehending the scale and seriousness of the threat. They weren't alone. I nudged the young woman next to me on the departure lounge sofa and showed her a photo of the giant evil god drifting past Mars, and the headline explaining that the world would be destroyed on Tuesday. She pursed her lips, tutted at it, and went back to reading an autobiography of David Walliams.

A big screen in the lounge was showing Lorraine Kelly's ITV morning show. The producers were looking for the fun showbiz angle on the story of the forthcoming destruction of the planet. Varg Vikernes, of the Norwegian black-metal band Burzum, was among the celebrities already expressing disappointment in their online blogs about the sudden end of all life. Lorraine had a link-up to him deep in the ancient Scandinavian forest, wherein he dwelt.

"I had hoped human civilisation would grind inexorably to a halt in violent disputes over land and resources," Varg told Lorraine Kelly, his white-painted face glowing in the primordial gloom, "plunging us back into a second dark age, pitting man against man, race against race, in a barbaric struggle for survival. This sudden end of everything, instantly, has no dignity to it, no nobility. We have been cheated of glory, betrayed by God." And Varg disappeared back into the womb-dark of Mother Forest.

Then Lorraine turned to her studio guest, the transvestite Irish comedian Brendan O'Carroll, titular star of the award-winning *Mrs Brown's Boys*, who said that the imminent end of everything was ". . . a fecking shitty thing to happen, and no mistake". People in the departure lounge laughed at the "fecking" bit. I don't think they were really listening to what Brendan and Lorraine were talking about. O'Carroll went on to mention his tour dates, but Lorraine said there would be little point trying to attend them as the world was certain to be destroyed on Tuesday. And they were all sold out anyway.

I flipped the channel to News 24. In an effort to maintain balance, the BBC had finally found someone to dismiss the threat of Malignos the space titan. Appearing live from Oodnadata in the outback, where he was presenting an abandoned upturned tin bath to local people as a reward for good behaviour, Tony Abbott, leader of the Australians, said: "This space-god looks like a poofter to me in his nancy-boy hat and shirt-lifter's boots. Send him down here and we'll kick his arse into the back of next week." An Australian tourist on one of the seats behind me applauded and laughed. "Go, Tony! Legend!"

I flipped again. On CNN a female news anchor was playing Sarah Palin footage of Malignos, and explaining the god's intent to destroy our planet. Palin laughed, shook her head and said, "There's only one god, ma'am, and I'm pretty sure he doesn't wear Princess Beatrice's royal wedding hat." I'm not a religious man any more, but I went to find the airport's multi-faith prayer room, suddenly moved to address the god I grew up with. But there seemed to be some argument going on in there about whose turn it was to use the prayer mat, and about which religion's prayers were going to be most effective in the light of the current crisis. I went to the bar instead and started drinking.

Later, as I walked back towards the departure lounge, I looked at all the books on the shelves of WH Smith, the classics in a little cluster near the floor. Hardy, Dickens, Eliot, Brontë. It seems trivial, I suppose, but it suddenly struck me that all this would be lost too, our finest thoughts, our noblest artistic endeavours. Then I saw a new Jeremy Clarkson book, *A Life of Certainty*, at the top of the bestseller shelves. Perhaps we are getting what we have deserved all along. We are scum. We can't even save the rhino from extinction, and the very thing we're killing him for, his supposedly magical horn, has no medicinal value whatsoever.

"Come, Malignos, come," I found myself thinking, "come now, and purify this filthy sphere in space."

Back on News 24 the forthcoming end of the world was already being bumped down the top-stories list. A paper that used to be run by Nazi sympathisers had said some bloke's dad was once a communist. The father of a famous lady's son wasn't who we had thought it was. A woman politician had nice shoes. Then Owen Paterson, the environment secretary, came on, to voice his opinion on the IPPTDG's confirmation of Tuesday's apocalypse. "People get very emotional about this subject," he said, "but remember that for humans the biggest cause of death is cold in winter, far bigger than sudden mass extinction due to the planet-eating ambitions of a world-destroying demi-god. I actually see this report as something we need to take seriously, but what it is saying is something we can adapt to over time, and we are very good as a race at adapting." I stood up and started shouting, "We're fucked. We're absolutely fucked." "Sit down and be quiet, sir," said a member of staff, "you're upsetting everyone."

What to do if millions of Romanian vampires pitch camp at Marble Arch

Observer, 5 January 2014

How quaint it seems, as I write in April 2016, that only two years ago the tabloids were worrying about Romanians, and Boris was exploiting the fear of them for political ends.

During the Thatcher era, wealthy British people leaving the National Theatre skirted British homeless people in the cardboard cities of the South Bank subway. Today, wealthy Arabs, Russians and Europeans, leaving the Princess Diana memorial playground, skirt Romanian homeless people in the Marble Arch underpass. Can there be any better proof of the astonishing progress London has made in three decades to become the truly global city it is in 2014?

Even as a professional comedian of twenty-five years' standing, I nevertheless find it difficult to know what angle to take on this week's much anticipated mass influx of Romanians. I am filing this column, in English, on the morning of Thursday 2 January, but by the time you read it, on Sunday the 5th, it may already be appearing only in Romanian, in an attempt to court some of the 29 million potential new *Observer* readers the soft right predict will arrive this week. From a business point of view, should I be pro-Romanian or anti-Romanian? While I won't be down at Luton airport handing out Costa coffees any time soon, I do nonetheless wonder which market should I work.

At the end of November Boris Johnson, Britain's first self-satirising politician, became an early advocate of the anti-Romanian business model, observing sadly: "We can do nothing to stop the entire population of Transylvania – charming though most of them may be – from trying to pitch camp at Marble Arch." Johnson's trademark tuck-shop wit makes him a formidable political orator. Johnson is like an iron fist encased in an iron glove, but on the knuckles of the iron glove are tiny child-like drawings of ejaculating penises at which even the son of a Marxist intellectual cannot help but smirk.

I am not a political speechwriter, and I hate to appear cynical, but when Johnson said most of the Romanians "may" be "charming", I don't think he meant this. I think Johnson was being sarcastic. Johnson chose to make Romania synonymous with Transylvania, a region of Romania comprising, at more than 7 million souls, roughly a third of the country's 20 million-plus population. In doing so, was he deliberately evoking fears of the blood-eating Transylvanian vampires of legend, deeply buried in the European collective subconscious? I believe so. For nothing Johnson does is accidental, even things that look like accidents. His wizard zip-wire prang of 2012 was choreographed by CBeebies' Mr Tumble, to exact specifications laid down by a team of spin doctors, in order to court the slapstick vote.

F. W. Murnau's silent 1922 vampire classic, *Nosferatu*, is frequently read as anti-Semitic, the hook-nosed, rat-fancying Count Orlok obviously a 1920s Jewish stereotype, as surely as Johnson's flesh-drinking "Transylvanians" represent the Romanians today. Johnson is mired in the folkloric, I should imagine. His evocation of the unholy dining habits of the Romanians is as deliberate as Enoch Powell's allusions to Virgil, and Powell's "rivers of blood" marks the same attitudinal watershed as Johnson's own dinners of blood.

In a way, it's a shame the Romanians aren't the vampires Johnson insists they are. If 7 million vampires were to set up camp at Marble Arch, we could at least fight them. Pitched battles between crucifix-wielding clergymen and razor-fanged aristocrats, of inexplicable sexual allure and indeterminate vintage, spilling out from the subways around the Animals in War memorial would provide a valuable boost for the tourist economy and show the practical value of the Faith Community™ in an increasingly and aggressively secular society that places no value on the spiritual ©.

Dracula must be destroyed. Not even Keith Vaz would argue against this, though he may offer him a gingerbread latte. But it's harder to know what to do with dozens of old people on crutches sleeping on the floor between bin bags full of rags or crammed by unscrupulous landlords into unregulated low-rent ex-council properties in market towns forgotten by party politics. You can't just creep up and drive stakes through their hearts, even though Johnson's calculatedly casual allusion to the vampire myths seems to be inviting Londoners to do so.

As a commercial traveller, delivering my humour content to customers nationwide, I don't think the service industries of Britain could cope without east European workers, even if they do feast on human blood, take gas form, attract vermin and poison our wells. From the lowliest Travelodge to the highest Hotel du Vin, every front desk I approach is manned by an eastern European, their literacy and numeracy skills putting them ahead of one-third of the British workforce.

The "Off-Liscenese" near my home and the "Babelon Cafe", Nicholson Street, Edinburgh, are just two examples, off the top of my head, of British businesses that have managed to spell their own names two different ways on the front of their own premises. And, while the extract from the lyrics of The Waterboys' "Fisherman's Blues", hand-painted on the wall of my room in the Morrison hotel, Dublin, sports a glaring misused possessive apostrophe, it is unlikely that the Bulgarian woman on reception was responsible, as her English was perfect.

We fear what we do not know. And what do I, I wonder, know about the Romanians? Well, like many people, Johnson included,

I should imagine, say the word "Romania" to me, and I think instantly of Ştefan Niculescu, Octavian Nemescu and Corneliu Cezar. We all accept that the Romanian electro-acoustic composers of the post-war era were decent, hard-working pioneers in their field. But it is not decent, hard-working Romanian electro-acoustic composers who will be coming here and undercutting decent, hard-working Polish immigrants who have spent ten years undercutting the decent, hard-working British workers at the hand car wash by the cemetery on the bypass, now closed. And I should be very surprised if British artists applying for grants to drop ring modulators down wells suddenly find there is a bald Romanian with a communist beard trying to gazump their funding bid. The last place in Europe a Romanian would come to pursue a career as a state-funded experimental artist would be Britain.

Of course, it is very easy for me, a middle-class man, economically shielded from any immediate negative impact of surges in immigration, to adopt a moderate attitude to the imminent arrival of 29 million Romanian vampire Gypsies coming to eat our children, but pointing this out won't stop the comments section under this article from going on and on about it. And I need an electrician. No one returns my calls.

Another goddamned appreciation of the late, lamented Bill Hicks

Observer, 1 March 2014

On the twentieth anniversary of Bill Hicks's death, journalists, many of them right-leaning libertarians trying to claim him for "their" side, wrote banal appreciations of his work, often characterised by a sort of fake American beatnik argot, of which Dominic Cavendish's in the Daily Telegraph, *barely tweaked below, was far and away the most embarrassing. The comedian Brendan Burns has kindly pointed out to me that I, like Hicks, am now the kind of overrated touchstone of quality critics and consumers who don't really know much about stand-up invoke as an indication of good taste.*

Twenty years after the tragic injustice of his goddamned death, isn't it time we canonised Bill Hicks as the best goddamned stand-up comedian contemporary broadsheet newspaper critics have ever heard of? If only for belatedly providing dozens of desperate hacks and pro-celebrity columnists working in the last days of the dying print media with the opportunity to crap out 1,000 words-plus of clichéd lazy banality, often in curious and inexplicable mid-Atlantic idioms, in every British newspaper costing more than £1.20.

The garbled hagiographies of the last week are doubtless what Bill P. Hicks would have wanted, whoever he was, I expect. I don't know. I was on a bill with him in Edinburgh sometime in the early '90s, but when he started going on and on about how he hated anti-smoking legislation I mistakenly thought he was just another Denis Leary clone and went off to the bar. But not knowing anything is no bar to writing a Bill Hicks's death anniversary column, it seems. So here goes:

Hicks came. Hicks saw. Hicks poured scornful, bilious, bileful scorn. Dude! Goddamned pancreatic cancer claimed that lone-some preacher's boy child to its cancerous bosom at the dagnabbit tragic early age of thirty-three. And broadsheet newspaper critics shan't see his like again – not in the main big four venues with the private media hospitality bars at the Edinburgh fringe, not from a press seat in the audience of a television stand-up showcase full of acts represented by the management arm of the production company that made it, not anywhere – in their lifetimes.

On the anniversary of his death, last Wednesday 25 February, broadsheet newspaper critics started smoking again, mixed up some of those legal high pills from Camden market in a sauce-pan of Waitrose cream of celery soup, and stared at their own melting, frightened faces in their shaving mirrors for two hours while listening to Hicks's orange-drink-packaging bit over and over again on repeat. They wept, remembering that they are now much older than they were in 1994, touched themselves down-stairs through wet driving gloves and breathed through gags made of clementines stuffed with Nicorette chewing gum. Great, so far as it goes, but all this was only a small token of esteem scaled against Hicks's immense talent. He made rare sense of the crazy roller-coaster ride we're all a-rollin' on.

Some people, I guess, might admire Hicks for the superficial allure of his self-destructive antics, which broadsheet newspaper critic eunuchs are secretly all jealous of: the smoking, the tight trousers, the kissing of women, the ridiculing of orange-drink packaging, the dangerously high platform shoes and the over-eating, all of which saw him lose his way. But Hicks wielded his comedy like a pointed stick with some dog muck on it, against an undead holocaust of orange-drink packaging and anti-smoking legislation and, in one riff, all of Billy Ray Cyrus.

It's no-prisoners-barred stuff. This Southern Baptist preach-er's son was the Shiva-esque scourge of society, but he pointed his dog-muck-smeared stick at his own failings too – his love of hardcore animal pornography, his fear of certain smells. And he was more than a stand-up comedian. He was a preacher. Dagnabbit, he was more than a goddamned preacher. He was a philosopher. Hell, he was more than a philosopher even. He was a prophet. Goddamit! Strike that from the record, your honour, if ye so please! Hicks was more even than a philosopher and yea even so more even than unto a simple prophet. He was a philosopher preacher prophet, a philosopher preacher prophet sage, a philosopher preacher prophet sage magus, a prophosopheacher sagus, no less, but dealing his sage-like prophetic philo-preachophy not in stone tablets sent down from on high in a bush, but in dick jokes shot out across a thousand pee-stained stages in the very worst dive bars of red-necked America. Hicks learnt his craft in places where people only went out to see live entertainment in order to attack and denigrate it, their hatred for performers exceeded only by their inexplicable desire to pay to watch them. We imagine.

Who is there that broadsheet newspaper critics have ever heard of who even comes close to what Bill H. Hicks was about? Frankie Boyle might have the same kick-to-the-nuts brain-freeze punch but it's too often focused through a filthy working-class Scottish ashtray lens that offends middle-class English critics' sensibilities. Russell Howard has been inspired by Hicks, and at his fulminating best – his recent riff on Golden Wonder Nik Naks a case in point – achieves the catalytic conversion that Hicks so often managed, like acrid cat's piss hitting offensively shiny linoleum. And when Peter Kay talks about higher planes of consciousness, there are clear points of comparison too. But who else except Hicks seems to have been injected as an unborn egg with such manifest semen of destiny to become the unfettered inner Leveson Inquiry of his own race, righteously baiting the uneducated, the ignorant, the fat, the poor, Billy Ray Cyrus and orange-drink packaging?

Broadsheet newspaper critics on the right imagine Hicks's

goddamned incredulity and dagnabbit derision would have sustained him against the holier-than-thou tyrannies of political correctness with which we have apparently been afflicted since his death. Indeed, to read some of them, you'd imagine that if he were here today, Bill Z. Hicks would have a weekly *Daily Telegraph* online blog alongside that bloke who keeps denying climate change and the one from the free-schools movement. But the fact is, the Right has never had anything cool to call its own in popular culture, and it never will, and it's too late to try and appropriate a dead man now, who can't defend himself against having some confused journalist's oiled fist rammed up his anus in an attempt to make him a ventriloquist's puppet for the anti-PC movement.

Hicks's first two albums have dated badly, with their adolescent potshots at inoffensive figures from popular culture and self-conscious rock'n'roll cool. But the bit on one of the later ones, where he uses Shane as a metaphor for American foreign policy, is a masterclass in performance, writing and softly spoken polemical sleight of hand. It ought to inspire anyone to do better, to be better. But it's easy to be a dead comedian, beatified for three hours of material. By twats and ghouls. The hard thing is to stay alive. And keep knocking out a new three hours every year. Gradually degrading the quality of your own obituary.

Sarah Vine sets a new bog standard. But will Mr Gove leave the seat up?

Observer, 16 March 2014

Sarah Vine boasted in her Daily Mail *column of sending her children to a state school, enjoying the moral high ground. But it was a selective Church of England school in an area of London ever more socially exclusive since her husband Michael "Adopted" Gove's party economically cleansed it. Whatever your position on the rights and wrongs of selective education, her comments were transparent bullshit.*

And yes, I did attend a fee-paying school. And yes, I did so on a part-scholarship and with a charity contribution based on my historic emergence from an establishment for "waifs and strays", and this in the 1970s, not the nineteenth century. I point all this out in columns whenever possible in order to minimise erroneous assumptions about my background, which are used to invalidate any genuine opinion I may appear to have; and also to play up to the idea that the person writing these columns would be drowning in middle-class guilt, which I, the person writing these columns, am, and as my children will be too, now and for ever more, if I raise 'em right.

My grandfather did drown flies in urine alongside me in Malta, but he was an RAF ground-crew member, not a combat pilot. On the same holiday, my mother watched some Maltese boys of my age, eight or so, unloading crates from a lorry, and compared my general incompetence unfavourably with their obvious practical skills.

Conservative politicians, and their husbands and wives, have always been obsessed with toilets. Last week's *Daily Mail* carried a full-page picture of Sarah Vine, partner of the education secretary, Michael Gove, emerging from a "bog standard" public toilet in Westminster, waving an ordinary toilet brush and declaring that her family will be using public toilets in future, and not the private facilities selected for the ablutions of the families of her husband's Etonian colleagues.

It's easy to be cynical about a politician's spouse using their family to score political points, but finding the original picture of Vine emerging from the Westminster toilet online, before Conservative HQ had cropped it, reveals an image every bit as damaging as that famously suppressed photo of George Osborne poking a proboscis monkey with a pencil.

True, Vine is holding an apparently ordinary toilet brush, of the sort ordinary people like the late Jade Goody or that woman who put the cat in the bin might use, but zoom in on it and it appears that the handle is made from the ivory of the severely endangered African forest elephant, which sells at a million pounds an ounce, while the bristles have been fashioned from the tail hairs of the virtually extinct white rhino. Is this the sort of toilet brush that would wave in the hand of, for example, ordinary folk like Jimmy Pursey from Sham 69 or rap's Dizzy Rascal?

Meanwhile, the tiny brown flecks on Vine's toilet brush are revealed not to be the excrement of ordinary people, like Ray Winstone or Dappy, but tiny flakes of Green and Black's organic Maya Gold dark chocolate, the most expensive chocolate in the world. And the transparent sheet of toilet paper flapping from it is not the tracing-paper type we might see wiping the bottoms of working-class heroes like White Dee or the late Bob Crow, but is in fact a gossamer-thin whisper of silk, provided by the top people's department store, Peter Jones of Sloane Square, official silk supplier to Michael Gove's family's bottoms.

View the picture in full, and Vine is not emerging from a "bog standard" public toilet at all, but from the marble edifice of Green Ernie's Church of England Toilet for Girls in Westminster, one of the least socially inclusive toilets in England. While the toilet is nominally open to the public, the majority of its customers are given keys on religious grounds, and a quarter on their ability to work the hand-dryers properly, and when you have factored in the exclusivity of its location and the wealth one would need to move into its economically cleansed catchment area today, the political exploitation of Vine's egalitarian toilet choice begins to look crass. What would Jesus do? It's impossible to say, but like the new pope, he would probably have chosen the tracing-paper toilet tissue on purpose.

That said, it is difficult to criticise anyone for the choices they make where their family's toilets are concerned. The Free Toilets Movement, championed by the BBC TV personality Toby Young, aimed to liberate toilets from the interference of the state, allowing toilet users to make their own choices as regards soap brands, toilet-paper texture and whether the graffiti should be in Latin, like in Pompeii. In setting up the pioneering Hammersmith Free Toilet, Young won hearts and minds by explaining there was no guarantee that, once his new experimental toilet was built, his own family would even be allowed to use it. But then, just at the last minute, the rules changed and they were.

(In the interests of full disclosure, I must admit that I made enthusiastic use of fee-paying private toilet facilities during my teens, having been granted access to them via a bursary for "waifs and strays", and as a result of scoring highly in a test of my abilities to drown flies while using the boys' urinal trough. In the further interests of further full disclosure, I should also admit that I was privately tutored in this skill, during a family holiday in Malta in the mid-1970s, by my grandfather, who had been a gunner in the RAF in the Second World War.)

While it's difficult to censure Vine for making use of a system that was open to her, it's harder to accommodate the exploitation of that choice, of that cultural and geographical privilege, for political ends. The ginger tomcat from down the road came in through our cat flap last night and defecated, twice, in the kitchen. It appears to have the same electronic cat-flap collar key as our cat, and so has unlimited access to the house. I saw the first piece of cat excrement, by the radiator, at about 8 a.m. this morning while giving the children their porridge. I cleaned it up, mopped the floor with disinfectant, and washed both of my hands, then slapped them together three or four times and shook them out twice, the international Oliver Hardy gesture for having completed an unpleasant task.

Later on, my wife, having seen the second piece of cat excrement, by the window, which I hadn't noticed, accused me of deliberately ignoring it. She said I had left it for her to remove, having misunderstood that when the three-year-old told her that Daddy had "seen the cat poo", she was referring to the first piece of cat excrement, which I had already dealt with. It was not even nine o'clock and already our day had descended into the usual accusation and counter-accusation.

But I bear the ginger cat that defecated in our kitchen no ill will. It did nothing wrong. There is no active moral dimension to the cat's choice of toilet location. Finding itself in our house, in an increasingly gentrified part of Hackney where less well-off cats will soon be a rarity, it merely took advantage of the best toilet facilities available to it. The cat is without blame. What would have annoyed me would have been if the cat had then written a thousand-word piece for the *Daily Mail* implying that the lovely kitchen it was privileged enough to be allowed to defecate in, by virtue of the accident of its postcode and its electronic collar access key, made it in some way morally superior to other cats.

The maggots that changed my life (and the future of the Tory party)

Observer, 23 March 2014

Grant Shapps was another politician of this period who, like Gove, seemed inherently absurd to me, to the point where he became a kind of comedy character independent of his actual self. After the March 2014 Budget he sent a tweet saying, "Cutting the Bingo tax and beer duty: To help hardworking people do more of the things they enjoy." He was then accused of having a patronising attitude to ordinary people.

There was a maggot-vending machine on Tollington Park when I lived there in the '90s. I never saw anyone using it. In my first few years in London, doing temp jobs in the day and open spots at comedy clubs late in the evenings, I made all sorts of odd small-hours friends that I never see now: a "techno-pagan" of Indian parentage; a man I never saw sober who could recite whole Herbert Huncke poems; a woman on acid who everyone thought must be crashing in the shared house's sitting room at someone else's invitation, but who it turned out no one really knew; and PJ, who ate light bulbs, and who may or may not have been Terry Scott's cousin and Ben Dover's stunt double. I miss those days.

From 1989 to 1991 I lived in Finsbury Park, decades before it began to show signs of gentrification. I'd get home late from unpaid stand-up try-out spots, and it was hard to hold down a day job. At the end of my street, outside a hardware shop on Tollington Park, was a contraption so unusual that each night, in a state of adrenaline-driven imbalance, I would find myself staring at it in the small hours in bleak fascination. It was a maggot-vending machine, faintly glowing, dimly humming, and stuffed with millions of live maggots throbbing gently en masse in a barely warmed state of collective suspended animation. As a younger, and more impressionable, man I couldn't help but find it vaguely profound.

One hot July night in 1990, around 1.30 a.m., I was staring at the maggot machine as usual, a contraband comedy-club can of Carlsberg in hand, thinking about the maggots as metaphors for something or other, when my musings were interrupted by a sharply dressed young man, of around my age, emerging from a van bearing the legend "House of Maggots". "Excuse me, sir," he said, politely, "maggot maintenance," and he wheeled over a pallet of plastic cool boxes. Unlocking the maggot machine he began to pour gallons of immobilised maggots into it, topping up the depleted stock within.

"Can I have a look, mate?" I asked. "I walk past this machine every night and I've wondered how it works." "By all means," said the man, and helped me up with a politeness and confidence that my prejudiced assumptions hadn't led me to expect in a man who vended maggots. Beneath me, millions of maggots pulsated slowly in comatose contentment. "I keep them just warm enough to live," he said, "but not hot enough to get excited, nor cold enough to expire. Here, pour this on them. It's their food." The man handed me a sachet of yeasty-smelling flakes and I sprinkled it over the ignorant maggots.

"You're out late," the maggot man said, as he locked up the machine. "I'm trying to be a comedian," I replied. "I get back late from all these try-out gigs and the buzz keeps me awake. It's making it hard to hold on to temp jobs." "Oh," the man said. "Can you drive?" One cup of tea at an all-night cafe in Crouch End later and I became House of Maggots' second-ever staff member.

Each night after my try-out gigs I would get a train up to Watford to meet Grant, who patrolled his patch (principally London, and vast swathes of Norfolk and Suffolk, where early-morning anglers gathered by his machines in lay-bys and car parks), nocturnally maintaining his maggot empire. Like me, Grant had left further education a year previously, having studied finance at Manchester Polytechnic. One morning, setting off early on a fishing trip with an uncle who had forgotten to pack live bait, Grant spotted a gap in the market that his business brain could exploit. And House of Maggots was born.

There was less traffic in the night-time, and between midnight and morning Grant and I swiftly circumnavigated his machines in a minivan full of permanently chilled larvae. Pretty soon our roles were established. I did all the heavy lifting and driving, while Grant sat in the passenger seat doing paperwork, maintaining his swelling maggot supply lines. Grant's enthusiasm was infectious. I liked him, though we rarely saw eye to eye on politics. Mick Jones from The Clash was Grant's cousin, and we'd blast his tapes from the tinny stereo, singing along to the words while debating the sentiment.

"How can you like The Clash", I asked Grant, "when you're obviously a Tory entrepreneur?" "Easy," he answered. "A protest group like The Clash? They're extremely valuable. The disgruntled proles go and see them on a Saturday night, get drunk, jump around, and feel like their grievances have been addressed. Then they're much happier going back to being wage slaves for the rest of the week." I laughed. Back then I assumed Grant was joking. "Out you get," he continued, "and don't forget to feed the maggots."

One night, as I was topping up a maggot machine in a lay-by near Thetford, an angler arrived to fill a Tupperware box with comatose larvae. While he made small talk he threaded the fattest maggots onto a succession of hooks, spiking them between two black, eye-like markings on one end. It seems silly to write about it now, but when I got back in the van with Grant I felt a twinge of conscience. "Grant," I said, "don't you ever feel bad about this? We spend the absolute minimum on maintaining those barely alive maggots, just so someone can buy them and then throw them to their deaths?" "My dear fellow," he said, buoyant as ever, "the maggots are comfortable, and they're fed, and they're warm-ish. They are serving an economic purpose. Their pointless existence is being monetised. I validate them."

When I got my first unpaid half spot at the old Comedy Store, on the east side of Leicester Square, in December 1990, I told Grant I was quitting, and he kindly came to see the show. The hot Saturday-night sweat box was stuffed with drunken revellers, packed together at 2 a.m. in tight rows like sardines, though I got the feeling Grant saw them as something else. I stumbled through a typical anti-Tory alternative-comedy set and Grant handed me a good-luck card. When I got home I realised it contained the most eloquently written letter of encouragement and £50 in cash. I never saw Grant again.

Grant left House of Maggots, by then a successful outfit with nine employees, in 1997, when he stood as a Conservative MP, but remained a director until 2009, three years before he became chairman of the Conservative Party. The skills Grant picked up in marketing maggots seemed to have deserted him earlier this week, when he blundered onto Twitter with an ill-judged graphic about the Budget that swiftly sent the social network into melt-down. But I liked Grant back then and I still like him now, despite never actually having met him. Grant just wants all hard-working people to be content, fit for purpose and able to do more of the things they enjoy.

"Stewart, I have to say that Grant's generosity of spirit shines through a lot more than yours in this article. I also have to say that I have never heard the word 'prole' used seriously in conversation about the working class: ever. Just maybe he was hamming up your prejudicial thoughts about him (you admit to prejudice after all) as a way of connecting with you, despite your clear opposition to his values. Values, what's more, that gave you paid work tailored to your needs at the time. You might want to reflect on that before assassinating characters in order to publicise your gigs." Robert Kelsey WSY

Why I'm a leading contender for the Great British fruitcake bake off

Observer, 4 May 2014

It's difficult to remember now, but in the twelve months leading up to the 2015 election, UKIP were big news, a major political party, and gold dust for lazy liberal comedians like me. But the Tories absorbed UKIP's most appealing attitudes and promised, foolishly, a European referendum, and the party more or less melted away. I can't even remember what inspired the column below. It was probably something to do with the perception that UKIP were being given a hard time by the so-called liberal media, whatever that was, and being called fruitcakes. I appear to have cut and pasted and then rewritten various speeches by UKIP politicians and supporters, including the anti-women's trousers tycoon Demetri Marchessini, the "gays cause floods" bloke David Silvester, Godfrey "sluts" Bloom and Nigel Farage himself. At the time of writing, April 2016, I feel it will be a shame if we end up leaving Europe because Cameron caved in to these twats. And I am writing this in France, where I came to get away from British people.

As home-made fruitcakes continue to rise in the nation's ovens, the political and culinary establishments are sinking to even greater depths to smear them. In some Birmingham schools, traditional Christmas cake, the famous fruitcake of English festive celebration since Dickens's day, has even been banned. But moist fruitcakes composed of dried fruit, flour, margarine, eggs and spirits have made delicious British teatime treats for centuries. What better combination of tastes is there than a pint of foaming ale, a Totally Wicked e-cigarette and a slice of flavoursome fruitcake? But could a fruitcake represent British interests in the European Parliament? Many believe so.

I have always delighted, quite innocently and without malice towards anyone, in fruitcakes. Fruitcakes are literally in my DNA. Anyone that knows me will tell you I am rarely to be found without a slice of fruitcake or, indeed, an entire fruitcake, concealed somewhere about my person, or upon that of my wife, who should be following respectfully behind me.

Indeed, during a midlife-crisis mania for baking a few years ago, my gooseberry drizzle was so enthusiastically gobbled up by a Greek tycoon at a fundraising cake stall that I was forced to subject him to the indignity of a swift Heimlich manoeuvre. Having been slapped heartily on the back Demetri spat out not only the fruitcake, but also ten thousand pounds in cash, which I swiftly pocketed, along with the fruitcake fragments and a copy of his fascinating book, *Women in Trousers – A Rear View*.

I bloody love fruitcakes, though. Sometimes my fruitcakes mania reaches such a peak that, having sourced the fruitcake ingredients, I haven't even the self-control to wait to bake them, and on more than one occasion my wife has found me hiding in the en suite, swilling a mixture of dried fruit, flour, margarine, bicarbonate of soda and some egg around in my mouth with brandy, mainlining fruitcake mix into myself like a bloody madman.

I like British fruitcakes most of all, made from indigenous British fruits, like a red apple, for example, and have no time for foreign fruitcakes: the Italian *torta alla frutta*; the French *gâteau aux fruits*; and the Jamaican ackee pancake. I think if Jamaican fruitcakes come to this country and don't like mixing with our fruitcakes, why are they here?

I just like to eat fruitcakes made from fruits I am familiar with and comfortable around. I shouldn't be forced to eat fruitcakes made from foreign fruits from Bongo Bongo Land, and indeed I never am. No one is. (I am partial to the Irish Halloween fruitcake, barmbrack, but find I can never stomach much more than the top right-hand corner before it starts to make me feel queasy.)

On balance, though, despite these caveats I would declare myself an enormous fruitcakes fan.

Sadly, work commitments, and a repetitive strain injury to my drinking and saluting arm, mean my days stirring the mixing bowl at the fruitcakes front line are long gone. My wife, who is a German lady with little time for British fruitcakes, is not prepared to bake my fruitcakes recipes for the small financial incentives I offer her. She buys me instead ready-made fruitcakes from Aldi, defying my will at every opportunity, the slut.

Women should be banned from buying fruitcakes in shops. Women used to make fruitcakes for thousands of years. Did you know that until 300 years ago a woman seen buying a fruitcake would be executed? They don't taste as nice as the home-made ones. Mass-produced fruitcakes don't excite men. Only home-made fruitcakes excite men. If they stop making fruitcakes, then men are going to stop fucking them, do you understand?

And may I tell you with great respect that if men don't make love to women, the western world is going to disappear? When you get married, you promise to look after the other person for the rest of their life. You certainly don't promise that you're going to go to Aldi to buy fruitcakes. If you bake fruitcakes on Friday and bake fruitcakes on Sunday, you can't say Saturday is Aldi. Once a woman accepts, she accepts, and especially when she makes a vow on her wedding day.

Fruitcakes must be home-baked. But some people go out at night and they pick up five, ten, fifteen different fruitcakes in one night. They just all go out looking for supermarket fruitcakes. That's the way it is. The scriptures make it abundantly clear that a Christian nation that abandons its home-baked fruitcakes will be beset by natural disasters such as storms, disease, pestilence and war. I wrote to David Cameroon in April 2012 to warn him that disasters would accompany the sale of supermarket fruit-cakes. It is his fault that large swathes of the nation have been afflicted by storms and floods. No man, however powerful, can mess with Almighty God with impunity and get away with it.

My local Waitrose stocks an award-winning *panforte*, a variety of fruitcake from Tuscany, apparently. I rang up my close friend Tim Rice, the lyricist of *Jesus Christ Superstar*, and shouted at him: "Can someone explain please how *panforte*, a Tuscan fruitcake, has won an award in Great Britain? This is no longer a nation that I recognise as my own." Today, I must take whatever fruitcakes crumbs of comfort I can find in the fruitcakes of others. And thus it was with no small degree of excitement that I heard the news, last Thursday morning, that 38 per cent of British people were considering voting for fruitcakes (home-baked) to represent British interests in Europe.

The possibilities were thrilling. Suppose a fruitcake won? I wonder how big a fruitcake would have to be for a small and slender man like myself to hide inside it? If I was to conceal my body within the fruitcake for a whole day, while it was shipped out to Brussels, would I need an air supply, beer to drink, fruit-cake to eat, Totally Wicked e-cigarettes to suck on, and some of Tim Rice's most rousing music on an iPod to inspire me? ("Take That Look Off Your Face" from *Tell Me on a Sunday*, probably.) If I dressed up in my home-made uniform, would the epaulettes, ceremonial daggers and cap badges set off the metal detectors? Imagine! Imagine the looks on their stupid faces. They think they have voted in a harmless fruitcake and then out I jump! Ha!

"Another shill for bourgeois Liberalism." Edmund Beurk

Sex and drugs? Real rock rebels are into tax-efficient accountancy abuse

Observer, 18 May 2014

Last week, it was confirmed that Gary Barlow, Mark Owen and Howard "The Duck" Donald, the key talents of legendary rock'n'rollers Take That, hid £63 million in the Icebreaker tax-avoidance scheme. Barlow's crime may cause short-lived shame, but it could guarantee the Take That frontispiece an eternal place in the rock'n'roll annals that his music (a regular presence on David Cameron's Spotify account) might not. Sid Vicious, Pete Doherty and Screaming Lord Sutch can step down. Gary Barlow is now the most offensive rock'n'roller of all!

Rock'n'roll has always given young people the means to offend the petty sensibilities of society, from Elvis Presley's lascivious legs and Freddie Garrity's cruel dances, via the furious bile of punk rock'n'rollers The Jags, Bad Manners and The Pork Dukes, to the sexual explosives of Bucks Fizz's Eurovision thighs, Miley Cyrus's plucked chicken wrecking-ball lick and Dennis Roussos's diaphanous sack.

But for me, and many other part-time pop-cultural critics, rock'n'roll as an art form of offence appeared to have reached its apogee in the work of the late GG Allin. Allin delighted the American hardcore rock'n'roll scene of the late '80s and early '90s by performing naked, having swallowed vast amounts of laxatives, before bellowing violently misanthropic lyrics, maiming himself, defecating on stage, throwing his excrement into the crowd and inflicting often actionable degrees of physical damage on audience members. But at heart, Allin was still an entertainer, pledged to put on a good show for the paying public, no different to TV's Dara O'Briain or World War II's Dame Vera Lynn.

Though he had always promised to commit suicide during a show, a defeated Allin finally walked off stage in Manhattan in June 1993, sporting just soiled briefs, his body smeared with blood and droppings, and into a fatal heroin overdose. Gary Barlow, in contrast, performed before the Queen at her Diamond Jubilee concert wearing a scrupulously clean thong, received an OBE for his services to charity in 2012, and once climbed Kilimanjaro with Fearne Cotton for Comic Relief, the latter an image more disturbing than anything a google of Allin will throw up.

But, to paraphrase an old vaudeville act, who is the real sick man? Is it GG Allin, singing "Bite It You Scum" in dirty knickers, beating himself over the head with the microphone until his skull bleeds, masturbating furiously and kicking audience members in the teeth? Or is it Gary Barlow of Take That, in his suit and tie, conscientiously following his accountant's advice to invest in a tax-avoidance scheme, while soliciting other people's money for charity and denying the most vulnerable members of society the benefit of his personal financial contribution? It is Gary Barlow. Obviously.

In *Hated*, a documentary about his former employer, GG Allin's drummer, Donald "Dino Sex" Sachs, suggests Allin's scatological, sadomasochistic performances had some satirical purpose, or were a form of social commentary; that Allin intended to compare his own zany plop antics with "a society that's going crazy with violence". I wish that were true, though I'm not sure Allin's posthumous body of work has the rigorous theoretical scaffolding required to sustain a consistent ideological or aesthetic position. That said, there doesn't seem to have been much difference between Allin's private faces and his public faeces.

Gary Barlow is a far more complex character than GG Allin, despite also choosing to place his artworks within the broad field of light entertainment. Though convicted of an appallingly violent assault in 1989, Allin was nonetheless a kind of punk *bouffon*, and one that the clown guru Philippe Gaulier would have recognised, inviting us to hate him, self-consciously taking on the mantle of the folk devil. In contrast to Allin, Gary Barlow publicly accepted an OBE for his good works, despite privately playing his part in closing hospitals, schools, shelters and women's refuges across the land. Allin's life was a performance. Barlow's life is an act.

The paper trail linking Gary Barlow to a homeless man expiring in an empty building is convoluted. Allin's culpability follows a more obvious sequence of cause and effect. He ate laxatives. This caused him to soil himself. He then threw his filth around, and if it hit you in the face you might get an illness. But compared with Barlow's tax avoidance, Allin's actions seem simple, uncontrived, honest – noble, even. His onstage offences were transient, as ephemeral as the sudden impact of a ball of dung in the eye. But who knows at what age Barlow began planning to present the public face of a charitable do-gooder, while secretly scheming to deprive the weak and vulnerable of succour, if indeed he ever did so? To quote Karlheinz Stockhausen's oft-misunderstood comments on the 9/11 atrocity, Barlow's career might be the devil's "greatest work of art that is possible in the whole cosmos". Allin aimed to be the ultimate rock'n'roll degenerate, but as an icon of filth, Barlow has surpassed him.

To be charitable to Barlow, we might perhaps see the same sort of satirical purpose in songs like "Back for Good", "Shine" and the other ones, all of which now taste of ashes and earwax, that defenders of GG Allin attribute to songs like "Kiss Me in the Gutter" and "Suck My Ass It Smells". In creating this "Gary Barlow" character who raises money for charity while simultaneously trampling our shared values into the urinal trough, was Barlow in fact (like the comedy of Jimmy Carr or Ricky Gervais at its best) holding up a mirror to society, magnifying our hypocrisy through the lens of his own actions? Who can say? But the fact remains, today's young people, anxious to offend as ever, need to embrace the opportunity Barlow has offered them to discover an avatar of offence that is entirely appropriate to our corrupt era.

Grubby T-shirts of Vicious and Cobain and Doherty all seem so twentieth century. In the current climate of cuts and austerity, drugs and violence are silly schoolyard crimes compared with massive corporate and individual tax avoidance. In 1976, Vivienne Westwood made T-shirts of a violent masked criminal. Couldn't some enterprising young fashion designer today employ Barlow's Cameron-endorsed visage as a similar cipher for off-the-peg prêt-à-porter moral transgression? How brilliantly and thrillingly offensive would it be for today's teens to parade around in T-shirts bearing the smiling face of Gary Barlow OBE?

"Who the hell is Dennis Roussos?!? DEMIS ffs!!" Lockie Baws

The search for the nation's identity: my part in Cameron's odyssey

Observer, 15 June 2014

Some background. Birmingham schools were suspected of promoting Islamism, and a debate on British values ensued; Rory Stewart, the acceptable face of the Conservative Party, did genuinely ask me to join a human chain of friendship across the Scottish border, but I suspected this might make things worse; my friend, the comedian, and former Balamory *actor, Miles Jupp, is the only person I know who has been immortalised as a wash mitt; and I was once asked onto a Radio 4 discussion about blasphemy with the Muslim Council of Britain's Inayat Bunglawala, after Muslims had issued death threats to Danish cartoonists. Rabbi Sachs was in the green room and embraced Inayat, saying, "How can we address the terrible wrong that has been done to your beliefs?" He did not embrace me, though a terrible wrong had been done to my beliefs too.*

On Wednesday evening a high-level spook I had known vaguely at Oxford, a former Etonian and a Bullingdon Club chum of David Cameron's, rang me up with interesting findings and a resistible offer. "You've been following this Birmingham schools thing, Lee?" "Yes," I replied. "It's outrageous. No child should have to go to school in Birmingham." "Very funny," said the spook. "But what do you make of it?" "Well, Doug," I answered, "it appears that where education is concerned, all faiths are equal, but some are more equal than others." "Don't be smart, Lee. People's lives are at risk. This could kick off into a bloody civil war. Luckily, Dave's got a plan."

Indeed he had. Like a man distracting his children's attention from a terrible car crash by pointing at a funny pig, David Cameron had deftly skirted the ideological collapse of the education system by saying all schools had to teach British values, and then disappearing back into his office before anyone had the audacity to ask what that actually meant.

As he monitors all communications of any sort all the time, Doug had noticed that my stand-up comedy act was much discussed online by the sort of fidgety middle-class liberals inherently sceptical about notions of patriotism. Doug wanted me to fill a gaping hole in an emergency celebrity think tank in Westminster the following morning, aiming to produce a workable definition of British Values as quickly as possible.

This definition could then be translated into Welsh, Gaelic, Cornish, Polish, Bulgarian, Romanian and Urdu, printed up on massive boards mounted on the front of intimidating armoured personnel carriers, and driven around areas with high immigrant populations by masked gunmen, instructed to shoot on sight anyone who so much as tutted at them.

There was no fee for the focus group, but unlimited Fanta and party eggs were to be provided for all the celebrities, and each of the entertainers was to be given a £4 voucher to spend in the House of Commons bar at the end of the day. The token could not, however, be exchanged for sparkling water or continental beers, which were to be paid for at a till linked directly to an account in Luxembourg, as part of an arrangement organised by the chancellor.

It was not the first time I had been invited to help shore up British national interests. Earlier this year, the famous adventurer Rory Stewart had asked me to be part of a continuous "Auld Lang Syne" of E-list celebrities, their arms linked along the border in a gesture of Anglo–Scots solidarity. I was to take my place on Adrian's Wall, joining hands with the Scottish folk singer Dick Gaughan and a life-size wash mitt of Archie, the Laird of Balamory.

Gaughan, a staunch nationalist, declined, and the foamy

Archie mitt became saturated with tepid bathwater and collapsed in on itself, uselessly. Besides which, my own opposition to Scottish independence had by then collapsed too. In the light of UKIP's success I now rather wished that I too could become independent of Britain and Farage's bewildering policy void. Nonetheless, anxious to defer bloodshed in my home town of Birmingham, the city of a thousand faiths, I accepted Doug's offer.

The next morning, Thursday, I found my letter box compromised by a free copy of the *Sun* newspaper, which was aiming to win new readers. In the wake of UKIP's success and our forthcoming national football fever, 22 million patriotic editions of a special England issue were delivered free to unwitting households all across Britain. Some made landfall in beatnik hipster urban zones such as mine, where the paper was so rarely seen by human eyes that it had assumed a folkloric air, like the Sasquatch or the kelpie.

I was to be charged later that day with defining a national identity – Britishness – and the collective good was at stake. Tangentially, the *Sun* was struggling with a similar conundrum. The paper was trying to define Englishness, through the thoughtful writings of my fellow celebrity columnists James Corden, Tony Parsons, Jeremy Clarkson, Katie Hopkins and Rod Liddle. If anyone could wrestle this age-old problem to the mat, it was this dream team of clockwork opinion monkeys. Perhaps I could learn something that would be useful later that day.

For Parsons, the English are "gentle, tolerant . . . and love animals and freedom . . . and hate people who aren't polite". Parsons's definition of Englishness sounds like a transcript of the envelope upon which Ricky Gervais worked out his Derek character. Hopkins maintains she's English because if you cut her to the core, her blood's "red, white and blue", which presumably means Katie washed her England flag along with a non-colour-fast Conservative Party HQ sauna wash mitt. Corden appears in the paper in knitted tie, his face painted with a cross of St George, looking like the Man at C&A version of the Christian soldier who goes crazy and dynamites the Cajun's shack in *Southern Comfort*. The image illustrates his column. There is no need to read his column.

A *Sgt Pepper*-style *Sun* collage of 117 definitive English people included James Corden, Simon Cowell, Boris Johnson, Michael McIntyre, David Cameron, Jeremy Clarkson and Nigel Farage, but no Mark E. Smith, William Blake, Mary Wollstonecraft, Ted Chippington or Pauline Black from The Selecter, which my superior version would have boasted. At which point during the preparation of the artwork was Gary Barlow crossed out? When did they realise they'd forgotten to include Rik Mayall, who narrowly escaped this unasked-for honour?

Doubtless the *Sun*'s choices exemplify Englishness to someone, but not to me. It was as if ideals of identity were almost entirely subjective. Making David Cameron's dream of a definition of Britishness a living reality was going to take some doing.

I arrived at Westminster at 8 a.m., ready for a day of defining national identity with the other key British celebrities hurriedly assembled by Cameron's advisers: Inayat Bunglawala of the Muslim Council of Britain, Judaism's Rabbi Sachs, television's June Sarpong, *Top Gear*'s Richard Hammond, thought's Brian Eno, women's PJ Harvey, history's David Starkey, comedy's Leo X. Muhammad, Scotland's Lulu, Northern Ireland's Van Morrison and Wales's Gorky's Zygotic Mynci. Rabbi Sachs embraced each of us in turn at length, weeping; Hammond began sucking hard on a Calippo; Van Morrison took off his wellington. The debate had begun.

Want to know what's really killing Christmas? Just ask Ben Stiller . . .

Observer, 14 December 2014

People blame the death of Christmas as they remember it principally on "political correctness" and never on commercialism, capitalism, mass media, the redefining of the traditional family unit, the existence of more than just three TV channels, or the simple fact that they aren't five any more and it isn't 1972. It isn't Islam or gays that hawk out the very sky of Oxford Street itself to advertise crap every December, is it? I paid to take my kids to see Night at the Museum 3 *and it was lazy shit.*

Every year since I can remember, it seems something has been killing Christmas: commercialism; multiculturalism; secularism; or that political correctness of the "gone mad" variety that they have now. This is not a new idea. An ancient cave daub, dating from 10,000 BC, on the walls of the Grotte de Niaux in southern France appears to show a Neolithic man tutting at a cave child who has ignored a perfectly serviceable flint in order to play with the leaf it came packaged in. Like an elderly Christmas reindeer that can no longer illuminate its own nose, Christmas continues to cling to life, damp December tinsel fluttering in a February gutter. But this year I feel the fatal body blow may finally have been dealt.

On 16 November the three members of the shamed defensive tax-planning unit Take That arrived in London to turn on the Regent Street Christmas lights. This year the Christmas lights take as their theme the third film in the successful *Night at the Museum* franchise, *Night at the Museum 3: Secret of the Tomb*. And nothing says Christmas like a trio of broken dead-eyed tax-avoiding husks pulling on an imitation joystick purporting to throw into life dozens of enormous illuminated images of Ben Stiller's face, hanging obscenely in the once-empty air, a stale and unprofitable space between the buildings now at last actively monetised, thank Christ. Merry Christmas. Merry Christmas. God bless us everyone.

Stiller, the star of *Night at the Museum 3: Secret of the Tomb*, is in town to promote *Night at the Museum 3: Secret of the Tomb*. Stiller and I have mutual acquaintances, principally in the podcasting community admittedly, but I ask his people if I can meet him, cynically hoping he will say something facile about London's festive *Night at the Museum 3: Secret of the Tomb* Christmas lights that I can spin out into a space-occupying *Observer* column.

Stiller elects to meet at a Soho pancake joint. The comedian is, it turns out, obsessed with pancakes, confessing, "It's the one vice I have left. As soon as I get to a new city I say to the runner, 'Show me the pancakes.' I like to go to a new pancake store and sniff each of the pancakes in turn before I choose one. If I could die and come back as a pancake, I would. I wish my nutsack was full of pancake mix so I could make my own on demand. Christine made undershorts out of pancakes at Thanksgiving. I felt really happy wearing them but in the end they just weren't practical and after a few days they rotted away. *C'est la vie*, my friend, *c'est la* fucking *vie* already."

Stiller, dressed casually in trousers, socks, shoes, underpants, shirt, jumper and jacket, orders a large plain pancake with no syrup, and a mug of pancake mix, which he downs in one, slamming the mug hard on the table afterwards like a shot glass. "Hoo hah!" he shouts, sweating and suddenly agitated, "Bisquick!" Stiller wipes stray mix off his lips using his uneaten pancake as a napkin, and clicks his fingers to the waitress for more mix. "Do you think maybe you could warm it up this time, honey, if it's not too much trouble?" he barks, Hollywood style, before turning his ire on me.

"Don't think I don't know why you've brought me here, Stew Art," he begins. "You think I'm a joke, don't you, Mr Too-Cool-for-School? I'm the once-radical innovator of *Reality Bites* and *The Ben Stiller Show*, the comedy voice of Generation X, reduced to shilling for serving three of a mainstream movie franchise that appears to have done a marketing tie-in deal with a major religious festival. That's what you think. Well, do I look that dumb to you, I mean, do I? Maybe, just maybe, I've been playing a long game."

The pancake mix, warm this time, arrives, and as Stiller drinks it down, staring at me, he continues between hearty gulps. "Ben Stiller is in the mainstream now, Stew Art," he whispers, menacingly, "in deep. And the power and influence this position affords Ben Stiller has allowed Ben Stiller to embark upon the first of a series of pornographic spectacles which, when viewed through the lens of history, will reveal Ben Stiller as the greatest satirist that ever lived, a person whose very life became a conscious commentary on global corruption. More mix!"

The pancake mix arrives. Stiller barks at me, "What's my most famous scene?" I hesitate. "Say it. Don't be ashamed." "Well," I admit sheepishly, "it's when your penis gets trapped in your flies in that film." "That's right, it is," he agrees, "and you know what, I played it brilliantly. I tried to make a face that wouldn't preclude my character being either circumcised or uncircumcised, so the scene would play for maximum comic effect in all territories, irrespective of their penis traditions." "Yes, I'd often thought you must be doing that," I agreed, "it's very clever."

"It is clever," Stiller reiterates, "but I know that when people look up in London and see the *Night at the Museum 3: Secret of the Tomb* Christmas lights, they aren't going to be thinking about peace on earth, goodwill to all men and all that jizz. No, like it or not, they're going to be thinking about a guy's schlong trapped in his zipper. I just torpedoed Christmas. And you deserve it. You say Christmas is dead, and you blame immigrants and imaginary liberal cabals imposing non-existent PC diktats, but all along it was capitalism, man. And now I've engineered a situation that ought to make that totally obvious, holding up the mirror to your corruption, but you're so blind."

"So you're living your whole life henceforth, the promotional duties, the lights, as a satirical critique that will only make sense in the future? You're masterminding everything?" I ask. "Not everything, Stew Art," Stiller replies. "Sometimes a creative talent like me sets an idea in motion and it takes on a life of its own. I didn't ask for three tax avoiders to throw the switch. London chose Take That. But it's too, too perfect. If I'd planned that, it would have seemed too heavy-handed, sledgehammer subtle. But London chose Take That, and with no sense of it being the crowning obscenity. Some days you're just lucky, I guess. Try the pancake mix. It's delicious."

I've had it with comedy awards – and so has my bounty hunter alter ego

Observer, 21 December 2014

I am a stand-up comedian. Last Tuesday, I attended the British Comedy Awards, my first since 1991. Today the awards are an edited Channel 4 highlights package from a Wembley warehouse, but back in '91, in their second year, they were a prime-time ITV Saturday-night live spectacular in a big South Bank studio. I wrote for Radio 4's *On the Hour*, which was up for best radio comedy, a category which, like best live comedian, has now been dropped to make space for TV faces. Broadcasters are no longer required to honour their general arts-coverage remit, so there's more time for revenue-generating film of newsreaders eating insects. Slaves, rattle your chains. Are you all enjoying your new freedoms? What a difference twenty-three years makes.

I was working the next two times I was up for British Comedy awards, nearly two decades later, and absconded. But people had raised money for the rights to release the third series of *Stewart Lee's Comedy Vehicle* commercially, which was nominated this year, so I thought I should go, as it's hard to make the stake back in a world where the public expect to steal all content for nothing.

Besides which, I have become the sort of person who declines to attend events on principle, but where my absence is not noticed anyway. When I won two British Comedy awards in 2011, it wasn't mentioned in any newspapers. And my 2012 BAFTA acceptance speech was cut from TV, perhaps because I told the presenter, Kate Thornton, that acclaim was a random phenomenon, like cloud patterns, into which you read significance at your peril.

Nonetheless, the thought of going to the British Comedy Awards was terrifying. In a possibly psychosomatic state, the flesh on my lower left leg had taken on a Play-Doh texture, and I could move it around in clumps beneath my skin. Could the thought of having to sit alongside celebs I'd done routines about have brought this on? Or was I a new kind of human, like Sir Ian McKellen or Janelle Monáe? Then I thought, what if I don't go? What if I sent a different version of myself instead, more confident, better dressed?

Hiding in plain sight, barely in regulation black tie, I arrived at Wembley in a tassled Native American jacket, rodeo shirt, braided bola necktie and snakeskin boots. I was a half-breed tracker, a bounty hunter, behind the lines in enemy territory. I ploughed straight through the mandatory photo-ops corridor un-photographed, the Ghost Who Walks, and into the hospitality room, where I shook hands with people I'd ridiculed and sipped red wine, his drink, not mine. And when Jonathan Ross slagged me off from the stage the outlaw me was still reading the awards programme unaware of what was said. The camera caught this, and I transcended the whole charade. "Are you laughing at my mule?"

They got to my categories, best male TV comic and best comedy entertainment programme. Lee Mack got the first, and Graham Norton the second. And I realised I'd been lying to myself. Through a mixture of indefensible arrogance and mathematical logic, I had assumed, without acknowledging it, I'd win both. I'd won both for the second series, three years back, and the third series was demonstrably better than the second, so what had changed?

Don't misunderstand me. I don't think for a moment I am the best stand-up in Britain, and if this was an award for live stand-up, and I was up against any of the hundreds of inspirational acts I see on the live circuit, then I would never have been arrogant enough to assume that I deserved anything. But this was TV stand-up, live stand-up's idiotic attic-bound relation, and a world through which I soar like a mighty eagle through a cloud of diseased gnats.

Lee and Graham accepted their awards on video. My acceptance speeches, which, I realised with a sudden regretful surge, I had composed unconsciously in my head that week, had things positive and not untrue to say about the other nominees, but Lee said nothing and Graham said he didn't even know who he was up against. I was shocked. I realised I had convinced myself I was here to help the DVD investors, but I had been entangled by vanity and ambition. I had chosen to attend the British Comedy Awards, which, once attended, could not be unattended, like the worm-ridden dog egg in the infant-school playground which, once seen, cannot be unseen.

There were six people on our table. The bottle of red had disappeared, and with it my cowboy–Indian creation. I had turned to pear cider in search of answers and soon I was me again, fearful and drowning. The button popped on my rodeo shirt. It wasn't mine to wear. Jack Whitehall won king of comedy for the third year running, and I found myself shouting out "Shame!" and, inexplicably, "Class war!" When the filming ended, people started asking me to do interviews, but I growled them away because he'd gone and I was just me. I couldn't find my wife and descended into a kind of prima donna panic attack, like the husband in *The Vanishing*, and then we grabbed a cab, the last helicopter out of Saigon, and got home and watched a '70s George Carlin DVD, and in the morning my zombie leg was human again.

On Wednesday I went to do a benefit show at the Bloomsbury. None of the stand-ups there were even aware the awards had happened, and when I saw the TV coverage later that night, my shouting had been surgically erased and vast swathes of the night seemed unfamiliar. Was Danny Dyer, who suggested slashing your errant girlfriend's face with a knife in a lads' mag agony column, really invited to hand out best comedy entertainment programme? My mind was blank, as if I had shut down, like the mice in our hallway that go catatonic as they wait for the cat to kill them.

It seems unlikely there will be another British Comedy Awards. In the end, they chased the capricious populist audience with their phone-ins, even as the former award-winners' votes drove them towards neglected gems such as *Toast of London*, and ended up in a curious no-man's-land between *Nuts* and the *Independent on Sunday*. Even Jonathan Ross couldn't save them. It was interesting to attend twice, a quarter of a century apart. But I know now that I will never, ever go to anything like that again. Maybe the bounty hunter will come out of the wardrobe. I'll need to lose some weight to get into his trousers. Good. I could do with looking after myself a bit. I'm in this for the long haul. There are no short cuts.

"You didn't win an award because you're not funny." Petrol Head Paul

Farty TV and BBC3

Chortle, 21 January 2015

I wrote this for the comedy website Chortle. *It wasn't really aimed at the general public. A consortium of two production companies, Avalon and Hat Trick, was trying to force the BBC to sell it the BBC3 bandwidth, in contravention of various charter agreements, after it was announced that government cuts meant the channel would be dropped. In the end, when it became clear the government's ultimate aim was to destroy the BBC as a whole, the pair's plans were quietly forgotten. There were bigger problems than the disappearance of BBC3 ahead for massive production companies looking for shop windows for their own talent.*

The redoubtable independent production company, Farty Television, has offered £100 million to take over the digital channel BBC3, which is facing a radical online-only future due to government assaults on the licence fee.

Though public fondness for BBC3 rests largely on the reputations of quality programmes like *Gavin and Stacey* (Baby Cow), *Pulling* (Silver River), *The Mighty Boosh* (Baby Cow), *Little Britain* (BBC) and *15 Storeys High* (BBC), Farty Television's cheap and cheerful BBC3 filler (*Snuffle Farty's Good Farts* and *Live at the Farthouse*) has been a vital ingredient of the channel's identity, and a tragic part of its appeal to the elusive sixteen- to sixteen-and-a-half-years-old demographic.

Farty Television's BBC3 shows have usually been heavily weighted towards featuring farts managed by Farty Television's sister company Farty Management, the farts' fees often going towards servicing debts incurred while working in Edinburgh with Farty Television's live wing, Farty Promotions. But the ongoing existence of a public marketplace, such as BBC3, for Farty Management's farts remains vital.

If Farty Management's farts catch the public imagination, they can be sent out on lucrative tours, where the farts are released into vast sports auditoriums for delighted audiences to smell. Farty International can't allow the fart-elevating platform of BBC3 to disappear, as it is a vital fan wafting their farts towards the open mouths of the public.

Beyond BBC3, Farty Television's programme portfolio is vast in width, if not always rich in quality: *Farty Fartball* (BBC2), *Smelly Farter Farts* (Paramount), *The Fart Zone* (Paramount), *Unfarted* (ITV), *Fart Gentlefarts Fart* (Sky), *The Fart Show* (BBC1), *I Love My Farts* (BBC1), *Farty Phil's TV Fart* (ITV1), *Farty Old Farts* (BBC2), *Farty Farton's Well Farty Farts* (BBC3), *That Sunday Night Fart* (BBC3), *Farter* (BBC Radio 4), *Fart Hunt* (ITV1), *Fart, Fart and Fart* (BBC2), *You Can Chose Your Farts* (ITV1), *Fart to Fart* (BBC3), *Farts for Lunch* (BBC Radio 2), *Touch Me, I'm Farty Farter* (BBC3), *The Three-Day Fart* (C4), *The Fart Gang* (BBC2), *The Farts on a Plate* (C4), *Three Farts in a Fart* (BBC2), *Farts Now and Then* (UKTV), *Farts and Farters* (BBC1), *Animal Farts and Farters* (BBC1), *The Nightmare Fart Next Door* (C5) and *The Nightmare Fart Next Door Extreme* (C5).

Perhaps Farty Television are aware that being able to slap a BBC logo on their product would, despite the ongoing attempts of free-market evangelists to discredit and destroy the idea of public broadcasting, give it a credibility abroad and at home that its content alone might not. But would the BBC3 brand be part of the deal anyway?

The Farty company, and its many subsidiaries, are built in the image of its founder, Donald Farty. Farty prides himself on the fact that even though he is now the director of a successful multinational content provider, he still has a nose for farts. Donald Farty remains involved at grass-roots level in the entrapment of new farts, and is still excited by the process. "If I am out in a bar or a toilet and I smell a smelly fart, or see one coming out of someone's bum, I gulp it up into my mouth and run home with the fart stuck in there. Then, at home, I burp the new fart out into a screw-top jar and trap it so I can explain the benefits of Farty Management to it. Sometimes, in the end, the farts escape, or leak out, or lose their smelliness, but the brilliant thing is there are always new farts out there for me to catch. And there always will be. There will always be farts. I think so anyway."

Farty Television's plans for BBC3 promise that "all existing contracts would be honoured", indicating that any of the channel's current deals with independent content providers would be safe, though crucially it says nothing about renewing or extending them. And when it says "all original commissions would be made by UK companies", which UK companies would these be? Perhaps some of the many other smaller independents, which have all been assiduously bought up by Farty Television over the last decade or so, such as Farty Smelle, Fartbox, Flaming Farts and Topical Farts.

Perhaps Farty could appear to fulfil any broadcasting-industry obligation to make contracts with a host of other content suppliers, while in fact just channelling more and more farts quietly through his own back door. There is, of course, no suggestion that this is what the company is intending to do. The ancient BBC forefather Lord Reith, clearly unfamiliar with modern notions of hot-desking and the virtual office, rose spinning from his tomb today to demand that whatever fixtures and fittings remain of BBC3 be destroyed as a precautionary measure, to prevent their appropriation by what he sees as the enemies of Reithian values.

"No blade of grass, not a pane of glass, not a plug socket or a doorknob or a light fitting must remain," he bellowed, shaking his gory locks. "Destroy it all. Raze BBC3 to the ground lest she fall into the hands of these rapacious railroad privateers. And make no mistake, Farty are pirates. Their extension of a helping hand towards BBC3 is merely a greedy digital land-grab disguised as an act of philanthropy, no more convincing that Vladimir Putin's concerned humanitarian excursions into ailing former Soviet states. To accommodate Farty's empire-building ambition in what was a publicly owned arena would be a betrayal of everything the BBC stood for, worse than the David Attenborough baby polar bear scandal and when those actors all mumbled in that historical drama last year. If I wasn't already dead I would kill myself."

Can it be right that Conservative cuts to the licence fee weaken areas of the BBC so that they can no longer be serviced fully, and yet these areas still remain attractive to private companies? Then, having been made non-viable by the government, these assets, despite having been established by public funding, are suddenly attractive to, and then sold on to, the government's friends in big business to exploit, depriving the public of seeing the benefits of their own decades-long investment? It's happened in every other area of British life, from postage to energy to transport to education to health. It appears to be a deliberate strategy. Why shouldn't it happen in the, if anything even more important, area of youth-orientated comedy television too?

Or was Farty's proposal even serious? Perhaps not. In the last few weeks Farty's PR wing appears to have hired some bright spark from the Vladislav Surkov school of propaganda, distributing disorientating headline-grabbing stories that land with heavy impact in an increasingly desperate and ephemeral news pond, but which, while placing Farty in the public eye, may not serve to distract from the standards of much of its product and the nature of its business practices.

"Secondary ticketing" might be legal, but that doesn't make it morally right

Observer, 8 February 2015

Look, this isn't that funny, but it is true, and nothing has changed since it was written.

Culture secretary Sajid Javid has said that ticket touts are "classic entrepreneurs" and their detractors are the "chattering middle classes and champagne socialists, who have no interest in helping the common working man earn a decent living by acting as a middleman". Fill my flute with Dom Perignon, comrade, as we raise the red flag and toast Vanessa Redgrave. Because £20 tickets for my current tour have been touted to confused online consumers at nearly 400 per cent more than their face value, none of which either I or the theatre see, and this Moët & Chandon Marxist isn't happy about it.

I am a stand-up comedian. Due to a decade of tri-annual BBC2 exposure, dogged Dantean circuits of provincial comedy venues, conscious manipulation of vulnerable broadsheet opinion formers and undeserved good luck, I am now popular enough to have caught the eye of touts or, as we now dignify them, Secondary Ticketing Agents™. As Eric Cantona said twenty years ago on a celebrity fishing trip with Tom O'Connor: "When seagulls follow the trawler it is because they think sardines will be thrown into the sea." Well, I'm pulling my sardines out of the sea and putting them back onto Eric Cantona's trawler. Or something.

I try to keep my tickets down to around £20 in the big theatres, and avoid ones, such as the Ambassador Theatre Group chain, where I can't. This is not a huge sacrifice. I will put prices up if I suddenly want a velvet cloak or a bejewelled cock ring. But I am doing fine. In the last twenty-four hours alone I have bought muffins, a second-class single to Colchester, two quality newspapers, a dish of luxury nuts and a garage-punk CD called *Back to the Grave 9*. I now live beyond my wildest dreams, although admittedly, until recently, my wildest dreams involved one day owning a table.

£20 is about as low as you can go in theatres, which need to make a significant slice from their standard percentage of the take. For your local taxpayer-subsidised theatre, low-tech high-return junk such as stand-up comedy, discredited TV psychics and ABBA tribute acts float more worthwhile artists with identifiable skills – dancers, actors, puppeteers and ex-members of The Stranglers doing acoustic tours. And public subsidies in the arts temples of ballet, classical music and opera are supposed to provide cheaper tickets for everyone, not to create back-door profiteering opportunities for Sajid Javid's dodgy mates.

My old manager is of the opinion that comedians are only popular for a short time, and that in that time they should try to accrue as much as possible. Being a comedian was a kind of confidence trick, it seemed, that the public would eventually rumble. Then the comedian would be run out of town by an angry mob who had realised that this charlatan's stories were not necessarily true, his jokes were just meaningless wordplay, he did the same fake improvisations every night and his personal anecdotes had been bought in wholesale from an uncredited writer on a £60 day rate.

But I think if you can keep prices down, and come back with new stuff every year, perhaps an artist can build an audience for life. I am a Bollinger Bolshevik, apparently, because I believe I should have a final say in what my tickets cost, in order to manage audience expectation of the work itself, to control perceptions of my own apparent avarice and to make sure that money that is spent on me by punters reflects the cost savings I and the venue have cut corners to make, and the public subsidies the venue may have received, all of which are designed to make entry to the show viable, so that all sorts of people can come along and think I am shit together.

I managed to track down the individual touts selling tickets for my London run of shows, and then banned them from further purchases at the theatre. Now one of them, a "company director", harasses me online. I wrote to Viagogo and StubHub to ask them to stop reselling my tickets at inflated rates, and they replied with standard emails. StubHub included the pointed insert, "Stewart, I would also like to mention to you that the act of reselling tickets is legal in the UK."

I went into StubHub's London outlet to reason with the man on the desk about the difference between "legal" and "moral" when it involved overcharging a person by up to 400 per cent. But it wasn't his fight, I felt sorry for him and he had obviously been trained to stick to a script involving repetition of the phrase "We just provide a platform". I did eat a lot of sweets from a pot on the desk, though, free, which was, I suppose, legal, though not strictly speaking moral.

I wrote to Sajid Javid, twice, but he never replied, so I sent a sarcastic email saying: "Perhaps we could go to the House of Commons bar? Are the drinks there subsidised? If so, then you won't mind me snaffling a few bottles and reselling them out in the street at a 400 per cent mark-up! I'm a 'classic entrepreneur'!"

Then, as a former rock critic, I got a mass email from Iron Maiden urging fans to support the All-Party Parliamentary Group on Ticket Abuse, led by MPs Mike Weatherley and Sharon Hodgson. Crack open the Cristal! The touts may have Sajid Javid in their back pocket, but they cannot defeat Iron Maiden. Bruce Dickinson is a qualified pilot and international fencing master. Iron Maiden have their own giant zombie robot, three lead guitarists and a bespoke bottled beer. I won't be drinking it, obviously, as I am a Louis Roederer revolutionary.

Iron Maiden also have the kind of loyal lifelong following to whom they mean a lot, and who deserve not to be fleeced. In miniature, Sajid Javid's approval of touts is part of the same ideology that sees every available inch of public life exploited for profit, every transaction monetised at every possible point, from energy to entertainment, often at the expense of those least able to afford the surcharges. How can Javid legitimise touts, making access to the arts prohibitively expensive for many, and yet also be the culture secretary responsible for the simple act of getting people through the doors to see stuff? It's Orwellian doublethink that is beyond mockery. Which is why this column wasn't very funny. I blame the government.

Privatising BBC3 would be as pernicious as Isis destroying Iraq's historic sites

Observer, 15 March 2015

When so-called Islamic State destroyed historic sites in Iraq, I was wary of making judgements of other cultures, and gave these exuberant young men the benefit of the doubt. Perhaps shattering the statues was mere high spirits, like when Greeks trample wedding crockery? Or perhaps it was the fault of MI5?

Of course, we also sacrifice our heritage to ideology. Say goodbye to Paolozzi's Tottenham Court Road murals, trashed by the terrorists of Transport for London; to Oxford's ancient Port Meadow horizon, occluded by death-cult developers; and perhaps to the BBC, the greatest cultural achievement of any twentieth-century democracy, soon to be poleaxed by free-market fundamentalists as pernicious as the statue-smashers of so-called Islamic State.

Admittedly, the BBC has not been good at preserving its history. In 1990, when I first visited White City's iconic doughnut, since sold off to a "Luxembourg-based consortium", I saw Hamble from *Play School* abandoned in a skip, Del Boy's van rusting under an awning and the decomposing body of Lord Reith propped up in a mobile toilet.

The BBC mislaid much of its finest footage: the moon landings; The Beatles on *Top of the Pops*; and the Troughton-era *Doctor Who* serial "Embarrassment of the Inseminoids", where Doctor Who lands on Mars with a sign on his Tardis saying "Martian Benders" and punches Jamie in the sporran when his tea arrives cold.

In the wake of the licence freeze, the BBC plans to move the youth channel BBC3 online and halve its budget. As a middle-aged, middle-class man, I hate pretty much everything on BBC3. *Snog Marry Avoid* is just one of many BBC3 show titles that resist parody. The channel has the creepy vibe of a sleazy art teacher trying to coax sixth-form girls into the pub. But BBC3 isn't aimed at me. And it shouldn't be.

That said, it has its evangelical supporters, prepared to do anything to preserve it. In January my '90s manager, Jon Thoday of Avalon, maker of *Russell Howard's Good News*, and Jimmy Mulville of Hat Trick Productions, which has an impressive record of critical hits, floated a philanthropic proposal to buy the channel for the nation, a bit like when those nice Greeks sent those Trojans that lovely wooden horse which worked out so well for everyone.

In a piece authored for public-broadcasting enthusiasts the *Sunday Times*, the sages described as "talented" the BBC3 controller who contracted Avalon to make *Live at the Electric*, for which the channel intended to "assemble the hottest acts on the brink of breaking through to the public consciousness". A demonstrable majority of these hot acts were managed by the management wing (Avalon Management) of the production company (Avalon Productions) making the show, their journey into public consciousness smoothed by their management's control of BBC3's public-consciousness gateway. It's like a pig farmer being paid to make a publicly funded prize-pig programme featuring his own pigs, when he owns the podiums on which the prize pigs are appraised. And it's a fabulous taster of how the Avalon–Hat Trick BBC3 might work.

A crucial part of this Jörmungandrian cycle is that companies that manage acts need to persuade TV execs to pay them to make shows featuring these acts. But if you could buy your own ready-made channel, you could broadcast your own acts whenever you liked, ramping up profiles and coining in your percentage of subsequent live work. In its client Al Murray, who has now formed a genuine political party, Avalon might even have a parliamentary presence, as well as its own TV channel. Perhaps one day our political and media scene will be as respected as Italy's.

Outlining his hopes on Radio 4 last month, Mulville, anxious to emphasise the importance of a BBC3 that he "happens to believe in", skirted the fact that BBC1 was enjoyed by ten times more young people than BBC3, saying, "I happen to have young children in that demographic," and dismissed BBC4 as "basically BBC2 for Oxbridge people". But I happen to have an immediate family who never experienced the privileges of further education, and they love BBC4. As an Oxbridge snob myself, I find the channel a bit lowbrow, but it calms me after reading Old Norse and playing chess against cyborgs of my former professors.

Mulville, who happens to have attended Cambridge, is typical of a certain kind of media magnate who, despite enjoying the benefits of a liberal education himself, sees the proletariat as pigs to be farmed, leaning over the balcony like some Groucho Club Marie Antoinette, dismissing the peasants' demands for more Lucy Worsley with a cry of "Let them watch *Hotter than My Daughter.*"

The main obstacle to the duo's buying a bargain-priced BBC3 appears to be acquiring the frequency it is broadcast on. The easily accessible channel 7 of the EPG spectrum is reserved for public broadcasters. "We would need the help of the BBC to convince the government to allow that," they conceded on Radio 4. I thought of the emergent oligarchs of collapsing communist Russia, snaffling the ideologically dismantled infrastructure, the BBC an ailing hog, drawing out marks on its own back for butchers who maintain they only wanted to preserve its meat for the nation. "We happen to love bacon." The 300,000 signatories wanting to save BBC3 weren't necessarily signing up for the carve-up.

Lawyers love loopholes, and prey on a precedent. If the BBC3 frequency is, unprecedentedly, reallocated, then public broadcasting is holed below the waterline, the whole thing is up for grabs and we'll lose the very idea of public broadcasting to the free-market fundamentalists within a decade, as surely and shoddily as we lost the Post Office. Maybe BBC3's would-be buyers and the BBC Trust don't realise this. Maybe they realise this all too well. Maybe, fundamentalists of the free market, that's what they want?

And if I went to talk to someone at the BBC Trust about this, would I find myself faced with another government-friendly west London billionaire, and end up floating face down in a £5 million sub-basement swimming pool?

We need a BBC Trust that comprises communicators who have pursued ideas for their own sake, not necessarily for gain. Grayson Perry, Lenny Henry, Mary Beard, Brian Cox, Caitlin Moran, Jarvis Cocker, Meera Syal, Victoria Wood, Rowan Williams and Tinky Winky. And yes, this is my proposed shortlist for the next Doctor Who, that curious, questing, idealistic creature who embodies everything we so want to believe should also define the BBC.

"Sometimes, just sometimes, the *Guardian* is beyond parody."
Tim Montgomerie, Conservative blogger, Twitter

If Grant Shapps was made by little green aliens, what's left?

Observer, 22 March 2015

Grant Shapps was a gift that kept on giving, now alleged to have owned multiple identities to flog his tatty online business schemes. I wrote this in a hotel room in the ruggedly beautiful town of Dundee, where I was doing shows, having driven over the Cairngorms, lightly dusted in snow, to the accompaniment of the first four Led Zepellin albums, which I had never heard before. Filing my column, doing the shows, drinking some of the whisky I bought at a distillery in the day, googling mad quotes from Grant Shapps and filleting them into existing UFO lore, the story sort of wrote itself. I thought life was about as good as it could get.

Last week, I betrayed the homosexual parenting community. At Elton John's insistence I tried to boycott Dolce & Gabbana, which was a great sacrifice for me, as other designer underwear makes my testicles look old.

As I have been appearing at a theatre in Dundee it has been difficult to find any Dolce & Gabbana outlets to boycott. Instead, I located a second-hand copy of Joe Dolce's "Shaddap You Face" single in Groucho's records on the Nethergate, and pointedly refused to buy it.

But it has been a troubling week. News events, coupled with the liminal experience of spending time in Dundee, have conspired to make me doubt my own existence. And that of others. And that of all matter. It is the fault of the government.

Earlier this week, the Conservative Party chair Grant Shapps was revealed to have operated, even while an MP, a variety of ethically translucent Internet business funnels under the alias of Michael Green, pseudonymous author of a book called *How to*

Get Stinking Rich. Grant Shapps even wore a badge saying he was Michael Green at a 2004 conference, though apparently this was a joke, but one so subtle that many people took it at face value. Now he knows how I feel writing these columns.

Green, a non-existent man, marketed software that steers Google search engines towards particular information, manipulating our perception of reality. Fittingly, most traces of this Michael Green's HowToCorp company have since been erased from cyberspace, perhaps by his own software, jammed in reverse gear with an imaginary spanner.

How disorientating. Some twenty-five years ago now, in 1990, a young Grant Shapps hired me as the sole employee of his profitable live-bait vending business, House of Maggots, which I didn't over-firmly deny in the *Observer* last March. Grant Shapps and I spent many a moonlit night at popular Suffolk angling spots, filling roadside fridges with comatose larvae, discarding maggots that failed to thrive, talking about our dreams. But who was the Grant Shapps that I imagined I knew all those years ago?

In August 1989 Grant Shapps had a car crash near Wakeeney, Kansas, on Interstate 70, his companion probably falling asleep at the wheel. Speaking to the *Welwyn Hatfield Times* in 2011, at the opening of a refurbished McDonald's in the region, Grant Shapps confessed: "I was in a coma for the best part of a week and when I came round I recuperated in a Ronald McDonald home. I've always been grateful to Ronald McDonald." Could this bizarre incident be significant?

The spring of 1989 saw a surge of UFO sightings in Kansas, clustered principally around the town of Russell, sixty miles west on the Interstate 70 of Grant Shapps's subsequent accident. The UFO-spotting season closed spectacularly in November 1989 at Goodland, 111 miles east, on the same road, when two women were abducted by aliens and left unable to account for three hours of their evening. And in between those two spates of alien activity, geographically and temporally, lies Grant Shapps's own crash and coma. Could this be the point at which the reality-moulding entity known as Michael Green somehow took possession of the future Conservative Party chair? Did Grant Shapps's Kansas blackout provide a gateway for the little Green man?

Given this Michael Green's self-professed ability to use software to rewrite our perception of our own history, and our own reality, I wondered if there ever was a "Grant Shapps", as we understand him, at all? Grant Shapps's Wikipedia entry is known to have been regularly and favourably massaged by unseen hands. But are these hands alien hands? Are they green? Could this Michael Green have inserted a rebooted "Grant Shapps" character, who never really existed, into our reality by a similarly deft manipulation of online records?

And what kind of name is "Grant Shapps" anyway? Say it a dozen times. Roll "Grant Shapps" around your tongue. It sounds, as does Douglas Adams's pitch-perfect Ford Prefect, like the kind of name an alien would choose in a bungled attempt to appear human. And so does "Ms Stockheath", one of Michael Green's supposedly satisfied online customers, and a name no one in the world has ever had. Ever.

Writing in the *London Review of Books* in January, Andrew O'Hagan showed how easy it was to use online resources to build a non-existent man from the ground up, who eventually took on a viable virtual life. And, of course, members of the police have famously created similar false identities in order to have sex with *Guardian* readers and befriend Mark Thomas.

Is Grant Shapps the creation of this Michael Green? And if so, who are we? Has this Michael Green, or this Grant Shapps, micro-engineered a virtual world in which we also believe we exist, when in fact we may not? Are we just ciphers now, clumps of sentient meat, plugged into sockets, farmed by Michael Green or Grant Shapps, but for what? Data? Energy? For some super-being's sick fun? Are we maggots dreaming of Grant Shapps, or is Michael Green a vast consciousness that dreams Grant Shapps daily into being?

I leaned against the outside wall of a public toilet near a building site on the banks of the Tay and rang a mobile number Grant Shapps had given me twenty-five years ago, in case of nocturnal maggot emergencies. Back then it had connected to the brick-sized car phone in his maggot van. Now a trim buzz broke off suddenly and Grant Shapps, identifiably and audibly Grant Shapps, snapped, "Who gave you this number?" Instead of asking for Grant Shapps, I said: "Is Michael Green there?" "Michael Green is here," came the reply, "but who and where, I wonder, do you imagine you are, my meddling maggot?"

And then everything went wobbly. The surface of the Tay seemed to shimmer, the grey light rolling over the estuary from Tentsmuir Forest frazzled and burned, and the Tay Bridge buckled and bent. The brick wall at my back melted and my internal organs fused, air in my guts and liquid in my lungs. In the purple cloud above the boiling river I swear I saw the face of Grant Shapps, or Michael Green, or maybe even God, looking down and laughing, his hands full of wriggling maggots tumbling into his open mouth. "Am I dead now?" I cried.

"Come on," said my tour tech, James, snapping me out of it, "we have to get to Inverness today." And everything went flat again. And we drove north across the Cairngorms dusted with snow, looking for all the world exactly as one would imagine mountains would look.

"When arthritis hits your hands, you'll feel very sorry for having wasted such a precious time writing all that nonsense." Ricardo

If we send the migrants back, who will cook my late-night steak?

Observer, 5 April 2015

The Observer *asked me to write weekly columns about the 2015 election campaign. Given a set of parameters I couldn't really deliver the goods, and lapsed into the kind of uninspired personal anecdotal rambling that characterises columnists I don't like. For the most part, I've not included the election columns in this book, and many of them became swiftly irrelevant, based, erroneously, on the assumption, shared by many, that the Tories could not win again. How long ago April 2015 seems now; and how many of the presumed strengths of post-war British society are being systematically dismantled and determinedly discredited.*

In 1944, the *London Evening Standard* sent Betty Knox, of the popular music-hall trio Wilson, Keppel and Betty, to cover the Normandy landings. Knox's impromptu one-woman performance of their famous Sand Dance, a rip-roaring montage of ancient Egyptian imagery and racially insensitive soft-shoeing, was delivered under heavy bombardment on Gold Beach, and so bored the humourless Germans watching from the cliffs that they eventually abandoned their final operational 75 mm gun out of sheer *Weltschmerz*. Knox had been employed to report on the costly liberation of Europe from a comic perspective, but her very presence on the beach may have altered the outcome of the war itself.

Likewise, the *Observer* has asked me, a stand-up comedian, to pen a weekly column on my experiences of Britain in the run-up to the election. I agreed to this knowing that I would be on tour at the time. I imagined I would use my zingers to take the nation's temperature from stages all around the land, and then report back from the front line with news of how laughter told me how real people felt about the real issues in the real regions, far from north London, where we all live, obviously.

But whether I am in Inverness or Reading, my audiences are comprised exclusively of left-leaning middle-class *Guardian* readers, often in same-sex, mixed-race and interfaith relationships, and I quickly became aware that I have learnt little I wouldn't already have known from merely talking to myself. My crowd, painstakingly carved over nearly three decades into the exact image of me, reveals little new.

And so I learn more from casual conversations with people I encounter along the way. Every single member of staff in every single hotel I have stayed in since January has been an efficient eastern European immigrant, apart from in Perth, where, tellingly, the indigenous Scottish staff were unable to locate the room key for two hours. When it finally turned up it had been coated in batter and served up as a delicacy to an American tourist in search of her roots.

I fear a UKIP victory will turn every hotel in Britain into an enormous one-star-on-TripAdvisor catastrophe, run by useless British people, failed by the state, who can neither add up nor speak, offering me breadsticks instead of keys, squashing sausages into the toaster at breakfast and putting the complimentary bottle of mineral water into the en suite toilet to chill. And then doing a big wee on it.

A young Polish night porter in Guildford enthused about what a fantastic place Guildford was, as if he had discovered some mythical Shangri-La, but as he was unable to cook me a late-night steak I punched him in the face for thirty seconds to teach him a lesson and remind him whose country he was in. But if we send these people back, who will make our food in the night on minimum wage?

I arrived in Truro on the day of St Piran, Cornwall's patron saint, and riffed on our perceptions of good and bad nationalism.

Crossing the Tamar I saw black-and-white national flags were waving, but in opposition to very real financial oppression by English incomers, as opposed to those St George flags that unfurl against the often imagined monetary drain of EU migrants. That said, the tradition that every English visitor present on St Piran's Day must spend the night naked and sealed inside a giant pasty full of hot spiced meat seems harsh, and St Piran has pockmarked my perineum permanently.

In Oxford the lady on the stage door talked about her son going to college in Coventry, and I said how few of the people I knew would have studied if it had cost what it costs today, and how the circumstances, and attitudes to education as an end in itself, that saw generations of people from different backgrounds into and through university no longer exist. And she countered my abstract worthy meditation on social privilege by telling me she had grown up on Oxford's Cutteslowe estate.

In 1934, after clearances had moved former slum-dwellers into new council housing appended to a prosperous suburb, the prestigious Urban Housing Company unilaterally erected a succession of two-metre-high spiked walls across the public roads to keep the working classes out of their betters' sights. And these stayed in place until 1959. The Beatles were coming, and punk rock, and contraception, and the Open University, and student grants. Those walls wouldn't have stood a chance anyway.

But I rather admired the Cutteslowe Walls. There had been no pretence in Cutteslowe. Today politicians make grand statements. But things are perhaps even less porous.

"'My audiences are comprised of'? Try 'My audience are composed of', or 'My audiences comprise'." Hareox2

"'Useless British people'? I am curious why such text is permitted when critical comments about say, some religions, is ruthlessly expunged. We really do have one rule for some and a different rule for others." Timtim1

"A bit off topic but, will UKIP be able to succeed against the whole of the Main Stream Media? I fear not. We are headed for a world fascist government." Acrion

"The only late night steak I'd like to see Stewart Lee involved with is the one he should be burnt at for this insensitive article. Some of us can't even afford a steak, late night or otherwise, thanks to the metropolitan elite, the EU and Labour!" Mr Stan

"Typically smug attitude from a privately educated out-of-shape-Morrissey comedian whose jokes don't even have punchlines. Cook your own steak. Why should I be out of a job because a foreigner will cook steak more cheaply than me? Disgusting." Esistgeschlossen

Truly, this man was the son of God. And I don't mean David Cameron

Observer, 12 April 2015

Easter is the time of eternal symbols: the fictitious egg-abandoning rabbit; the female mantis, biting off its mate's head during a loveless copulation; and, perhaps most profound, the newborn orphan lamb's greedy suckling at the laughing prime minister's eagerly proffered teat, a scene re-enacted every Easter by a local actor in the village of Chadlington, before a barn of frightened Oxfordshire children and their sympathetically lactating nannies.

Centuries pass, nature's ancient cycles overlaid by each epoch's successive blooming of ephemeral religious belief. But this year Easter was the time of election campaigns and, tired from my stand-up tour but obliged to file the second of my "a comedian observes the election" columns, I was vulnerable to symbols.

On Good Friday I took my children to Trafalgar Square to witness a re-enactment of Christ's Passion. Jesus, a charismatic Russell Brand figure from biblical times, excited a populace desperate for answers, but seemed reluctant to give specific ones, preferring to pronounce mysteriously about wineskins, his profound thoughts eventually forming the basis of an enduring bestseller.

The production was given a surprisingly contemporary air of tragedy by the twenty-first-century passer-by's tendency to wander along, pose for a selfie with the agony of Christ as a diverting backdrop, and then wander off again to the Trocadero centre. "Here's me and Josie with the expiring Saviour." Father, forgive them, for they know not what they do.

My own Easter epiphany, during the actor-Christ's actual crucifixion, was itself compromised by a lady from the theatre company handing me an out-of-date leaflet saying, "Buy tickets for

The Life of Christ and receive 20% off *The Nativity* if booked before 31 March 2015." How dare they do this in my father's house? The actor who played Jesus was brilliant. He had to get down off the cross, clean his wounds, re-engage with the character, and then do the ninety-minute show again for the 3 p.m. matinee. Truly, this man was the son of God.

The last time I'd stood all day in Trafalgar Square was twenty-five years and one week ago, in the poll tax demonstration, my buttocks squashed against the Imperial Units plaque by phalanxes of mounted police, unaccountable in those pre-camera-phone days, clumsy protesters bumping their teeth out against truncheons right, left and centre.

Today we know that most of the supposed troublemakers were probably undercover police officers. Indeed, my first marriage fell apart four years in when I discovered that "Jean", whom I met that very day beneath the trampling hooves of a horse named Raisa, was in fact junior police constable Alan Ripley in blond dreadlocks and a Back to the Planet T-shirt, with his winky tucked permanently between his legs.

Current legislation would make it impossible to arrange a similarly sized protest today, though driving a tank through central London to reinstate a punchy TV personality can be organised at a moment's notice. And the massed re-enactment of Jesus's maddeningly obtuse calls for social justice, in front of thousands of members of the public, was also fine, as no one ever listened to anything Jesus said anyway.

Though necessarily painted with broad strokes, the epic production showed how the gamesmanship of religious leaders and Roman administrators led to Christ's crucifixion. But I found myself seeing the Saviour's face not in that of David Cameron, despite the lamb-suckler's attempt to portray himself as our political messiah, but in the face of another idealist who, like Jesus, found himself caught in a political crossfire. You know him.

His name is Nicholas William Peter Lemsip Nutkin Horsebrass Bladderwrack Clegg. The man better known to you as Nicholas "Nick" Clegg.

Nick Clegg too was betrayed, not by a kiss in the Gethsemane garden, but by a handshake in the rose garden. And, selflessly, Nick Clegg sacrificed his career, if not his life, to keep Cameron's most savage Conservatives muzzled, so that we might not suffer quite as much as we might have done otherwise. And given a choice between him and some actual criminals, you would choose the latter, and abandon him to his fate. Nick Clegg. King of the Liberal Democrats. You did not recognise him when he came.

And now I wonder, what of that suckled lamb, the unwitting political pawn? The naked children climbing the Giant's Causeway on the cover of Led Zeppelin's *Houses of the Holy* were so traumatised by their childhood association with the group's first dodgy album that they all grew up to be attention-seeking TV chefs – Stefan Gates, Gregg Wallace, Rusty Lee and the Hairy Bikers. In ten years, when you see a violent and red-faced sheep drunkenly bleating its shame in a Cotswold field, will you recognise it as, like Nick Clegg, just another casualty of this filthy campaign?

"Utter drivel. Congratulations." Mark Turner

On the A1, at the border of England and Scotland, a miracle unfolded . . .

Observer, 24 May 2015

This column marked the start of a six-month absence for Observer *regular David Mitchell, and from here until mid-November I felt like a proper hack writer, turning in 1,100 words a week, irrespective of whether there appeared to be anything to write about.*

In the end I approached the task as a kind of method-acting job. What if I was a hack writer who had to hit both word count and deadline before moving on to the next slab of filler without worrying too much?

Every Thursday, the day before deadline, I sat myself in the cafe that I write in, with black coffees lined up around my laptop, and, having spent the preceding few days turning over ideas in my mind, proceeded to try to bash the offending article out in the five-and-a-half-hour space between school drop-offs and school pick-ups. If only I had been allowed to smoke and sink shorts, I would have conformed to the romantic idea of the columnist that I had in my head, before I knew what the job really entailed.

Even more than before, it wasn't the real me Stewart Lee that wrote the columns. I handed the work over to this pragmatic deadlines-freak, and he knuckled down and got on with the job in hand in a way that I, a perfectionist finessing every word, never could have done in the time allowed.

It was the seventy-fifth anniversary of the Little Ships, when 700 private boats sailed to the rescue of British servicemen marooned in Dunkirk, and the Conservatives had just won the election.

Are we naturally selfish? Or do we have an innate sense of empathy for our fellow living things? The radio journalist Herbert Morrison watched the *Hindenberg* come down and announced, "Oh! The humanity!" And once I stood outside a pub on the canal in Camden and watched a crowd of drunken men laughing and cheering as five seagulls pecked a fluffy baby duckling to death. I said nothing. But I suddenly understood why *Mock the Week* was so popular.

Perhaps there is hope for our species, despite the popularity of TV comedy panel shows. On Friday I witnessed at close hand the first flowering of the spontaneous collective act of compassion that has since dominated celebrity social-media feeds all week-end, reaching critical mass at around 2 p.m. on Saturday, when the sheer density of tweets caused Danny Dyer's nut to freak out, and saw Ricky Gervais append the heart-warming story to a breakdown of Netflix viewing figures for *Derek*.

Soon after breakfast on Friday morning I had crossed the Scottish border, driving north between stand-up shows, from the St Cuthbert's Players Playhouse in Alnwick up to the Kate Middleton Memorial theatre in St Andrews, where the young Prince William's eye first fell upon his future bride's Scaramouche in a performance of Ben Elton's *We Will Rock You*.

Gradually, on the southbound side of the A1, an enormous convoy of vastly varied Scottish vehicles appeared to take shape, streaming endlessly towards England, honking in celebration as they passed. But why? Not having a car radio, eschewing the iPhone and unable to buy a copy of Friday's *Guardian* that far north, I wasn't able to make sense of the incoherent events. I pulled off the road to watch at Ayton, by the sign for Q's Cat Motel, which was where I ran into Steven Moffat.

I had met the Scottish *Doctor Who* writer–producer once before, at a BBC think tank. I had suggested a new long-running drama series about a little old man whose face and body stay the same for millions of years, but whose buttocks are played by the buttocks of a succession of currently fashionable character actors, as the decades progress, of all races and genders. Needless to say, my idea was rejected by the fearful "suits", concerned, doubtless, about appearing too "politically correct", and in terror of losing the licence fee under a Tory government.

And now here was this Moffat again, by chance, at a cat motel off the A1 in Berwickshire, checking in his prize Persian, Erato, in anticipation of a long journey south. Perhaps Moffat could explain to me what on earth was going on. "Ian Rankin direct-messaged me and told me that Wattie from the Exploited was on Twitter encouraging all Scots to form a relief convoy," Moffat explained, "and then Miss Barbara Dickson phoned me up in tears saying we had to mobilise the Scottish public. I asked myself, 'What would Doctor Who do?' Doctor Who would help. I know that better than anyone."

In the sudden and unexpected political shift of the green island we all call home, the liberal left south of the border had been marooned, abandoned without hope. The Scottish celebrities' heartstrings had been twanged and, overnight, their fans and followers had used social media to spring into action. I ran to the road and watched the first of the flotilla of little vehicles beginning the return journey north, their available space crammed with escapees.

All Scottish life was there, taking to their Highland homes those with nothing left to lose. A tweed-clad Loch Lomond laird in a spluttering vintage car turned his head towards the back seat to laugh with a gaggle of London schoolkids avoiding academy status and the dead hand of Gove; half a dozen turbaned Scottish Sikhs, in a mobile festival-catering wagon, partied with north-bound Brighton lesbians, fearful of life under an equality minister who voted against gay marriage; and a whisky-nipping gillie at the wheel of a Land Rover softly stroked a young Yorkshire vixen and her sleeping cubs escaping the repeal of the hunting ban.

I repositioned myself on the central reservation to continue to observe the convoy. Edinburgh Muslims, chefs from the Mosque Kitchen, drove a delivery van usually laden with cash-and-carry rice, and planned their pause for Friday prayers with the family of left-leaning north London Jewish academics they were taking with them, thinkers and readers for whom life in England was about to become intellectually intolerable; Heriot-Watt students, dressed as vampires, had re-routed the Haunted Auld Reekie Tours bus they worked on at weekends on an unscheduled excursion, and now swapped alcopops with southern arts and humanities graduates, finally accepting that they had no future in a culture that saw the outpourings of the human heart as nothing more than missed opportunities for monetisation; and farm trucks from the far north, thick with the ground-in dung of prize Highland cattle, trundled towards the tartan utopia, their fenced flatbeds now thronged with teachers, poets, artists, dreamers, the poor and the unprofitable.

And then, as I crossed back to my car, there came the most moving sight of all. Celtic fans and Rangers fans, working together, taking turns to steer a hastily commandeered ambulance north, nursing the brows of dying old folk, bed-blockers from beneath the border, soon to be set adrift by the ongoing privatisation of their home visits, their tragic plight dissolving age-old sectarian differences. And all these noble Scots, it would transpire, had set their ancient grudges aside to assist those condemned to suffer by the unwieldy splitting of the democratic deck. I got back in the car and followed the convoy north.

As the makeshift caravan stopped at Dunbar for the night, the practical limitations of Wattie from The Exploited's vision became apparent. The volunteers' vehicles discharged their human cargo into a succession of hastily commandeered campsites, Dunbar Camping and Caravanning at the golf course, and Belhaven Bay by the reservoir, which were soon overwhelmed. "Is this what you wanted?" I asked Wattie, who was using a stolen golf club to direct the traffic. Wattie looked weary, his red Mohican wilting a little. "I'm no genius," he said, "but I looked at those poor people and I knew we had to do something. I don't have a plan. I don't even know what we're going to do tomorrow. But at least we did something. You know what they're calling this? The Miracle of Dunbar. Not bad, eh?"

"What a stupid article." Chance DuBois

From pagan rituals to the Queen's speech: the more things change . . .

Observer, 31 May 2015

Sometime between quitting drinking two months ago and the evening of the general election, I developed the ability to travel through time. Or rather, it appears that time has developed the ability to travel through me.

That said, if you remember when '70s donkey-jacket socialism dissolved in the acid of '80s Thatcherism, then the instinctive forward shambling of Labour's collapsed front bench, like the dead husks of Italian B-movie zombie shoppers still shuffling towards the mall on muscle memory alone, certainly has a chilling element of déjà vu.

I am old enough to recall the last time Labour looked this broken, before Blair swooped down upon its expiring body, a predatory sexual opportunist with a pick-up-artist manual in his manbag, sniffing a vulnerable, drunken divorcee in a Holiday Inn bar, his temporarily unencumbered ring finger toying with the olive on her plastic cocktail stick. "Honey, I know how to make you feel wanted again."

But it isn't merely the chemical misfiling of old memories in my brain's in-tray that makes me wonder which way I'm travelling through the time stream. Twice in the last six weeks I have experienced the sense of an actual temporal shift in my immediate surroundings.

In the sunlit remnants of Fountains Abbey, North Yorkshire, one morning last month a nave of hooded monks rose briefly from the turf before me and then faded permanently from view, like ghostly Liberal Democrats, their dry mouths chewing inedible hats as history dismissed them.

And last Wednesday afternoon, at the ruined Roman temple of an ancient river spirit in the Forest of Dean, mumbling votive supplicants holding effigies of limbs they wanted mended moved momentarily around me towards an ambivalent deity and his dog servants, across a mosaic pavement, long since moved to a museum, now doubtless volunteer-operated on a greatly reduced budget.

I appreciate that these events were merely malfunctions prompted by the chemical rebalancing of my consciousness, but these days the implausible past seems more vivid than the impossible present. If reality were a broken TV set, I'd be beyond turning it on and off at the mains, banging it hard with the flat of my hand instead, hoping the picture would somehow look familiar once more.

Leaving the still resonant rites of pagan Lydney behind me, I drove back along the Severn to watch Parliament open on the news. An old woman with a hat of shimmering jewels, the human embodiment of a fragmenting nation, crossed her capital in a coach of gold, Selene's moon chariot, trailed by plumed horsemen, half Sandhurst, half flamingo.

The gem-encrusted empress's entry to the airtight decision chamber was announced by an emissary in pantyhose, who banged his rod upon an opera-house toilet cubicle door, an aroused and aggressive transvestite drunk, home late from the support group, his keys mislaid.

Sat upon Demeter's golden throne of indifference, Madam Allotrope Hat droningly intoned a speech dictated to her by her captors, the sexless plutocrats on the right of the house. This impregnable dynastic cabal's ancestral wealth was built on Norman bequests, received for betraying the ancient Britons, establishing ongoing precedents.

The pedigree bloods sat opposite the people's other representatives, powerless straw men strategically placed to enact impotently the now empty ritual of imagined opposition; deflating beachball heads with *Art Attack* googly eyes, tied at the neck to the collars of dead men's charity cast-offs, stuffed with shredded manifestos in an illusion of substance, awaiting the oncoming bonfire of their values.

Everyone in the chamber appeared to be in character, fulfilling various symbolic roles, from Diamondhead herself to the flower-draped southbound Scots, playing the part of a poorly rehearsed Greek chorus, ignoring the conductor, cacophonously crashing its cues.

And there was the sin-eating scapegoat of Little Clegg, who was supposed to have dragged himself off into the desert to die, to dissolve the transgressions of his people inside his own rotting carcass, but had instead the temerity to return and vomit up all the undigested sin again in front of his indifferent former partners, burying their barely noticing nostrils in scented nosegays.

Even Ed Miliband, absent from the TV coverage, appeared not as himself, but as a corporeal cloud of shame, hanging suspended above the proceedings like a stupendous cotton-wool fart. His would-be successors tried not to gag with revulsion, even as they blundered for faint words with which to praise him, at once not untrue, and yet not unkind, while dreaming of alternative realities in which his clearly more capable brother had brought home the bacon sandwich unbitten.

Only Michael Gove, the Lawgiver, appeared unapologetically as himself. He arrived to play his part in the pantomime clad in an enormous black velvet oven glove inlaid with mysterious runes, accepting from treasure-haired Nerthus his mission to eradicate the Rights of Humans. Like the orangutan science-priest in *Planet of the Apes*, Gove believes these humans to be some kind of inferior species, who have been getting away with their mischief for far too long, and who have now to be dealt with, before they further spoil the crops and foul the drinking water.

Analysis of all this cryptic mummery was provided by the BBC's chief political journalist Nick Robinson, himself an increasingly representative figure. Having undergone successful lung tumour surgery before the election, his recovering voice currently a whisper, Robinson now stands for the Conservative government's, and the new culture secretary's, vision of the BBC itself.

The BBC news nowadays is a barely audible miniature portable television set, standing on a stone sideboard, its insight drowned out by the honking of guests at a private kitchen supper in a private Chipping Norton cellar. And yet the possibility that this voice might one day still be allowed to squeak on, under reduced circumstances, continues cruelly to be entertained. For now.

I thought of the rituals of Nodens in that forest glade, which my apparent madness had granted me a glimpse of that afternoon. And I laughed at the great god Pan, as his great green masquerades dissolved into parliamentary procedures. I looked from Nodens to the news and Nick Robinson, and from the news and Nick Robinson back to Nodens again. And Nodens, even in despoiled statue form at the gates of Lydney Park garden, his nose smashed off, his face caved in, seemed somehow more convincing.

"The ritual of Guardianista reporter having a dig at anything that holds society together. Here with the added bonus of royalty being involved. Nothing new here then . . ." JezJez

"Anything can sound stupid if you make up nonsense about it and write it down using utterly inappropriate language." Dominic Stockford

"The conflation between ancient 'British' deities and cults transmitted to the isles with the Roman Empire means there was a missed opportunity to stretch your apology further, Stew!" The Fury

FIFA, Eurovision, the BAFTAs . . . the poison is all around us

Observer, 7 June 2015

My cousin and his Russian wife pointed out to me that any newspaper article that mentions Russian politics, including a few earlier ones of mine, is then critiqued below the line by commentators clearly in the employ of the Kremlin. I decided to bait them from within this piece, written in the wake of BAFTA, Eurovision, a racist football sex scandal and the FIFA corruption scandal's first stirrings.

As a tiny child, I fell in love with the pageantry and camaraderie of the Eurovision song contest. But my infant innocence was shattered as early as 1969, when, barely eighteen months old, I watched Norway's Kirsti Sparboe crawl criminally into last place with her swinging slice of Carnaby Street pop "Oj, Oj, Oj, Så Glad Jeg Skal Bli" (Oh, Oh, Oh, So Glad Your Skull Bleeds). From that day forth I no longer believed in the existence of a supposedly just God.

Nonetheless, throughout my adolescence I followed Eurovision blindly. I made my own Eurovision Top Trumps, carved my own Eurovision chess set (with Terry Wogan as the king) and baked myself a tiny clay Eurovision thong. I chose Eurovision, almost provocatively, over the things an '80s teenage boy was supposed to enjoy, like torn-up pornography in a wood, the New Wave of British Heavy Metal or football. In retrospect, I have only myself to blame for being kicked into the sixth-form urinal trough every day and then urinated on. And that was just by the teachers!

What an appalling thing football seemed to my youthful, Eurovision-formed sensibilities. And what an appalling thing football has remained. And what strange and self-deluding accommodations football's followers and practitioners must have to make with their beautiful game's racism, its violence, its avarice, its sectarianism, its corruption, its misogyny and its Andrew Lloyd Webber and Ben Elton musical.

The world of football is a world in which the phrase "racist orgy" really exists, and genuinely applies to an actual thing that actually happened. The phrase is not just a random meeting of deliberately tasteless words Hadron-collided together in the human subconscious for the sheer sick pleasure of their absurdity, such as paedophile frogspawn, anti-Semitic wool or colonic wasps' nest.

And last week's football players' racist orgy wasn't even spoiled by the racism. On some level, the racism appears to have improved the orgy for the young Leicester sportsmen spreading their international goodwill around in it. It's as if at some point during the orgy one of the rich football players thought, "What this orgy, already involving an arguably morally dubious power imbalance between millionaires from the developed world and poor Thai women, really needs to make it absolutely perfect is some overt racism!" It is only fair that Leicester City's mascot, Filbert Fox, is forthwith forced to Patpong to play ping-pong.

But what threatens to finally bring football down is not a racist orgy, but the plain old-fashioned human greed of FIFA, the Football Illegal Funnelling Association. Of course, in retrospect, it's obvious no just system would award the World Cup to Qatar, a country named after a sinus phlegm blockage, or, worse still, to Russia, which lacks even the distinction of sounding like a mucus-based illness, and which always generates dozens of below-the-line comments from full-time, Kremlin-controlled Internet posters, masquerading as annoying *Observer* readers, whenever I mention it in print and online.

One may as well give the *kosovorotka*-marinading wazzocks something incomprehensible to feed to their bewildered brainstems. To me, then, Vladimir Putin is a giant prolapsed female worker bee that sucks hot ridicule out of langoustines' cephalothoraxes. Let's see what crunchy, expansionist lavatory honey this notion causes the parthenogenetic Russian keyboard wendigos to inflate for us this week, in the shadow of Paul McGann and his art gnome. Happy now?

FIFA's decisions may yet be revealed as the result of backhanders as obvious as Chuck Blazer trying to sneak up on an unattended tray of Krispy Kreme doughnuts. But corruption is everywhere. For example, these days individual Eurovision songs' respective scores reflect only the shifting geopolitical allegiances or entrenched national prejudices of the voters. And since the high-water mark in '96 and '97 of Gina G's religiously ecstatic "Ooh Aah . . . Just a Little Bit" and the tectonic emotive surge of Katrina and the Waves' "Love Shine a Light", it appears some foreign agent has drugged the infinite number of monkeys we had working on our annual entries.

At the centre of this toxic bubblegum farce lies the laughing, mocking, sneering face of one man, soaked in duplicity like a sin-smeared human pikelet: the Jack Warner of Eurovision, Graham Norton. Surely it can't have been only on my face that eyebrows were raised when *The Graham Norton Show* beat my own *Comedy Vehicle* in the category of best comedy and comedy entertainment programme at last month's BAFTAs? A man failing to ask Gary Barlow about tax avoidance and tipping a member of the public out of a chair, better than my artfully crafted work? Surely there was some mistake. And yet this Norton, like Blatter, chose to accept the award as if he deserved it.

Of course, like those of Sepp Blatter, Eurovision's tentacles are long and covered in suckers, and it is very useful for the organisation to have a public face that brings BAFTA-winning credibility to its tawdry TV competition. Just as Sepp Blatter paraded a grieving Nelson Mandela at the 2010 World Cup final in order to ennoble his vile carnival of ball control, so the presence of BAFTA-winning Graham Norton, TV's Nelson Mandela of celebrity chat, at Eurovision lends the disgusting singing event a legitimacy it no longer deserves.

Eurovision is nothing more than music's FIFA. But what can be done with the bent football body now? Obviously this discredited organisation can't be allowed to run a football franchise, but is it right to squander FIFA's vast infrastructure? On the morning news last Tuesday, a nitrous-oxide-eyed Nicky Morgan, currently licking round the rim of the Gove-poisoned chalice of the education secretary post, announced that all "failing" schools would now be made into academies. An ignorantly on-message Morgan was unable to say how many academies are failing, though in September an Ofsted survey of twelve schools run by the Academies Enterprise Trust chain found half of them less than adequate, and she had no suggestion as to who might take these disastrous establishments over.

I think that rescuing failed academy schools is a job for FIFA, whose robust and flexible approach to business and ethics would appear to make them the perfect partner for the messy mallard mating-squabble Morgan's department clearly proposes for the school system. A good fit for the fundamentalist free-market future being rolled out unopposed by the government, FIFA could be swiftly rebranded as something positive, like Faith in Failing Academies, and set to work. Worse people than Sepp Blatter have already been sold a stake in the future of your children.

"'Oj, Oj, Oj, Så Glad Jeg Skal Bli' is translated as 'Oh, Oh, Oh, So Glad Your Skull Bleeds'?!? The correct translation is 'Oh, oh, oh, so glad I shall be'." Quaestio

"Even if Putin bee, he stuggle for better colony much better
for world than western wasp colonialist Lee tries to flag wave."
Eggboiger

"When Ukraine egg tousers, Putin up the strong like bull though
Lee underpants socialist Wendy-baggers." Nervinjapan

"Russia is very well doing without your Opra Winfrey western pornography and youre decadent music. More lies about
Ukraine which was only the size of a biscuit before transexual
won." General Dreedle

"Your doughnut dogma can't disguise the Russian peoples
undimmed love for its president, champion of sensible shoes and
a lonely flat full of cats." Jon56780

Top Gear: can any mortal control this foul, pulsating orifice?

Observer, 21 June 2015

When I write stand-up or prose about things like Conservative politicians, right-wing newspaper columnists, Top Gear *presenters and sports business folk, it is fun to make it as mad as possible. These sorts of people bat away comment with carefully constructed put-downs, with a punchy word ending in a hard consonant at the end of the sentence, following a rising, and finally resolved, sneery inflection. But the one thing they can't understand, despite their oft-avowed claims to a collective sense of humour, is pure silliness.* Top Gear *was marooned following Jeremy Clarkson's punching of his producer, and Chris Evans was up for his job. I think the public's blaming of the bloke Clarkson punched for being punched will be looked back on as a watershed moment, a historical barometer reading of the exact point where the heart of the nation hardened beyond healing.*

The Britpop DJ and breakfast-television innovator Chris Evans is a brave man. But perhaps he has a suicidal streak. Or maybe, more nobly, he has discovered a belated desire to do some good in the world, as if to atone for the crimes of his past, before walking willingly to his inevitable doom. Like Gene Hackman's crazy priest in *The Poseidon Adventure*, Jesus Christ from the New Testament or the nuclear clean-up crews at Fukushima, Chris Evans's odds of surviving the job he has taken on are not encouraging. But he is doing something that needs to be done, for all humanity.

Because, for years now, a vast, gaping inter-dimensional sphincter, the size of a gothic cathedral rose window, has throbbed and dilated silently at the heart of the BBC buildings on Upper Regent Street, belching fossil fumes and foul thoughts from a dark realm of negative space. I saw inside the pulsating meat oculus once, caught unawares as I stumbled across the Dave channel late at night, drunk. There, between Lee Mack's laughing face and Robson Green's leaping fish, compelling footage of the fetid portal's sickening interior unfurled endlessly into the small hours. I saw it so you don't have to.

In a fiery lake, through a carbon cloud, precious saplings were torn from their roots, the many and varied peoples of all the Earth were denigrated with arcane curses now largely vanished from the lexicon, inverts were sodomised with presumptuous jibes, a half-blind statesman was branded a "one-eyed idiot", and a poor slave, penitently proffering a tray of sandwiches, was punched in his tiny face, to the indifference of drunken onlookers.

To me, it was a vision of hell as vivid as Camposanto's wall-daubed *Triumph of Death*. To others, it is merely banter, harmless banter. I clicked rapidly forward to the relative comfort of *The Nazis – A Warning from History*, but once seen, the space-sphincter's contents could not be unseen.

No one at the BBC can quite remember when the evil muscle portal was first opened, or when it began to be a problem for the broadcaster. Elders of the organisation, bent double upon their sticks like the ancient Eric Gill patriarchs adorning their architecture, say the hole of hatred began life innocently enough as some kind of motoring consumer programme, once reputedly presented by the likes of Quentin Willson and Angela Rippon, though all evidence of this has been destroyed.

Matters came to a head last year when, after an especially violent rumble, the fractious sphincter suddenly ejected a massive torrent of bile from deep within itself, out of the cellar where it dwells, through the hot-desking communities of the BBC and into Langham Place, carrying strange creatures alive and dead from inside its horrifying maw (a two-headed turtle, a flatfish with pendulous lactating breasts, and a mummified cat that looked like Steve Howe from Yes).

In the shadow of All Souls Church a giant transparent squid, which had been spat out from within the sphincter, suddenly blistered in the sun and burst its guts, spilling out a succession of rusted car-registration plates, each carrying coded insults to the war dead of vanquished nations. Thankfully, an independent internal investigation decreed all this mere coincidence, and the exonerated hate-sphincter continued its malicious throbbing undisciplined. This was, perhaps, the moment at which all chance of controlling the entity was lost.

In the liberal press, the usual bleeding hearts called for the poisonous vacuum to be sealed with hot wax. But, removed from public opinion in their lofty Islington ivory towers, they could not comprehend the sphincter's allure. The prime minister himself confessed a fondness for the foul opening's charms. Chillaxing at night, wine goblet in hand, Dave tunes into Dave and gazes vacantly at the ever-dilating aperture's flickering but seductive pantomime of hate. Temporarily tranquillised, like all the duct's followers, he is purged of his own covert evils by witnessing overt cruelty made flesh.

To close the portal permanently would make an already wounded BBC, itself a fixture of the culture secretary's kill list, vulnerable to the criticism that it does not reflect the public it is charged to serve. To leave the depraved sphincter open and rumbling risks the release of further terrible evils into the world, the chance of international diplomatic incident and the shame, as the Earth chokes itself to death, of being on the wrong side of history.

The toxic sphincter is like Hitler's bunker. Left open but unattended it will become a focus point for the untrammelled rage of the very worst people on Earth, numbering billions globally, who believe an imaginary liberal conspiracy prevents them sending their children into school on public feast days dressed up as golliwogs, Enoch Powell or the knights of the Ku Klux Klan.

To placate them, the BBC's vibrating cesspit of vile stupidity needs to be allowed to appear to continue to function, but within safer limits. Someone needs to wade into the stinkhole's slimy opening, stand knee deep in the filth that pours from it and regulate the flow. And that person, it appears, is Chris Evans.

Like Han Solo in *Star Wars: A New Hope*, Evans is, historically, a mercenary figure, selling his considerable skills to the highest bidder, spouting populist rhetoric, while wearing a loose-fitting, but ultimately transparent, waistcoat of apparent rebelliousness and puckish individuality. But maybe the crisis caused by the endless toxic discharge issuing from the BBC's subterranean bile-valve has forced Evans's hand.

Previous denizens of the hate-hole were a generation removed from Evans, in attitudes if not always in age. But Evans, despite his regrettable friendships with many of the earlier guardians of the pit, is a product of the post-punk Age of Enlightenment. While his mid-'90s TV persona parroted the contemporary New Lad agenda, it at least appeared to do so with some degree of irony. But will Evans's reflexive, nuanced echoes still sound so strongly when his words have only the soft, filth-smeared flesh walls of the abominable sphincter to bounce off?

The chalice Evans has accepted is poisoned, and there is some old wee or something on the bit where you hold it at the bottom, and that wee will probably go on his hand. But I give Evans my blessing, despite the fact that I, as a multi-BAFTA-award-winning BBC star myself, have been anxiously awaiting the call to accept the detoxification job that he has finally been offered.

"I really don't think I have ever read such an appalling load of pretentious nonsense EVER!! This explains why I seldom if ever read the *Guardian*, it's standards are so low today as to make it's opinions irellevant." Harry Merrick

"I think it's time to finally ditch the *Guardian*. This piece of self-serving polemic drivel, would've firmly belonged in the *Sun* or *Daily Star* when I first read the *Guardian*. Unfortunately, it would seem that the editors have lost the plot and let Stewart Lee pass off his own inner jealousy of Clarkeson and in fact any other of his journalistic industry who have done better than himself. Enough. Goodbye." Gary Clarke

"Reads like the ramblings of a madman." Fuego999

"What a waste of my life reading this article was. I am utterly and profoundly devastated – not to mention disappointed in ones self – that it took me to approximately half way through the fourth paragraph to realise what a load of biased, unfounded and new age 'PC' load of garbage this article was." John B

A passport to my lovely garden? Dream on, you wretched souls

Observer, 28 June 2015

I have a house with a garden now, in London, something that was beyond my wildest dreams until very recently. Obviously I feel guilty about it, as I do not believe my success is "deserved", and I don't see how anyone can be so blinkered as to believe that their privilege, and other people's deprivation, represents some form of deserved justice. And yet the Conservative world view enforces this idea, just as the migrant crisis ought to make us all realise that our own relative security and wealth are just accidents of geography and birth.

I broke this piece down into stand-up, and it hung around the try-out gigs for the fourth series of Stewart Lee's Comedy Vehicle *for about nine months. The executive producer loved it because it was funny on paper, like a newspaper article, but in performance it always sounded too "written", despite me trying to conversationalise it night after night for the best part of a year. It had been written as prose, not stand-up, and it's surprising how little I have been able to raid from the thousands of words making up the columns I have written to use in the live act. Apart from the odd line here and there, nothing carries across.*

Late in my life I have become the owner of a house with a garden. But there are very few gardens in the area of the inner city where I live and naturally my garden has become a focus of envy from the deserving poor.

Last Sunday I was in my garden, drinking fine champagne from the bottle and playing croquet on the lawn with my pantalooned children, when I began to notice some of the people with no gardens from other less salubrious parts of the borough straddling my fence. They were probably jealous of my lawn and flowerbeds, and wished they could have them, which they can't because they are mine and I must deserve them otherwise why would they have come into my possession?

I squirted the grasping interlopers in their puzzled faces with greenfly spray and then poked them off the fence with a hoe, sending them tumbling down into the fly-tipped mattresses and old nappies below in the council flats' parking area. Then I went off to smash up some champagne bottles so I could fix broken glass to the top of the fence, in order to lacerate off the interlopers' buttocks and genitals should they try to climb the fence again, the vile cockroaches. A newt lives below the steps up to the house. I am kind to it.

Later in the day I became aware that the North London Hang Gliding Club were holding their monthly glide-past in the sky above my garden, with the usual and inevitable consequences. Soon the bodies began falling, the mortal shells of poor misguided souls who mistakenly hoped they could find their way into my garden from the air, and had clung to the glider wings, like kittens gone viral on Twitter, but not cute enough to earn their own hashtags.

Luckily, I had already taken the precaution of suspending cricket nets from the tree branches that hang over the garden to catch the falling corpses, which I then threw into the compost to decompose out of sight. My neighbour, who is Australian, has taken to bribing the glider pilots to have their flying fun further south, so that any stowaways make their fatal final landfall in the nearby boroughs of Islington or Camden, rather than onto our immaculate lawns, solving the immediate problem.

At around teatime I was wearing small tight white tennis shorts and drinking champagne again, while playing swingball with a TV producer friend from the media, when I heard a noise coming from the old sewer below the patio. The ongoing escalation of these constant interruptions, all in one afternoon, remember, was rapidly becoming tiresome.

Handing Alan my champagne and racket, and crouching down on my bare knees by the manhole cover, I heard a voice say, "Please can we come in your garden? We haven't got a garden where we live." And I said, "No, get back in that sewer, you no-garden people. I'm very sorry that you haven't got a garden but this is my garden and I deserve it." And I walked away. But the tapping continued.

I listened again. "Please, it's really horrible in the sewer. We've been crawling through it for days. And back at the other end of it there's no food and a man trying to behead us." This changed things, I suppose. A straightforward narrative based on simple avaricious envy of my garden had been complicated to encompass a basic human desire for survival, a trickier thing to dismiss out of hand.

But as I considered the problem, the manhole lid started coming off. Luckily, I managed to force the woman beneath it back down into the sewer, kicking her in the face and punching her. And then I slammed the cover back down, at least buying myself a little more time to ponder the moral dilemma her plea had posited.

Then, still wrapped in thought, I put a really big flowerpot on the manhole cover so that she and the other people without gardens couldn't get into my garden through their hole. This solved the problem to an extent. They still hadn't got gardens but at least they weren't in my garden. They were trapped in a sewer underneath my garden, dying, which was better, I think. And also, their deaths would hopefully deter any other people without gardens from trying to come through the sewer into my garden, which they can't, because it's mine.

I wondered if it was really humane to have people trapped in a sewer and dying just for trying to get into your garden. Then it came to me. The real cruelty lay in my allowing people to go into the sewer in the first place. So I found an old drainage plan on the Internet, noting that the sewer surfaced somewhere out on Hackney Marshes, which had recently been occupied by a sadistic fascist death cult hell-bent on the murder of anyone they disagreed with even remotely, which was unfortunate, but hardly my fault.

I got into the armoured 4×4 I use for the school run and drove round to the sewer opening, where the people without gardens were getting in, and poured petrol all over it and blew it up in a massive explosion, so that all the people without gardens who had been going into the sewer could stay where they were and die there from being starved and beheaded, like they were supposed to, rather than dying in a sewer on the way into my garden which is mine.

And then I thought, if only there were something I could do to make the whole world fairer so that the people trying to get into my garden didn't feel the need to try and get into my garden in the first place. But there just isn't, I suppose.

And so I laze in my garden, champagne glass in hand, the bubbles popping in the sun, as the fence wobbles and buckles, and bodies block out the light as they tumble into the cricket nets, and the manhole cover over the sewer rumbles and grumbles. Later I will raise the fence an inch or so and stick more glass on the top of it, and roll another old flowerpot over the manhole cover. And before bed I will tighten the nets once more and empty the day's catch into the compost. But for now, I will swing here in my hammock, sipping my champagne and sniffing my freshly mowed lawn in the dying of the midsummer day.

"I never read most boring article on *Guardian*. Editor are becoming lazy without reading impose these kind of boring article on reader." Raghuvansch1

"Presumably you bought the property through a normal, legal transaction having also come by the money to do so legally. Perhaps you earned it through socially useful work. Perhaps you won some of it in a legitimate gaming contract, such as betting on a greyhound. Perhaps you earned some money and invested it in a business, which provided goods or services to fellow citizens and employment for others, while also offering a return on your capital. Or maybe you inherited some from close relatives who came by it themselves in an honest way. There are lots of ways you could have accumulated the money to buy a modest property without needing to feel shame. Perhaps you have been misled into thinking that you and your family working hard at an honest job and enjoying some luck from time to time (as well as suffering the vicissitudes of existence according to the laws of chance and fate) is a source of dishonour, for which you should offer up a public display of sarcastic self-flagellation. Perhaps, in short, you have read the *Guardian* too much." B26354

"Changes come no matter what one person can do to stop them, and the world will keep spinning its burdens of joy and sorrow until it becomes too unbalanced, and it all winds down and stops." Vadata1940

It's too late to save our world, so enjoy the spectacle of doom

Observer, 5 July 2015

In the middle of a week of record temperatures, as if unaware of the irony the business community celebrated the consolidation of its attempts to force the government's hand to agree to a third filth-generating runway at Heathrow, tipping all species on Earth towards extinction. Everything will die soon, except for cockroaches, and Glastonbury favourite The Fall, who will survive even a nuclear holocaust, though they will still refuse to play their '80s chart hits.

In Norfolk on Thursday, the tarmac melted, and ducklings became trapped in sticky blackness. When a lioness whelped in an ancient Roman street, Caesar thought something was up. Here, solid matter transmuted to hot liquid and swallowed baby birds whole. How surreal do the signs and warnings have to become before we stop in our tracks? Are whales required to fall from the sky? Does Tim Henman have to give birth to a two-headed cat on Centre Court?

CBI director John Cridland says: "The government must commit to the decision now, and get diggers in the ground at Heathrow swiftly by 2020." Head of the Institute of Directors Simon Walker says: "There can now be no further delay from politicians." And Segro chief executive David Sleath merely bellows: "Get on with it!" like some selfish *Top Gear* presenter demanding his steak dinner after dawdling, the planet itself the powerless BBC employee he punches in the face.

The business community has thrown its executive toys out of the pram, and now there are chrome ball bearings on strings everywhere, tripping up unpaid interns and making life difficult for immigrant cleaners scrabbling under desks on less than minimum wage. David Cameron, an electoral promise to oppose the third runway sticking in his throat like an undigested salmon bone, can only duck his cowardly head and hope some terrible atrocity or a Wimbledon win wafts our attention away.

When I was a child, my grandmother always referred to our pet dog's excrement as "business", so to this day, when I envisage "the business community", I imagine a vast pile of sentient faeces issuing its demands while smoking a Cuban cigar, an image that seems increasingly accurate as the decades pass.

The destruction of all life on Earth is inevitable if fossil fuel use continues unabated. (Legal, please advise. Are we allowed to say this now without being shouted down by Nigel Lawson?) The business community's genius move in the third runway debate has been to change the dialogue from an argument which should have been between building a runway and not building a runway at all, and trying to restructure our society to avoid the need for a third runway, into an argument about where exactly it was best to position this massive portent of our world's forthcoming doom. It's like offering an innocent man who doesn't want to be hanged the chance to be poisoned instead.

As with fracking and the academification of all schools, decisions have already been made behind closed doors by forces beyond our control. Heathrow's third runway will happen. Assurances about air quality are meaningless. The UK has already been threatened with £300 million a year fines by those meddling Brussels bureaucrats for our terrible British air, and Boris's solution in London was to spray adhesive around the city by night to try and stick the pesky pollution particles to the pavement, like a lazy duplicitous boy pushing his mess under his bed rather than tidying up his room.

And in fifty years will there be anyone left to remember what it was like before a sterile and toxic environment gradually became the norm? Can it only be four decades ago that every summer-holiday trek along A-roads to South Devon caravan sites left our Morris Marina windscreen smeared thick with now-disappeared invertebrates, that sparrows swarmed around morning milk bottles, that sticklebacks and minnows spawned in every park pond, that hedgehogs gathered at night in suburban gardens and lay flattened in their thousands on roads every morning, and that an actual hare ran out of the encroached common land of Palmers Rough, on the fringes of Birmingham, to be chased by my grandfather along Arnold Road in that same Morris Marina, a sight that would seem as surreal today as escaped hippos wandering the streets of some collapsed eastern European capital?

The absence of abundance is already accepted. The metaphors of the nature poets, mapping human hearts through once commonly understood imagery, are irrelevant and impenetrable.

> The sun of Winter,
> The moon of Summer, and all the singing birds
> Except the missel-thrush that loves juniper,
> Are quite shut out.

I'm sorry. The missel-what? Can the juniper be monetised? Is this missel-thing for sale? Our children already have no stable baseline from which to calibrate the loss of all that lives. It's game over.

Bearing this in mind, I finally find myself reluctantly agreeing with the business community. There is no time for delay. Let's build the runway. Let's choke the Earth. Let's get this damn thing over with, for what can be avoided, whose end is purposed by the mighty gods of business? Hasten our demise, let our children be the last of their sorry line, and spare their unborn descendants any further suffering. We will not save the rhino. We will not even save the hedgehog. How can we save the world?

But if you can purge cheap sentiment from your mind, how exciting and fascinating it will be to watch as the world becomes uninhabitable. It's almost worth going on a health kick to survive another sixty years and see everything immolated. How many humans have had the awe-inspiring opportunity to witness such spectacle, the end of all that is?

But something of us should be preserved, I think, for posterity. Perhaps the village of Harmondsworth and its residents, instead of being demolished and paid off at 125 per cent of their homes' market values, should be sealed within a vast dome and shot spacewards, to drift on the solar winds as a museum of mankind, saving something of our society at the point where it finally became unsustainable.

Under a vast skein of convex glass Harmondsworth floats beyond Orion's Belt, its ancient tithe barn, Betjeman's "cathedral of Middlesex", still and safe under the stars; local resident Graham Wibrew, his once imperilled kitchen extension complete, watches the comets and thinks of home; and the bells of eleventh-century St Mary's toll the eternal hours silently in endless empty space.

> But far more ancient and dark
> The Combe looks since they killed the badger there,
> Dug him out and gave him to the hounds,
> That most ancient Briton of English beasts.

> Edward Thomas, "The Combe"

Cameron's monkeys are feasting on the BBC's nuts

Observer, 12 July 2015

In this column I have mistakenly used essentially the same Marie Antoinette joke I used in another column, also included here, four months earlier. In the interests of full disclosure, I leave it unaltered.

In January 2014, when a critically endangered water lily was stolen from Kew Gardens, the former Conservative MP Louise Mensch tweeted on her Twitter: "Got to say what's the point? Ordinary plant hardly worth saving." The Conservatives can't even see the point of flowers. It's asking a lot to expect them to see the point of the BBC. It doesn't even attract bees.

As a student in the late summer of 1988, I was backpacking in the far south-east of Turkey, blissfully unaware in those distant, pre-Internet days that an undeclared civil war against the Kurds was now covertly under way. Not knowing I had anything to fear, I floated with vacant impunity through military manoeuvres and migrating masses, danced at an illegal Kurdish wedding, and happily ate a bag of nuts riddled with green worms. There is much to be said for stupidity. Ignorance was strength.

But on a minibus on a dark dirt road out of the frontier town of Diyarbakir, a Turkish man from Istanbul, with artificially curly dyed blond hair and a Samantha Fox T-shirt, loudly declared the Kurds dirty dogs, and deep-veined regional rivalries suddenly exploded into violence. I, wearing salmon pink Aladdin pants, intervened clumsily, as knives flashed in the aisle. "Let's just cool it, OK, guys? Peace, yeah?"

Then someone noted my accent. "British!" said the men, putting away their weapons and laughing. "BBC! Del Boy fall through bar! Funniest scene ever. Licence fee very good value at twice price."

It was a remarkable moment, and one made even more remarkable by the fact that the classic episode of *Only Fools and Horses* in which Del Boy falls through the bar was not even broadcast until four months later, yet the BBC pratfall was already accepted globally as a benchmark of quality entertainment in places miles from anything the Conservatives would recognise as civilised.

But the Conservatives' assault on the BBC continues apace, doubtless to the delight of the shady media moguls with whom they regularly share clandestine Cotswold kitchen suppers, yachts and borrowed police horses. And like all the Conservatives' carefully chosen targets – foxes, lilies and abstract ideas like beauty, truth, fairness and empathy wherever they are to be found – the BBC is either unable or unwilling to speak out in its own defence.

That incoherent howling in your garden at night? That's foxes forcing their primitive vocal cords to articulate the argument against David Cameron's sherry-swilling friends dismembering them for fun. Incoherent as it is, this nocturnal yowling remains more convincing than anything anyone at the battered BBC has felt able to say to justify the internationally respected, world-class broadcasting organisation's own ongoing existence, at a cost to the individual annually equivalent to around 200 iTunes downloads.

The BBC's five-year funding was supposed to be in place. But on Monday, in the sort of shady behind-closed-doors negotiations we were assured wouldn't happen again after they did exactly the same thing last time, the government suddenly had the BBC 20 per cent down on the deal, due to the apparently non-negotiable withdrawal of OAPs' licence-fee subsidy. Like Marie Antoinette, unaware of the difference between nourishment and subsistence, Cameron leans from the Versailles palace window and declares, "Let them watch Eamonn Holmes."

On Tuesday I stopped in at the BBC comedy offices, only

recently a vast wing of White City's iconic doughnut building, but today a small room above a 7–11 on Marylebone Road, from where all the unit's globally lauded content is produced. A blabber-mouthed producer, high on petrol fumes and Pret A Manger breadless prawn sandwiches, explained the circumstances behind the killer budget decrease. Apparently, BBC director general Tony Hall had been forced at cattle-prod point into a sheep-shearing shed by the Conservative culture secretary, John Whittingdale, and quite simply bullied.

Whittingdale, a massive fan of the twenty-first-century horror-movie genre of torture porn, had strung Hall up over a meat hook and repeatedly spat into his face while dressed as an old woman, in an attempt to make him cry, punishing the innocent peer for Whittingdale's own hatred of quality arts and politics coverage, a misguided act of transference cruelly reminiscent of the latest Rihanna video.

But Lord Hall's willpower had proved strong, perhaps due to him being the only girl on the high-school camping trip to the forest who wasn't a downright filthy, pot-smoking slut; so Whittingdale had menaced him with some little gnashing mechanical dentures that jumped up and down by themselves on plastic webbed feet, biting at Hall's penis, and then with clockwork, fez-wearing musical monkeys in waistcoats that smashed their cymbals hard on the baron's testicles.

The consensus view in the corridors was that Hall's emergence from Whittingdale's corrugated-iron lair with a loss of 20 per cent further BBC funding may look lamentable, but it was only the lord's legendary negotiating skills – deployed calmly and collectedly, even as the culture secretary's phlegm and mucus crystallised on his noble, opera-loving face, while mechanical monkeys pulverised his scrotum – that meant he had his genitals merely mutilated, rather than chopped off entirely and eaten by leading Conservatives.

Hall's eleventh-hour rescuers, the eel-wrestling he-man Steve Backshall from *Deadly 60* and the scuba-diving BBC Trust chair Rona Fairhead, have since let slip that the culture secretary already had fava beans pan-frying on the hob when they bashed his shed door in, and that had they arrived even seconds later things might have been much worse.

David Cameron's embossed dinner invite, meanwhile, had clearly been dispatched hours earlier. Look closely at live parliamentary coverage from later last Monday and you'll see an aide hand him an envelope, and upon opening it the prime minister licks his tiny lips and mouths to himself the simple word "Delicious!"

In an attempt to stop the story escalating, Lord Hall issued an official statement. Even though his penis had been mutilated by the culture secretary John Whittingdale's arsenal of sickeningly modified clockwork toys, his testicles remained largely unscathed by the ferocious musical apes and dancing teeth, and he conceded that "far from being a cut, this is the right deal for my genitals in difficult economic circumstances".

Last week, I found myself watching a repeat of the May meeting of President Obama and the naturalist and former BBC programme director David Attenborough. Slowly and patiently, Attenborough made the case for nature. Its value was beyond the monetary. It was where our imaginations lived. And once it was gone it was gone. He could have been making the case for the BBC.

"Why do I always feel with Stewart Lee that whatever point he is making (often ones I agree with) comes second to trying to impress everyone with how clever he is being?" 1969nbrown

"'I, wearing salmon pink Aladdin pants, intervened clumsily, as knives flashed in the aisle. "Let's just cool it, OK guys? Peace, yeah?" Then someone noted my accent. "British!" said the men, putting away their weapons and laughing. "BBC! Del Boy fall through bar! Funniest scene ever. Licence fee very good value at twice price.' Evidently the above writer does not recognise when he is being laughed at rather than with and if that is the sort of British culture he would like to see Britain best known for around the world then it explains why he is so supportive of the present dumbed down BBC." Unlywntd

"Ah yes – a bunch of third world types fighting each other with knives retreat in confusion when the white sahib in pink pants stands up and tells them to cut it out. I thought these *Guardian* types were against stereotyping, but I guess it's OK if they do it since they have their hearts, if not their brains, in the right place." JanwaarBibi

The government's witch-hunters are ready to reform the BBC to death

Observer, 19 July 2015

As this book goes to press, a year after the column was published, the writing is on the wall.

Due to its legendary nose for news, last week's *Sunday Times* was first to reveal the "eight experts" chosen by culture secretary John Whittingdale to "help decide the BBC's future", the Murdoch empire barely able to wait to share its horror at the venerable institution's latest humiliation.

And what a golden shower of talent Whittingdale has stitched together, a veritable human centipede of business-minded entities, in order to safeguard the nation's cultural heritage.

Dawn Airey is the former head of Channel 5, the launch of which in 1997 marked a colourful new chapter in British broadcasting. Some might say that asking a former head of Channel 5 to decide the future of the BBC is a bit like asking someone who draws ejaculating penises on the inside of public-toilet cubicle doors to curate the National Gallery, but she is sure to bring an interesting perspective to the negotiating table.

Dame Colette Bowe sits alongside her, chief press officer to the late Leon Brittan in the 1970s, and currently chairwoman of the Banking Standards Board. She must be brilliant, as bringing standards to banking is a tough job. Apparently, there's a Conservative MPs' Scruples Committee as well.

Darren Henley is a former managing director of Classic FM, which is like Radio 3 with all the problematic programmes filleted out, the perfect playlist to keep people calm while they wait on hold for hours for someone in a call centre to answer their phone. "Just one Cornetto! Give it to me! Delicious ice cream. From Italy."

Andrew Fisher is the executive chairman of Shazam, a smartphone app which identifies unknown songs, and with which he has made the world a much duller place, bereft of mystery; crushing the richness of human experience for economic gain, giving you what you want, right here, right now. Perhaps Andrew can now develop an app that can identify what someone has had for dinner from the smell of their farts?

His co-committee member, Alex Mahon, is a former chief executive of Elisabeth Murdoch's Shine Group, connecting her to the exciting world of government-friendly media businessfolk, Cotswold kitchen-supper snafflers, and police horse-sharers, and to those most likely to monetise the vacant space left in broadcasting should she and her colleagues have, regrettably, to reform the BBC out of existence.

In an atmosphere reminiscent of a medieval witch trial, where the three-nippled woman with all the cats is bound to be found guilty of whatever she can be tortured into confessing to, everyone knows the BBC has been doing something wrong, and must be punished, just as soon as some appropriate crimes can be agreed upon.

But no one so far seems to know what kind of BBC they want. Our metrosexual prime minister believes it should concentrate on the kind of HBO box set programming he and Sam enjoy when chillaxing at home, and which he imagines emerges fully formed from a salami-making machine in Los Angeles.

Others complain the BBC makes shows that are "too commercial", and clearly it would be better if the job of making popular shows, and indeed all television, was left up to Sky, since they are so good at it. But who could ever have dreamed that a show about an old man travelling through time in a phone box, a laugh-track-free sitcom set in a paper-company office, complete with cutaways to photocopier in-trays, and a motoring review show in which vehicle analysis is interspersed with actionably inappropriate banter would become commercial hits?

True creativity isn't an exact science. But is there anyone on the culture secretary's panel of business-friendly bean-counters who understands this? Indeed, the actual creative talents who have made the BBC the globally respected brand it is of late are notably absent from the negotiations.

Where is Armando Iannucci, a BBC-nurtured polymath now making box-set content for HBO? Where are Russell T. Davies, Mark Gatiss and Steven Moffatt, who between them made massively successful brands of genres viewers maintained that they loathed – nerdy science fiction, sexless literary detective stories and hardcore gay action? Where are Dick and Dom or *Horrible Histories*, educating children by stealth, and David Attenborough, who did the same to generations of adults? And where am I?

Like it or not, and I am not sure that I do, I am objectively the most critically acclaimed British TV comedian this century, and every one of my BBC series of the last decade has been either nominated for, or won, multiple BAFTA, British Comedy and Chortle awards. Any panel on the future of the BBC that includes a phone-app bloke over me is clearly not worth the beer mat it was hastily drawn up on.

The sad truth is, the reason none of the above artists, writers and communicators are welcome on the culture secretary's committee is because they see culture as inherently valuable in and of itself, not simply as a branch of business that is too naive to know how to maximise its profit margins. And there is no place for them in his process.

Last Sunday, after I read in the *Sunday Times* of the culture secretary's plans, I was stuck in traffic on the North Circular with the kids. A new young writer called John Osborne, who I hadn't heard of before, came on Radio 4 and told a half-hour story about childhood holidays that left all of us, aged four, eight and forty-seven, spellbound. The kids noticed I was crying and asked why.

I explained it was not just the quality of the work, but also that the government was dismantling the only broadcaster that would ever commission it. My eight-year-old said that if David Cameron did that, he would send him a collage of hundreds of photographs of dog muck. You cross creatives at your peril.

I've been watching a lot of spaghetti westerns of late. I developed a taste for them in the late '80s, when Alex Cox used to rave about them on BBC2's *Moviedrome*, informing me, educating me and entertaining me, as he did. Their big, simple gestures tell me everything I need to know. Robert Hossein's revenge tale *Cemetery without Crosses*, from 1969, has just been cleaned up for commercial release by Arrow films.

Maria (Michèle Mercier) arranges for the daughter of her husband's killer to be raped. But in a haunting, dialogue-free scene, her uncertain expression appears to convey a hint of regret that she let her desire for vengeance get the better of her conscience.

"I would be able to take this article much more seriously if it wasn't for this: 'Like it or not, and I am not sure that I do, I am objectively the most critically acclaimed British TV comedian this century, and every one of my BBC series of the last decade has been either nominated for, or won, multiple BAFTA, British Comedy and Chortle awards. Any panel on the future of the BBC that includes a phone-app bloke over me is clearly not worth the beer mat it was hastily drawn up on.' It's so pompous it actually made me wet myself. And honestly, I don't think you're very funny." Paul Vigg

"Nothing more enjoyable than a luvvy taking himself seriously. 'And what a golden shower of talent Whittingdale has stitched together, a veritable human centipede of business-minded entities, in order to safeguard the nation's cultural heritage.' Whereas comedian (and receiver of BBC funds) Stewart Lee is perfectly placed to comment . . ." Grauddown

"And can we have the NEXT special-pleading piece from a BBC beneficiary please. This one's done." Mmmmbisto

"Bitter, twisted and mendacious. If this is the best the BBCs supporters can do then it's in more trouble than I thought." Bigoldles

The Tories are using my holiday to change history

Observer, 9 August 2015

Professional columnists, who have to file the required wordage every week for ever, would never baulk at using a family holiday for material. I wondered if I could, without either giving anything away or sliding into nauseating flim-flam.

I have been on holiday in an isolated Pyrenean shack for two weeks. I enjoy not being approached by people who think I am the lead singer of UB40 all the time, my wife delights in juicy tomatoes and the kids love eating snails, befriending local snails and swimming with snails in the streams and lakes.

One day, having booked months in advance as required, we joined a party of twenty to venture through a secured airlock into an ancient cave and walk an hour underground to see the visionary animal artworks of our ancestors. The cave in question offers the only opportunity worldwide to see a prehistoric depiction of a weasel, which was something I had wanted to tick off my bucket list.

The guide told us, in English, that a British visitor had urinated in the hermetically sealed and temperature-controlled cavern the previous week, despite all the warnings about contaminating the cave paintings, and requested that any British people present please refrain from doing so, as the incident had left the archaeologists utterly distraught. It is always interesting to learn how others see us.

The art was so far beneath ground anthropologists assumed the artists never intended it for public display, so perhaps the urinating culprit was someone who felt the content providers should be punished for failing to monetise their work as part of a free-market economy?

I was suitably embarrassed by my compatriot's behaviour, but wondered what British person could have such contempt for art, history and human culture that they would deliberately book months ahead on an exclusive tour only to try and despoil the unique works with their hot urine.

Returning home, I checked the itineraries of the culture secretary, John Whittingdale, and his predecessor, Sajid Javid, but they had not been in France, and yet the fact that I assumed one of them must be to blame was an indicator of how events at home were playing on my mind.

I had been worried about leaving the country in the care of the new government, like a parent trusting their family home to unruly teenage children, only to return to find a fortnight-long laughing-gas party has destroyed every precious heirloom. Granny's commemorative coronation commode lies shattered in the garden; Auntie Gladys's Queen Mother-faced gas mask has been used as a bong; and the smashed remnants of the BBC have been stuffed into the lavatory and defiled.

I don't have an iPhone, and there was no TV in the mountain shed, so the news from home came in disturbing dribs from British newspapers picked up at the nearest town, seventy miles away, of which I found only two in the entire fortnight: a *Guardian* dated 24 July and an international edition of the *Daily Mail* from 28 July.

When you are far away and one copy of the *Daily Mail* is all you have to go on, the world distorts like a fairground mirror. The front page said a Labour peer had been taking drugs with prostitutes. It is to be hoped that George "Pencils" Osborne, when he is leader of the government, will take his thick brown pencil and ban from public office anyone who has ever had even the slightest connection with cocaine and call girls.

Meanwhile, on page 14, the demonstrably inaccurate writer Quentin Letts rubbished institutionalised attempts to encourage social mobility in an incoherent column that included the genuine sentence: "Middle-class parents are middle class because they have learnt what it takes to succeed."

The sentence, of course, does not bear a moment's analysis, attempting to assuage readers' guilt by assuring them their privilege is deserved. But it seemed so bizarre to me that such a sentence could actually be written without shame, only twelve days after I had left the country, only two and a half months after the Conservative victory, that I wondered what was really going on at home.

In his 1952 short story "A Sound of Thunder", the writer Ray Bradbury, after whom I named my hamster as a child, posits a form of time-travel tourism. Clients may visit any point in the past, but must stay on a floating metal walkway, for fear of interacting with history in such a way as to alter the future.

A time tourist, Eckels, is frightened by a dinosaur, falls momentarily from the path, and returns to the future with a butterfly crushed on the sole of his shoe, only to find the world now subtly changed. Everyone is speaking Latvian and people have penises for hands. Or something like that. It's thirty-six years since I read it.

Experiencing Letts's strange *Daily Mail* sentence, I wondered if the unopposed Conservative juggernaut's unstoppable forward motion meant that something indefinable was happening to the collective consciousness of Britain while I was away that would irrevocably alter the very idea of what could constitute truth itself, which would render the world to which I returned from my holiday as unrecognisable as Bradbury's Latvian penis-hands dystopia.

In the edition of the *Guardian* dated Friday 24 July, which I found abandoned in a campsite lavatory two days after I read Letts's column, I saw an article on the suspension of a UK ban on crop sprays containing neonicotinoids, thought by most scientists to harm bees.

On this occasion, apparently, the Department for Environment, Food and Rural Affairs abandoned its normal practice of publishing the minutes of its meetings in order to avoid "provoking representations from different interest groups".

I wondered what the sentence meant. It appeared to mean that Defra, which is now mainly run and owned by the commercial outsourcing company Capita, wasn't going to make available any information that it felt people might take issue with.

You get the result you want by concealing any information that might challenge that result? I am sure this sort of thing hadn't been acceptable practice when I went on holiday two weeks ago. Had somebody somewhere stepped off the path?

I was afraid. I phoned my father in Coventry to see if everything was OK. His accent seemed vaguely eastern European. He seemed to be having trouble holding the phone.

Suddenly, the rain came down. I sat under an awning and rolled my red wine around in my hand, Letts's column, the cocaine-bust exposé and the Defra story spread out before me. An electrical storm crackled over the Pyrenees, vast flat planes of light flashing behind the clouds, giving the impression of impossibly powerful forces moving somewhere out of sight.

"Nice article, but I don't think I'd read a newspaper I found discarded in a toilet – even the *Guardian*." Bigmickey2

"Cave paintings are crap and deserved to be pissed on." Id5279x

"Cave paintings are extraordinary. They show animal life in movement realistically and the economic means for continued human life from incredibly little materials, all originally invented. They see deeply into the psyche of early humanity." Parcelofrogue

"Another painfully pretentious writer. It's not possible to read past the first sentence without cringing. '. . . and the kids love eating snails, befriending local snails and swimming with snails in the streams and lakes.' Weird kids who eat their 'friends'!!" Jerrykryz

"Incomprehensible and probably neoliberal. He should leave the EU, join JC's Red Army and get some truth back into his life." Crazeecracka

Can we be absolutely certain Iain Duncan Smith is real?

Observer, 23 August 2015

Last week, the Department for Work and Pensions tsar, Iain Duncan Smith, was revealed to have fabricated a pamphlet featuring two entirely fictitious former benefit claimants, using Conservative Party stationery-cupboard scissors and an adhesive he emits from a weeping gland in his own perineum.

The level of happiness in the work-shy duo's photos, in which they beamed about the just withdrawal of their benefits, was utterly convincing. I wondered if the models featured had been told to imagine seeing Iain Duncan Smith fall into a wood chipper while wearing Michael Gove as a novelty meat hat.

And I realised that in so doing, I had fulfilled a *Daily Telegraph* reader's stereotyping of a modern comedian as someone who thinks images of unacceptable physical violence against public hate figures constitute a substitute for genuine wit.

But much as I would love to see the Conservatives make some catastrophic public-relations error that would permanently damage their so far untarnished reputation, I was not sure that Sarah and Zacgate was it.

There is, of course, a long history of public campaigns featuring ludicrous and fictitious characters designed to convey messages to the proletariat. Indeed, the last Labour election effort featured an unlikely puppet character called Ed, who wrote his thoughts in big letters on a semi-portable gravestone.

Historically, our masters have always imagined we lowly peasants will digest information more easily if it is written, for example, in a speech bubble coming out of the mouth of an imaginary squirrel pedestrian in yellow loon pants.

Yes, baby-boomers, there was no Tufty. The road-safety rodent was as unreal as Iain Duncan Smith's Sarah and Zac, if less cuddly. And perhaps the Green Cross Man's catchphrase – "Remember, I won't be there when you cross the road because I am a fictional character designed as a vehicle for public safety information" – should have alerted the children of the '70s to the non-existence of their favourite traffic-awareness superhero.

As an adopted child, my acceptance of my situation was greatly eased by early exposure to a book called *Mr Fairweather and His Family*. It was the beautifully illustrated story of a man, Mr Fairweather, who, having failed to find the emotional satisfaction he craved from getting either a cat, a dog or a wife, finally achieved it by getting an abandoned child off an old woman in a room full of cots in a grey government building.

Alcohol or drugs would doubtless have provided Mr Fairweather with similar consolations to fatherhood and would have been cheaper than a child in the long run. Nonetheless, the utilitarian fiction of *Mr Fairweather and His Family* was a superb piece of socially useful work I treasure to this day, and I remain eternally grateful to its titular and non-existent, ennui-ridden anti-hero Mr Fairweather, the Josef K of prescriptive childcare literature, for normalising my early years.

But not all fictionalised information-carrying characters are as popular as Tufty, the Green Cross Man and our jaded Mr Fairweather, with his disappointing cat, his unfulfilling dog and his unstimulating wife. People with long memories, who perhaps visited western Canada in the '80s, may nonetheless struggle to recall the once widely reviled public infotainer, Chilliwack the Aids Ptarmigan.

A plump cartoon gamebird in a Vancouver Canucks ice-hockey shirt, voiced by the legendary Canadian comedian Richard Lett, it was Chilliwack the Aids Ptarmigan's duty to instruct the gay communities of Alberta and British Columbia about safe-sex practices during the first Aids panic.

Over music provided by Ontario progressive rockers Christmas, a series of crudely drawn information films pictured stereotyped Tom of Finland-type lumberjacks about to get down to business in Rocky Mountain log cabins, only to find the Aids Ptarmigan fluttering around their heads advising them to act responsibly, squawking his catchphrase "We see thee rise!"

Needless to say, Chilliwack the Aids Ptarmigan swiftly became the butt of a thousand Canadian stand-up comedy routines, and his short-lived, sex-fearing reign of gay terror has been largely erased from cyberspace by censorious and retrospectively ashamed Canadian public-health bodies.

Given the long history of unconvincing public-information avatars, initially I wondered why it was that Iain Duncan Smith's Zac and Sarah had annoyed everyone so. Andy Burnham went as far as to say the DWP had been caught "red-handed", even as he and his moderate Labour co-candidates themselves assume the blurred penumbrae of implausible forgotten fictions.

Zac and Sarah may not be real, but perhaps they are not entirely unreal. I looked closely at their pictures in Iain Duncan Smith's false pamphlet. The pair looked as convincing as anyone. A woman I might have met at a library once. A man I might have kicked a ball around with in a south London park. And yet they were products of a propaganda machine.

I looked at Iain Duncan Smith on a YouTube interview clip. His skin covered his body accurately. Hair grew convincingly out of parts of his head and from patches on his arms. Teeth protruded from his gums. His ears were on the side of his face and his mouth opened and closed when he spoke. Was it, perhaps, all too good to be true?

The Right has a colourful recent history of fictitious personalities. Former Conservative Party chairman Grant Shapps was briefly thought to have been the unreal alter ego of a pseudonymous Internet privateer called Michael Green, and some even suggested the actual Shapps had been substituted by an alien clone after a UFO abduction in Kansas in 1989.

The Left has interrogated itself about its election failure, but maybe the battle was lost some time ago? This Zac and Sarah, the unreal people, selling a political fiction, maybe they are just the tip of the ice cube? Maybe it's all unreal, all the way down, the speeches, the photo opportunities? Actors move across a canvas. Paint splashes on a stage. Non-negotiable promises come and go.

I am in Edinburgh at the fringe festival. I walk to my venue, across town, at around midday. And every day, at the same time, I find myself moving east down the cobbles of the Royal Mile, against the upward flow of human traffic, in a vast throng of people. Actors press towards me, in animal masks and historical costumes, offering me leaflets and imploring me. How much easier it would be to turn away from my intended destination and move in their direction, flowing with them, like driftwood carried by a flood.

"Do you get paid for writing this shit?" Paul Harris

"I expect they will be queuing for all for five yards for this hilarious guff. Would last five seconds perhaps in the days of the gong show." Blueblood 62 (*sic*)

"I have to admit I googled Chilliwack the Aids Ptarmigan. I'm very disapointed to find no trace of him outside of this article." JozefK

Time to embrace the horrors of your Spotify playlist data

Observer, 30 August 2015

As *Observer*-reading ABC1 cultural consumers, our carefully culti-vated tastes in film, in literature and in oak-aged cheeses are the exquisite hand-crafted carnival masks that we wear as armour in the awkward middle-class dinner party of life. But the tragic con-sequences of last week's Spotify data hack continue to unravel. And we wonder privately what could be more revealing, more socially shaming, than exposure of the aching gulf between the music we claim to like and the music we actually listen to. I live on borrowed time. I'm not alone.

On Tuesday, a writer for the *Wire* magazine was sacked after analysis of her leaked playlists revealed that, despite passionate appraisals of post-Coltrane black-power ecstatic jazz, her favour-ite artist was in fact the late funnyman Bernard Manning's house band, Shepp's Banjo Boys.

And on Wednesday, a founder of the taste-making hip-ster website Pitchfork trimmed off his own beard after a num-ber of Nickelback albums appeared on his most-played profile. Nickelback's Chad Kroeger said, from within a jacuzzi of foam-ing Jägermeister, that he felt "vindicated".

Closer to home, our culture secretary John Whittingdale was forced into damage-limitation mode on Thursday after it emerged that he spent all of last year listening to nothing but an old BBC *Sound Effects of Death and Horror* album over and over again, though the powerful filth-maven seemed most ashamed by the fact that the record in question was a BBC product.

Pressed on this damning electro-acoustic revelation at the Edinburgh television festival on Friday, the semi-feral human claimed he had been trying to work out if the track "Eyeballs Being Gouged (17 seconds)" had a left-wing bias. And he concluded that it did, despite the eyes in question having been gouged by Nick Robinson as a Conservative-supporting teenage intern.

The *Daily Mail* and the *Sun* picked up on the fact that all the supposed sounds of maiming and amputation on the BBC's lucrative 1970s sound-effects series of long players were actually achieved by cutting up vegetables, rather than actual people, and that this was a betrayal of the promise of trust that lay at the very heart of the BBC.

Whittingdale, his lips honeyed with some kind of phosphorescent linctus, removed a single satin lady's evening glove and responded that had he known the sounds of mutilation he had been enjoying in private every night were in fact just chopped vegetables, then he wouldn't have derived so much pleasure from them.

"Only a pervert would choose to delight himself alone while listening to shredded fennel," protested the defensive culture secretary, definitively, over a Scottish supper, to a "feisty" Sue Perkins. Then, during the cheeses, Whittingdale hastily assembled an independent panel of openly corrupt newspaper barons, murderous highwaymen and low-life business vermin to farm out all BBC death and horror sound effects in future to competitive independent service providers and Conservative Party donors based in offshore tax havens, forcibly bound by an inflexible "no fennel" pledge.

As the Spotify revelations unspooled, I realised my own cultural currency was in danger. Although my main income stream remains live stand-up, I now exploit a number of secondary finance rivulets, unsentimentally fracking my assiduously cultivated record collection in the hope of transforming the intangible flatus of taste into the black gold of financial remuneration.

I have hosted live anniversary tributes to the venerable Scottish folkies Old Sawney's String Beans, the East German anarcho-punk band Kohlrübe and the cult Ohio power-pop group Voiding My Gussets, for which I received, respectively, some hay, a rancid swede and a plastic bag of tangled blank audio tape.

In 2010 I even fronted a doomed attempt to introduce actual jazz to the Cheltenham Jazz Festival, alongside the annual three-day boogie-woogie jam from Jools Holland, whose costly absinthe and Doritos rider consumed most of what should have been my fee.

Next April this self-inflated perception of me as a person of superior musical taste means I will take on the coveted twenty-first-century role of a curator, curating the hipster weird-beard drone-rock weekender Lady Godiva's Operation, held on this occasion at Zygotic Mynci Caravan Park near St Asaph, in north-east Wales. I am already in talks with Guillemot Penis Hospital and the pianist Irene von Scheizentank.

But now my future as a respected art/music facilitator hangs by threads in the light of the Spotify leak. I envy the bored busi-nessman whose mere marriage is in tatters since his infidelities with non-existent and inexpensive transsexuals were acciden-tally spewed from the Ashley Madison dating site. Because I know that although I have listened to *Trout Mask Replica*, *Locust Abortion Technician* and *Public Castration Is a Good Idea* once each in the last twelve months, my most played album this year is actu-ally *Platinum*, by the unapologetically unreconstructed American country singer Miranda Lambert. And now Spotify knows it too. And then so will you. So it's game over for me.

What can I say? Someone sent me a YouTube link to Miranda's nostalgia-lubed power ballad "Automatic", and its pre-digital prelapsarian vision of a southern-state Eden of Polaroid photos, handwritten love letters and teenagers taping the Top 40 off FM radio melted my stupid heart.

Like a sentimental old fool, I bought Miranda's album imme-diately, and a lifetime of meticulous cultural self-grooming was squandered in a moment of impulsive madness. Realising that drastic action was required to try and salvage what might survive of my reputation, yesterday I sent a message to my mailing list of blindly devoted fans, clarifying my untenable position:

> Dear All. You will know by now, that far from being the person I pretended to be, I am actually someone who enjoys the country singer Miranda Lambert's *Platinum* album. But you know what? At least two of the tracks are superb, it's a mainstream country record on which some of the songs are co-written by a lesbian, and there's a beautifully judged hanging cadence at the end of the cautiously life-affirming "Bathroom Sink" that I defy anyone to sit through dry-eyed.

> And then I realised. It's like Miranda sings to me in "Bathroom Sink": "I'm looking forward to the girl I want to be, but regret has got a way of staring me right in the face." The Spotify leak had liberated me. If we have no secrets, then we cannot be compromised. Finally, I was free, free to be who I really had been all along. You go, honey!
> And then I remembered, I don't even have a Spotify account. Ah. Too late.

". . . 'on which some of the songs are co-written by a lesbian' – My God, a lesbian??? Should they be allowed out in public, or to interact with other people, what next? Gay men on TV? Transgender Olympians?" Alexander Simon

"Champagne socialism comes in many vintages." IvorD

Jeremy Corbyn and I are the new Christs

Observer, 6 September 2015

Apparently, the Labour Party leadership contest frontrunner, Jeremy Corbyn, wants to dredge the decomposing corpse of Osama bin Laden from the seabed and then marry it.

And he wants to live with the dead body of Bin Laden in Islington, as if it were his gay-zombie husband, in a sick left-wing pantomime of the heterosexual Christian wedding ceremony. And this arrangement is also a perversion of Islam, which is, of course, a peaceful religion.

It was Monday morning. I logged off from the *Daily Mail* website. I only went on the damn thing to check whether migrants were currently a swarm of vermin or decent loving parents like you or I, or if leggy Israeli model Bar Refaeli would take the plunge in a tiny wraparound oriental miniskirt, and then I got bogged down in all this Corbyn necrophilia stuff. It's all so confusing.

Later, after I'd dropped the kids at school, I saw the cover of the *Daily Express* in a newsagent's and read that Corbyn had also said it was a tragedy that he and Bin Laden had not met during the latter's unfairly curtailed life, as Corbyn was sure that after they had become lovers, they would have sponsored a sloth at London Zoo.

I raised my eyebrow at the newsagent, a bearded Islamic man in long flowing robes with an inscrutable expression of fundamentalist certainty. But he said that whatever people did behind closed doors was up to them, as long as the sloth had given its consent and was not harmed.

Later, I attended a local radical artists' and writers' meeting in the last squatted tower block in Tower Hamlets. We were trying to decide how best to respond creatively to the political implications of austerity, and whether there was a place in our empty gesture for puppetry and dance.

Turning to sip my tea, I looked out of the window to see Tim Farron of the Liberal Democrats fly by in a hang glider, with a picture of Jeremy Corbyn kissing Bin Laden printed on its outstretched wings. Farron's pained democratic face suggested either constipation, sexualised religious ecstasy, the vain hope that someone would remember that he existed, or some fair and just proportional representation of all three positions. But a cat by the Museum of Childhood merely looked briefly up from burying its excrement on the lawn, as the desperate Cumbrian wafted himself westward towards Wapping.

The artists and I screwed up our agenda and discussed what we had seen. Of course, these days, rather than being reliant on squinting at the speeding news through the shit-smeared windscreen of newspapers, as it flashes by in full Doppler effect, we all agreed that we can use newfangled Internet technology to seek out and then freeze-frame the source of the supposed story.

"Had Corbyn really said the death of Bin Laden was a 'tragedy'?" asked a painter. "Not really," offered a young woman tapping at an iPhone. It appeared the veteran left-winger had used those words, but as part of a forward-moving collection of sentences, which contextualised them in the way that sentences in a supporting argument do, in order to lament the lack of due process in Bin Laden's killing, which Corbyn believed, rightly or wrongly, had ongoing global implications.

Anyone familiar with human language, such as a baby, a dolphin or a cleverer than average dog, would have experienced such a syntactical procedure before, perhaps involving nouns and verbs and various qualifying phrases. Only by decontextualising these words entirely were the *Mail*, the *Express*, the *Telegraph* and the actual genuine leader of the Liberal Democrats, Tim Farron, able to misrepresent Corbyn so absurdly.

The digitally enhanced, bionic GM news flies past us with such high velocity that within twenty-four hours the surface of the Corbyn teacup was again millpond still. Only occasionally did the becalmed Fairtrade brew in the chipped Corbyn mug begin to ripple once more, as Tony Blair's impotent ape footsteps pounded counter-productively on the tea tray around it.

Incoherently outraged, and yet in possession of a megaphone, the wounded and once powerful monkey god lashed out this way and that in a doomed quest for meaning. Or bananas. It's so difficult to tell since the creature no longer has Alastair Campbell to interpret for him. "We don't do bananas."

Like Jeremy Corbyn, I too have experienced the agony of decontextualisation. A DVD of a 2009 stand-up routine, in which I used depictions of violence against TV motoring journalists as a way of questioning their own right to operate outside accepted taste boundaries, ended with a direct, down the lens plea to *Mail* journalists not to decontextualise the images within the fifty-minute bit in order to misrepresent me.

But, brilliantly, this did not stop the *Daily Mail*'s Jan Moir doing exactly that. Moir's article was swiftly withdrawn from the paper's website, presumably when it became clear that my patented Jan Moir trap, baited with the stinking cheese of assumed outrage, had worked like a dream.

But apart from me and Jeremy Corbyn, there was another man, wasn't there, long long ago, whose wise words were often shorn of context by stupid fools and used against him. And perhaps that man had a beard, and maybe he wore sandals too. And perhaps he too came to lead his lost followers away from false idols towards the promised land.

And this lowly man, would he have gone among the people in fine Raja Daswani shirts like Tony Blair? No, he would have dressed like me, in an XXL T-shirt he got free from an indie band; or like Jeremy Corbyn, in a pair of itchy alpaca wool underpants knitted for him by his mother as a gesture of solidarity with the Sandinistas. And with all the oppressed peoples of the Earth.

I'm not saying, by the way, that Corbyn and I are the new Christs. But I don't have any say in what headlines the sub-editors and page-layout people choose to put on these pieces. I hope that "new Christs" bit isn't the attention-grabbing phrase that the *Observer* elects to pull out of this column.

Nobody on Twitter or "Comment Is Free" reads to the end of the pieces they are complaining about. And a headline like "Jeremy Corbyn and I Are the New Christs" will only serve to convince the Conservative content-provider Tim Montgomerie that *Guardian* newspapers have finally lost the plot, and send Baron Daniel Finkelstein OBE into a tail-chasing tailspin of baronic confusion. What's the point?

But in such moments of despair I think to myself, WWJCD? What would Jeremy Corbyn do? And the sadness just fades away.

"'The 'new Christs' bit is in bad taste and the author knows it. Why does he think he is, or even deserves, such a title? No one has annointed him, not is likely to. Poor Jesus: still abused by the ignorant after 2015 years." Kugelscreiber

"'Later, I attended a local radical artists' and writers' meeting in the last squatted tower block in Tower Hamlets.' – The cold winter evenings must simply fly by." PGV2012

"This article seems to have worked in the sense that it has led to lots of varied comments – brilliant satire or rubbish? I thought it was mildly amusing and clever at first, but it went on and on

and ended up being boring and repetitive. A much shorter article would have made the point more effectively" Keo208

"You were right on second thoughts. The article says precisely
nothing and nothing that hasn't been said commonly. Such arti-
fices promote only the 'appearance of cleverness by' pretentious
literacy' which is in fact illiterate, over content. The motivation,
however well intended, adds nothing to desperately needed simple and honest communications (which J/C. represents) in these
times. And is so powerful in juxtaposition to empty sophistry."
THKMTL

It's not easy getting laughs out of the migrant crisis

Observer, 13 September 2015

I am frequently criticised for writing stand-up about the process of performing stand-up. But it seems honest to me to do so, as my life is stand-up comedy, and therefore I am writing about my experiences, not pretending to be something I am not. Increasingly I found I could take the same approach to the columns, sometimes addressing head-on concerns about process and the appropriateness of subject material. Bits of this one ended up leaking into the stand-up for series four of Comedy Vehicle, *but the public mood relating to the migrant crisis changed so rapidly it was like a moving target that was impossible to hit.*

On Monday, David Cameron revealed that a Welsh Isis recruit had been killed in Syria by an unmanned drone, or defence secretary Michael Fallon, as the unmanned drone is better known.

The *Sun* responded with characteristic restraint, depicting the Welsh terrorist's head in cross hairs, alongside a coupon you could save for a chance to get your own unmanned drone and carry out the next killing yourself.

Amazon are in talks with Michael Fallon about a public–private finance initiative. Could an unmanned drone drop off a birthday copy of Richard Hammond's *Caravan Confidential* book at your dad's house in Kidderminster while en route to Syria to take out another Welsh terrorist? And would the chancellor be able to ensure that any savings made were passed on to Amazon shareholders as non-taxable dividends? And can we be certain that human error doesn't leave your dad's semi destroyed, while Isis murderers get to sit around in Syria having a laugh at how rubbish Richard Hammond says caravans are?

While I appreciate the need for drastic action, and commend the diligent drone on a job well done, I am not sure it is terribly civilised to actively celebrate the foolish Welshman's death. Nonetheless, Cameron's next step must be to kill one Isis recruit apiece from Scotland and Northern Ireland too, so as he doesn't appear to be targeting any of his English partner nations' home-grown terrorists unfairly.

On Tuesday I discussed with a Quaker acquaintance whether we should take refugees into our homes. The problem is my spare-room roof has fallen in, and now the whole attic conversion needs recarpeting, replastering and repainting. At the moment it looks like a bomb has hit it, and I became genuinely confused as to whether this was appropriate accommodation or not.

I wondered if a nice Syrian family might move in and do it all up for me, as I don't have the time. Then I realised that I was entertaining an arrangement that could conceivably, on some level, be described as crudely exploitative in the very worst possible sense.

Last Sunday, because I am much better than you, I took donations for the migrants to a collection point in Dalston. I did wonder what sort of booty the CalAid volunteers would harvest from our admirably diverse borough. Orthodox Jewish skull caps, Islamic hijabs, Quakers' white tights, gay bondage rubber gimp suits, feminist dungarees and ironic '70s soft-rock hipster T-shirts. And that was just in the bin bag I took down!

So you like jokes, eh, monkey boy? Well, since January, like some kind of horrible laughing fly, vomiting the enzyme of satire onto the rotten vegetable of human tragedy, I have been trying to work out how to do a stand-up comedy routine that addressed the migrant crisis. This was not an attempt to be deliberately tasteless or politically incorrect. I think political correctness is a good thing.

Indeed, I believe it was the broadcaster and thinker Toby Young who once said of me: "He essentially uses comedy to browbeat people into agreeing with his dogmatic left-wing points of view, taking what is the prevailing politically correct dogma of his generation and using comedy as an instrument to enforce conformity, not as a means of subversion." It's probably the most accurate review I have received, and one I regularly use on posters.

I need six half-hour stand-up routines written by December for my next BBC2 series. I had a workable thirty minutes on the go after Christmas about UKIP, and while I personally welcome the failure of the far right (see above), I was professionally worried that the amusing party might disappear after the May elections and render my new routine irrelevant.

Consequently, I actually spent much of March and April in Kent campaigning for UKIP out of pure self-interest, just to be able to keep the bit in, but all to no avail. Sadly, my serviceable "lining a cat-litter tray with an England flag" half-hour is now in the used-joke bin.

I am in a symbiotic relationship with The Appalling. The worse the world becomes, the easier it is for me to make fun of it for financial gain. My sofa was paid for with humanity's tears. Don't imagine I am proud of this process.

The migrant crisis is much worse than, for example, a large number of buses all arriving at once, so you would imagine it would be easy to write stand-up comedy about it. But I have been wrestling with the subject for months now. I'm not trying to make light of the terrible situation, but I wish Isis and Tony Blair and President Assad would think of some of the hidden costs of their actions. I'm just trying to make a living here.

From April to June I tried a bit where I pictured myself trying to stop hordes of migrants swarming into my garden to escape being beheaded in the garden next door. But it seemed too brutal to say aloud to paying punters who had innocently booked a babysitter for a fun night out in good faith.

In the end, I squeezed an *Observer* column from the idea, instead of delivering the words personally to confused, unsympathetic audiences. Back in those simpler times of summer, people were still unsure of what they felt about the migrants. Pundits spoke of vermin and cockroaches. And prime ministers talked of swarms.

Then a Syrian boy washed up on a Turkish beach, where maybe you had been on holiday. And on Wednesday you watched film of a Hungarian woman kicking a frightened girl and sending a fleeing man tumbling to the ground, his child in his arms. And over the last fortnight the migrant crisis moved in your minds from the realm of abstract information into a flesh-and-blood reality of palpable suffering.

Now, even David Cameron proclaims an emotional understanding of events. But only "as a father", not as a human generally, which might have been a more profitable outcome of the hours doubtless spent sculpting his statement. The drowned dead no longer swarm, it seems.

So the big boil is lanced at last. But how long will the fashion for compassion last? In ten minutes I'll leave this Premier Inn room and go down to the cellar of a Brighton cafe and read these words aloud to twenty-five people, to see if and why, at this point in time, anyone laughs. And then I'll start the rewrite. It's a living.

"'Feminists dungarees'. Really? A 'feminist' is anybody who isn't a dickhead. I don't see that many people in dungarees." Lydkid

"More evidence of the ongoing even worsening BBC bias to the left: this 'comedian' is just a left wing activist paid by the BBC for his sixth form level 'humour'. I suppose the BBC is now the propaganda arm of the Blob. When will the public get any chance to have this vast media empire put under some sort of democratic accountability? Whitingdale is clearly not up to this task." Peel

"Realise there are some thing beyond hilarity. Like children being washed up on a beach, starving frightened beyond belief in all of his young years. You think that's funny, you must be sick." Jane Laverack

"More narcissism dressed up as a moral conscience. With a little smugness to boot." Mickey LeBoeuf

Jezza the jester? He's here to satirise politics as we know it

Observer, 20 September 2015

As you can imagine, it is a constant source of irritation to me that I am frequently ridiculed in academic circles for my supposed over-reliance on cultural comparisons drawn from the world of the Native American shaman clown.

And yet, in the light of the ascension of Jeremy Corbyn, I find myself taking familiar soundings once more from the sacred miracle caves of the south-western mesas. But our story starts in north London, last week.

"She corbyned you, man," laughed a teenager on the 73 on Tuesday. On the top deck of Boris's faux Routemaster, despite being the third most critically acclaimed British stand-up of the century, I remain anonymous enough to eavesdrop. "To corbyn". It's a new verb, it would seem.

"You were corbyned, man, well corbyned." Listening in, I realised the phrase described a situation where one of the youngster's remarks had been deliberately misrepresented to some rival youths with the intention of compromising, perhaps fatally, his standing in their social milieu. It had only taken a weekend for the press treatment of the new Labour leader to make its way into the street argot of a younger generation.

"They corbyned Corbyn in the paper last night. They say he done that Diane Abbott once, back in the '70s when she was well fit," offered a young lad to his chums by Camden tube on Thursday. "Yes, but what's really appalling is that the *Daily Mail* columnist Sarah Vine", continued a well-scrubbed middle-class schoolgirl, "has apparently been doing Netflix and chill with Michael Gove for decades!"

And with that, the young Corbynistas stood outside the station miming projectile-vomiting into a dog-excrement receptacle, until they were forcibly moved on by a uniformed security guard in the pay of a vast property-owning multinational corporation.

Now, none of the above stories is true. But I feel what they tell us about Jeremy Corbyn is true. Post-digital, tech-savvy and able to google the sources of Corbyn's supposed comments, the vibrant young people on our capital's streets, their veins coursing not with genetically modified skunk juice, but with the thrill of The New Politics™, saw through mainstream media's misrepresentation of Corbyn immediately.

Why should Corbyn talk to Sky reporters? They'll only corbyn him. The voters of tomorrow share clips of Corbyn speeches on social media, without having to cut to Andrew Wilson raising his eyebrow quizzically and then making a sneery face, before he slithers away to rub himself on the rim of Adam Boulton's executive urinal.

There are big questions to be asked about the ethics of many of Corbyn's fellow travellers, but so far the questions being asked most loudly, and which are calculated by his enemies to do the most damage, are mainly about his top button, his anthem-singing ability, his ex-girlfriend from 1978 and some free sandwiches, which he may or may not have stolen from the hand of a dying Spitfire pilot.

And while Corbyn introduced members of Hamas and Hezbollah to Parliament using the ill-judged phrase "our friends", David Cameron is genuinely real-life friends with both Rebekah Brooks of News International and Rachel Whetstone of Uber, and had Jeremy Clarkson jump out of a cake naked at his fiftieth birthday party.

It is too soon to say whose "friends" history will judge most harshly. Ex-polytechnics have refectories named after one-time "terrorists", and commemorative slabs laid by Tony or Cherie will one day go the way of Jimmy Savile's gravestone.

Leaning over the shoulder of a *Daily Express* reader on the 341 on Monday, I saw a prune-faced content provider describe Corbyn as an "absurd Marxist". As a new philosophical doctrine, Absurd Marxism sounds viable to me, whatever it is. We already live in the oxymoronic era of Caring Capitalism, and that doesn't really seem to make sense either. If I were Corbyn, I would own the title of Absurd Marxist with honour.

Absurdity, with a small "a", has attached itself to Corbyn in a way that amplifies the ridiculousness of the world around him. He was mocked for making a vegan the shadow environment secretary. Yet under David Cameron we have had an equalities minister who was against equal marriage, an anti-environmentalist environment secretary and a culture secretary who loves torture porn and wants to dismantle the BBC. The government is ridiculous. Corbyn is its satirical shadow.

In many Native American societies the comedian, far from being a lowly fool who other children's parents think doesn't really have a proper job and so could host more play dates, is considered to have an important, almost priestly, function.

The Lakota clown, the Heyoka, lives his life backwards, washing in dirt, wearing his clothes inside out, shivering in sunlight, violating taboos and asking questions others dare not ask of those in power. Some plains people even gave their contraries, as these shaman clowns were known, important roles in battle, where their unpredictable behaviour and refusal to follow orders gave them massive advantages over their bewildered enemies. I cannot believe Corbyn has not made a detailed anthropological study of these comic visionaries.

At Taos Pueblo, New Mexico, in 2006 I was lucky enough to attend a massive outdoor Koshare ritual. Clowns ranged through the village, making erotic overtures to elderly disabled women, showing disdain for the beautiful, throwing food in the faces of dining Anglo-American dignitaries, hurling Christian crosses from the roofs of buildings, and doing all this to force onlookers to consider what kind of a society they wanted to live in, and to assess the professed values of the society they already had.

Mainstream media condemn Corbyn's actions. On social media, free from editorial interference, those same actions receive almost blanket approval. The satirical counterweight of the Corbyn shaman clown has forced society to enact its own Socratic dialogue. Should we bow to queens? Should we sing songs that profess spiritual and political beliefs we do not have? Should we speak to Sky reporters?

People on the right shake with fury at Corbyn, corbyning him mercilessly, while people on the old left tremble with anxiety over what further damage he may do to their already ruined party. But think of Corbyn not as a politician, but as a totemic figure, a contrary, a shamanic clown come to throw the system's failings into sharp relief, and I promise you can all enjoy his career as much as I am. The wailing. The gnashing of teeth. It's going to be hilarious! What fun we will have! Maybe some good will even come of it.

"Sorry, Stewart, I've never heard of you, so many of your comments made no sense to me at all. What I would say, though, is that it is precisely those things that the media ridicule about Jeremy Corbyn that made me vote for him as leader. Just as an example, the fact that he doesn't dress like a city whizz-kid all the time makes it easy to identify him from all the other politicians who, to me, look totally interchangeable." Laidbacklady

"Your whole story about the youths on the bus sounds like something you invented .So pathetic." John Doe

"So speaks the privately educated, Oxford graduate. Another one of the gilded elite." Cecil4

Cameron's piggy is in the middle of a question we're not asking

Observer, 27 September 2015

David Cameron was alleged to have put his penis in a dead pig's face when a student at Oxford University. None of us in the satire community had seen this coming. Louise Mensch continued to emerge as another reliable soap-opera character in the ongoing column experiment, who could be counted upon to do something stupid on social media from her faraway New York fastness. I wrote again about process and the notion of the obligation of generating content. Most people seemed to understand that this wasn't an attempt to belittle the migrants.

Long after their relationship ended, one of David Cameron's ex-girlfriends joined a nunnery, so wounded was she by their parting. It is hard to know what religious comforts the supposed pig at the centre of the *Daily Mail's* current allegations might later have pursued following Cameron's brief and perfunctory dalliance with it, primarily because it was already dead. And so on. And so on.

As a professional humorist, there is very little point, this week, in trying to write zingy one-liners about David Cameron, the Bodil Joensen of international politics. (Don't google this. Not safe for work.) Within two hours of the rumour breaking, the infinite number of monkeys of Twitter had written all the best jokes, winning the battle of wits by sheer weight of numbers. Well done. I concede defeat.

But the gravitational pull of unseen interests directing the movement of our perceptions of the pig rumour is all too obvious. It appears we must now view British politics, and the coverage thereof, as its own reality: a vast interrelated fiction comprising many parallel narratives, with our understanding of it shaped by some guiding editorial intelligence; like the Marvel Comics universe, the Eternia realm common to both *He-Man* and *She-Ra Princess of Power*, or the overlapping fantasy worlds of *Dallas* and *Knots Landing*.

The dubious pig story first appeared in a book by a wronged political ally of Cameron's, written in a spirit of spite and self-justification – though, we have to concede, is there really any other kind of book?

Nonetheless, it has been childishly amusing to watch the same trolls usually contracted to crow over the corpses of their defeated enemies struggling to defend their traduced leader. Was I dreaming or did the thinker Toby Young opine on television that the prime minister had "emerged well from the situation"? Perhaps. But he will never be able to eat breakfast in a hotel restaurant again. Or cuddle a pig in public.

Meanwhile, on social media, the expat plant-loather Louise Mensch cited an obscure 1981 street-punk B-side, tweeting "the story is rubbish, and if it isn't, to quote the Anti-Nowhere League, 'So f****** what?'"

But the League's "So What" ("I've fucked a sheep, I've fucked a goat, I've had my cock right down its throat") is perhaps not the ideal platform upon which to mount a defence of David Cameron, going on, as it does, to justify sexual relations with a schoolgirl in the same nihilistic spirit of mock moral relativism.

Derived from an overheard pub conversation between some jaded reprobates, "So What" is not intended to be embraced as a coherent philosophy for life, though the cover version metalhead Mensch presumably knows, that of her rock-manager husband Peter Mensch's protégés Metallica, is predictably stadium-shorn of whatever wafer-thin smattering of ironic nuance the original had.

Never mind. All Conservatives' interactions with culture of any form, from the very idea of public broadcasting itself down to a punk-rock B-side, end in confusion. They are like dogs listening to human conversations, the puzzled twitching of their heads sometimes mistaken for understanding.

One might be tempted to assume the pig tale is true because it is difficult to imagine most of the six Conservative MPs suspected of supplying it having enough imagination to imagine it. Jeremy Hunt, for example, couldn't imagine his way out of an imaginary paper bag, even if the bag had a hole cut in it in the exact shape of his own body, with arrows all round it and a flashing exit sign.

Michael Gove, on the other hand, does have a creative streak, and he and I both appear in the same 1983 anthology of verse by adopted middle-class teenagers, *Pathetic Bleats from the Cradle of Privilege*.

Gove is also a fan of the down-market horror scribe Dennis Wheatley, and though this looks classy next to the culture secretary John Whittingdale's voracious appetite for watching women die slowly in torture-porn horror films, Wheatley's sacrificial Satanic rites are rarely as lurid as Cameron's supposed sow abuse.

As an Oxford-educated classicist, Boris Johnson would, however, be familiar with the source material and critical studies required to conjure the bacchanalian vision engulfing the prime minister – Robert Graves's *The White Goddess*, James George Frazer's *The Golden Bough* and any number of visceral Greek and Roman tragedies. But what would be his motive?

I was never one for conspiracy theories, but today the sort of mushroom gibberish I loftily dismissed when it was spewed at me by an articulate crusty nicknamed "The Professor", hanging out the back of a converted peace-convoy ambulance at the Elephant Fayre festival in 1983, suddenly seems plausible.

Unnamed forces have moved against Cameron, as they inevitably would, eventually. The secret chiefs no longer have any need for him. He was always just a useful plasticine man with no real opinions, and no vision, remorphed periodically to fit the shape of prevailing trends.

Cameron is like Bob Kane's Batman, a two-dimensional cipher originally invented to amuse simpletons, subsequently invested with character and motivation as required.

To say Cameron is meaningless is to dignify him with the suggestion of anti-meaning. He is beyond meaning. And now the way is clear for whoever is really writing this story – Lord Ashcroft, Paul Dacre, or maybe even John Major, playing a long game – to have him replaced.

In case George Osborne gets any ideas, Boris Johnson is keen to pull rank. The mayor's spiky pun about "hookers", at last week's Influential Londoner awards, reminded Osborne that there is a shit-filled slop bucket of Damocles ready to rain down on him at a moment's notice, only deflected last time around by the quiet co-operation of the then *News of the World* editor, and future Cameron aide, Andy Coulson. Clearly, Boris the inveterate playground bully didn't get the post-Corbyn memo about everyone being nice to each other in public from now on.

Given what has been made to stick to Cameron, it is impossible to predict what the machine might use to destroy its next spent servant. If we were told George Osborne used to employ chained naked gimps as human pencil sharpeners, we'd probably go with it.

In a way, then, Louise Mensch was right, but for the wrong reasons. Does it matter if David Cameron did Netflix and chill with a dead hog? So what? What matters is who is telling us this, and why, and what power do they wield? But we've been so busy laughing at an amusing jpeg of Peppa Pig running away from the prime minister it's a question we haven't found time to ask.

"Eternia is a planet not a realm. Etheria, where She-Ra is primarily based, is a different planet." John Yard Dog

Now even *Bake Off* is being used to stir the pot on immigration

Observer, 11 October 2015

When a Muslim woman won the BBC's Bake Off, *the* Daily Mail *columnist Amanda Platell said maybe one of the other contestants would have won if they had "made a chocolate mosque". I wrote a piece about this, which became increasingly bogged down in self-awareness, though some of the one-liners did feed into my stand-up. In February 2016, during the last leg of the tour, when I laid off the material generated for* SLCV4, *an audience member in Leeds delivered two delightful, intricate and edible chocolate mosques backstage, which I brought out, to the delight of the audience. If nothing else, this column provoked baking that satirised the* Daily Mail.

On Tuesday the unflappable Conservative Party leadership hopeful Theresa May opined that high levels of immigration make it "impossible to build a cohesive society". To be fair, so do massive social inequality, a lack of affordable housing and systematic corporate tax avoidance on an industrial scale by the government's friends and backers. Ka-pow! Take that, Tory scum! Oh look. There's egg on your Savile Row suit. Never mind. Maybe a poor child would like to lick it off for their breakfast.

Social cohesion isn't helped either, of course, by the culture secretary's anti-BBC plans to kill off *Doctor Who*, David Attenborough and the stay-at-home mums' ecstasy-generation CBeebies heartthrob Mr Bloom, who provides private spring-onion-based fantasies that glue many a failing marriage together when the lights go out.

In fact, the best thing the Right has done for social cohesion lately was to spread rumours about its own ceremonial figurehead romancing a dead pig's disembodied face, which at least brought the country together for twenty-four hours, before the

goldfish-memoried populace promptly forgot about it, like fracking and that boy on the beach.

On the same day as the unflappable May's pronouncement on
immigration, the all too flappable public liability and professional
whey-face Jeremy Hunt struggled out of his scold's bridle and
made his annual emergence from behind his tree of shame to
declare that his wife was Chinese.

Then Jeremy went on to suggest we should all work harder, like
those Chinamen in the blue pyjamas and curly slippers they have
in cowboy films. But we don't want any of them coming here, of
course, however hard they work, unless it's as wives. That stupid
Hunt (*trad arr*).

Unpack Theresa May's anti-immigration statement and it dissolves into qualifiable anxieties about how schools and housing
and hospitals will accommodate rapid population growth. But it is
clearly phrased to compress down neatly into more alarming headlines, like the *Telegraph*'s brutal "Migration 'Harming Society'", and
designed to play well with hateful people historically ill-attuned to
nuance, such as Conservative voters and newspaper editors.

On the *Today* programme the same morning, the increasingly
flappable prime minister, David William Donald Cameron,
pig-headedly refused to distance himself from the comment. In
fact, he had clearly been briefed to endorse it, despite the fact
it can obviously be simplified to support a racist agenda. Dave
is either a cynic or an idiot. Either way, he's off soon to a brace
of directorships, a glacial Scandinavian box set and a heaving
cheeseboard from the bassist from Blur's Peripatetic Wigwam.
Some other mug can muck out the stable now.

While it's not racist to oppose immigration, is it still racist, in
2015, to be racist? And is it acceptable to make clanking cultural
generalisations? It was on 3 October that the *Daily Mail* content
provider Amanda Platell introduced the notion of a chocolate
mosque into the collective subconscious. But still, more than a

week later, Platell's enormous chocolate mosque continues to loom over my imagination like an enormous chocolate mosque, an image so absurd that it becomes a viable metaphor for its own self.

In case the news-blip passed you by, Platell made minor chocolate ripples by suggesting in print that a middle-class woman called Flora Shedden, and her chocolate carousel, were booted off the BBC's *Bake Off* cake contest in favour of Muslim mum Nadiya Hussain, gay doctor Tamal Ray and "new man" Ian Cumming, because she wasn't "politically correct" enough. Perhaps, wrote Platell, "if she'd made a chocolate mosque she'd have stood a better chance".

Let's subject Platell's statement to the same scrutiny May's will doubtless undergo this week. The idea that a chocolate mosque would have scored better than a chocolate carousel suggests a baking competition in which, as well as for the technical quality of the cake, points are also awarded for the meaning and cultural significance of the thing that the cake is made to look like.

The idea that Shedden lost because she didn't make a chocolate mosque would only hold water had she been in competition with other cakes that had also been baked into the shape of culturally, socially or politically significant icons, saturated with meanings designed to appeal to the liberally biased judges of Platell's fecund imagination: i.e. a sponge Unitarian chapel, a meringue women's refuge, a fudge abortion clinic or an icing-sugar Tom Daley. As this was not the case, and her fellow competitors' cakes were not baked in shapes smothered with inference, it is spurious to suggest that the outcome of the cake contest was decided on these terms.

An obvious subtext to Platell's story is that the other contestants were favoured, irrespective of the quality of their cake work, because they fulfilled some kind of politically correct quota, such as "Muslim mum" and "gay doctor". But the idea that this could be a deciding factor is undermined by the presence of the third baker, Ian Cumming, for whom the best denigrating epithet that the increasingly desperate Platell can find is "new man", a phrase last used pejoratively by a woman wearing leg-warmers in the early 1980s.

Indeed, we are all "new men" now. While Richard Hammond may, in a public and professional capacity, have failed to prevent his boss punching his employee in the face, he almost certainly changes babies' nappies and loads the dishwasher at home. Times have changed.

I am a professional humorist, and objectively the third most critically acclaimed British stand-up comedian of the twenty-first century. If I write a stupid thing, on some level I invite you to assume it was deliberate, and that I have, to some extent, created a secondary "columnist" persona, in which I take on the role of the sort of person who would write the absurd things that I am writing, such as this sentence for example.

Amanda Platell, on the other hand, is an actual *Daily Mail* journalist and a former press secretary to the genuine William Hague, a man who really exists, albeit indeterminately. There is no reason to assume we are supposed to take the things she says as if they were meant as satirical mirror images of received idiotic thought, unless, of course, Platell has been in extremely deep cover, consolidating the credibility of her chosen clown identity, for decades now.

If that isn't the case, then it seems the contrived and demonstrably invalid "chocolate mosque" idea was designed to inflame a particular sort of monetisable sentiment, also evident in the provocative headlines composted down from Theresa May's Conservative conference speech. "Here they are, coming over here, destabilising society and winning *Bake Off*. With their chocolate mosques."

"He gave the game away half way through: 'I am a professional humorist, and objectively the third most critically acclaimed British standup comedian of the twenty-first century'. The whole thing is a big joke!" Pessimist

"'Like those Chinamen in the blue pyjamas and curly slippers they have in cowboy films" – wow, you really wrote that ? Quite a demeaning racial stereotyping ?About a man whose wife is Chinese ? And you think that is funny ?" Jimmy66

"The North London left wing execs cannot even leave a simple cake contest free from their interference. They originally gave maximum publicity to the winner including BBC World and local stations." Jon9521

So David Cameron can tell lies but stand-up comics can't . . .

Observer, 18 October 2015

On Monday the content provider Boris Johnson positioned a typically triumphant column in the *Telegraph*. Having had a hail of multicoloured children's swimming-pool balls flung at him by suddenly energised disabled people in Manchester, the mischievous reaver explained to *Telegraph* readers that people throwing eggs and calling the Conservatives scum are the same as people who victimise Jews, Gypsies and homosexuals.

Then the one-time window-smasher declared that Tory haters merely transfer their own unhappiness onto the undeserving and innocent scapegoats of the Conservatives, before taking a sideswipe at Theresa May's pre-*Bake Off* immigrant bashing. The Bullingdon golem, his masters' enemies suitably roughed up, has swallowed his sub-lingual tablet and runs rampant in the Prague ghetto of the Tory press, bumping into potential leadership candidates and trampling their best-laid plans under his hooves like Japanese children.

But the mayor of London's comparing of egg-smeared Conservatives to the systematically eradicated victims of mass pogroms is so blinkered, insensitive and distasteful that it demonstrates perfectly why Johnson himself is scum; and why the calculatedly crumpled operator should be chained to a rock and have hot eggs pounded into his pie face for all eternity, waking each new morning to find yet more egg leaking endlessly into his eyes, discharging directly from the smelly anuses of perpetually hovering hen harriers, like some slapstick Prometheus of low-rent legend.

The press would have us believe Labour is swallowing its tail, a socialist serpent coiled in U-turns; and Tom Watson totters unsteadily, like a pile of CD singles by forgotten pre-Britpop bands – Mint 400, Bivouac, The Voodoo Queens – stacked precariously in a cluttered polytechnic entertainments officer's workspace somewhere in the north-east, circa 1991.

In the light of this disarray, Johnson's can't-be-arsed column is typical of the confidence engulfing the unshackled Tories rampant. And who can blame them? They seem free to operate beyond the law, beyond truth, beyond accountability, beyond good and evil.

When I record my multiple BAFTA and British Comedy award-winning stand-up routines for television or DVD, lawyers check the content. They are taking notes in my current run of theatre shows this week, where I prepare material for my next TV series, and I am enjoying the last few days of playing with phrases I know will not pass the BBC's stringent legal checks.

It is unlikely, for example, that I will be able to say the man Labour MP Emily Thornberry saw flying an England flag from his Rochester home was "obviously racist" because he "looked really racist", even though contained within the bit is an implicit critique of my own liberal prejudices about the appearance of a Kentish van driver. The irony-aware theatre audience understand this, but the problem with the BBC is that pretty much anyone is allowed to watch it, though the culture secretary is sure to sort this out soon.

But practical restrictions can become creative opportunities in themselves. In 2008, I wrote a parody of the then *Celebrity Big Brother* host Russell Brand dealing with racism on the show: "Ooh there's some bad racism and stuff like that going down today and no mistake, my liege. It's made my winkle go right small, it has. Oh yes it has, yeah, and my ballbag, my ballbag has gone up my bum. Here's H from Steps."

Lawyers for the DVD release of the live show it appeared in said it was so close to Brand's actual speech that I might be accused not of satirising him, but of misrepresenting him. Rather than cut the bit, I inserted an improvised interview where Johnny Vegas took me to task for feeling I had the God-given right to misquote people for comic effect. In an endless feedback loop this clip now appears, shorn of its parent show, on YouTube, where members of the public mistakenly perceive it as an unofficial exposé of my own insufferable arrogance.

Other legal issues have been more easily circumvented and I've often been able to hang onto the basic thrust of contentious routines by the substitution of a single word, such as "infer" instead of "read" (in a bit about perceived criticisms of me in a panel-show comedian's autobiography), or by changing "the Conservative Party" to "some people in the Conservative Party" (in a piece about their use of the slogan "If you want a nigger for a neighbour, vote Labour" in Smethwick in the 1964 general election).

Hilariously, in 2009 I was required to cut a routine imagining al-Qaida training dogs to fly planes, out of respect for Islamic sensitivities regarding dogs, only a few months before it was revealed that the same terrorist group had been experimenting with explosive-packed canine suicide bombers, irrespective of cultural taboos. You couldn't make it up! It's political correctness gone mad!!

Essentially, while I am allowed to exaggerate for comic effect (if it is considered by the lawyers that the exaggeration is obvious and clearly authored by an unreliable and biased character, i.e. me), I am not allowed actively to lie. And it struck me as strange, as I watched the eggs rain down on Conservatives this month, that my stand-up comedian's lowly stand-up comedy routines are held accountable to higher legal standards of truth and decency than, for example, a prime minister's conference speech.

Cameron's repeated smearing of Corbyn in Manchester, for supposedly saying 9/11 was not a tragedy, when he obviously did the complete opposite, is the case in point. Paradoxically, while the BBC can broadcast Cameron's lying speech in full, without any critical analysis or disclaimers, if I had written the same comments in a stand-up comedy routine the lawyers would tell me it could not be transmitted.

I suppose somebody in Conservative central did the maths and decided that the long-term benefits of associating Corbyn with a dishonestly decontextualised phrase about 9/11 outweighed the risk of Cameron himself being perceived as a fundamentally deceitful and manipulative liar; and that a sympathetically biased, or cowed and fatally compromised, media were unlikely to hold the prime minister to account for his lies.

To be charitable, perhaps Cameron genuinely thinks that, for the long-term good of the UK, Corbyn must be discredited at any cost, and that truth, ethics, decency are justifiable collateral damage. This is the kindest thing you can say about the unprecedented depths of dishonesty the prime minister sank to in his conference speech. And then Boris Johnson wonders why people threw plastic balls at him. If I'd been there, I hope I would have had the courage, fortitude and moral backbone to have thrown my own [word deleted under legal advice].

"'When I record my multiple BAFTA and British comedy award-winning standup routines for television or DVD' . . . Thank-you for putting this piece of absurd self regard early in the piece. Having sufficiently discredited yourself at that stage saved me reading several no doubt vituperative paragraphs of pompous faux rage!" Baldygoing

Royal kisses on the cheeks of a flatulent superpower

Observer, 25 October 2015

Ethical considerations were suspended as the Chinese president's visit to Britain offered too tempting an opportunity to develop trade relations. Meanwhile, my street was cleared to enable the movement of vast cranes converting former council flats into luxury apartments, bought off plan by Chinese billionaires. As usual, I looked at the paper, then looked out of my window, and mashed the stories up. I love writing stupid things about arses, farts and shit in the Observer. *I probably wouldn't do stuff like this on, for example, my own website, but the thought of it being in a national newspaper that is printed and distributed and read over breakfast amuses me. Context is not a myth.*

Last weekend, residents of our east London thoroughfare were told to remove their vehicles, clearing the route for an exceptionally wide and potentially hazardous load. Perhaps your mum, who I believe lives locally, had ordered a new pair of pants from Littlewoods?

Rising on Tuesday to a thunderous ding-dong, I saw "Free Tibet" protesters fleeing west, while nervous Chinese students waved identical banners reading "Welcome" and, in much smaller letters, "Made in China".

Dispersing the demonstrators, police ensured the welcomers were in place as the object of their obligations began its progress past my window. It was, at some 100 feet across, and mounted on tiny casters, nothing less than a massive Chinese arse.

With the silent authority of a vast totalitarian slug, the massive Chinese arse rolled over the buckling tarmac, shiny in the sun, with all farts coming out of it, speeding its gaseous progress towards Westminster.

Having flown in from China, suspended between four

Chinooks, the massive Chinese arse sat down discreetly at RAF Scampton, where it became the subject of an enthusiastic Lincolnshire cargo cult, and was then escorted into London by a fleet of police motorcyclists, clothes pegs discreetly over their noses against the arse's flatulent mechanism.

A human rights protester positioned himself before the massive Chinese arse, raising defiant fists. But two unremitting meat mountains, enormous Chinese buttocks, rolled unsentimentally over him, spitting him out behind, winded and battered.

"Did you see that?" I asked a policewoman. "A massive Chinese arse is crushing legitimate criticism." "Calm down, Mr Lee," said an undercover officer, recognising me from my multiple BAFTA and British Comedy award-winning TV shows. "Perhaps a ticket to tonight's ceremonial massive Chinese arse banquet at Buckingham Palace would buy your silence?"

I told him I could not be bought, having turned down an advert for Sharwood's Spicy Szechuan Stir Fry Melts on ethical grounds only last week. "There will be braised red cabbage, cocotte potatoes and timbale of celeriac," he bartered, waving an embossed menu of tainted possibility.

And so it was that, for truth and timbale of celeriac, I was seated at Buckingham Palace with the massive Chinese arse and his confidants, a host of delighted business people and some compromised dignitaries: Mark Carney of the Bank of England, George "Pencils" Osborne, David Cameron and, Christ-like in his accommodations, Justin Welby, Archbishop of Canterbury, supine among the sinners, the non-tax-gatherers and the non-dom non-taxpayers.

The Queen wore a white banquet dress, embroidered with beads by her dressmaker Angela Kelly, and a pair of old lady's knickers, the label sewn in by C&A. It was the first time she had worn the dress. The Duchess of Cambridge wore a bespoke red gown by Jenny Packham and a Chinese Rocks tiara, on loan from George "Pencils" Osborne. It was the first time she had worn the gown.

Instead of wearing a booby-trapped papier mâché head of the Dalai Lama, as was feared, Jeremy Corbyn wore a black jacket, white tie, white shirt, black shoes and black trousers, with black socks and white pants from Marks and Spencer's. It was the seventy-fifth time he had worn the pants.

On the subject of clothes, PEN Award-winning writer and academic Ilham Tohti appears to be wearing a blue anorak and a white T-shirt in the picture I found of him, but who knows what he is wearing now, as he is serving life imprisonment in a Chinese jail, as I would be if I wrote this piece there, even though it is only a silly thing about a massive Chinese arse.

Still, no time to worry about that now. The timbale of celeriac smelt delicious when I could catch a whiff of it, wafting in from the kitchen, through the low-hanging cloud of the massive Chinese arse's effulgent flatulence. And anyway, dinner was served. Fillet of west-coast turbot with lobster mousse, roasted loin of Balmoral venison in a Madeira and truffle sauce, braised red cabbage, cocotte potatoes and timbale of celeriac. To follow, and in celebration of the prime minister's heroic rejection of the sugar tax, délice of dark chocolate, mango and lime. And twenty-five almonds, some Space Dust, and a juicy red apple for George "Pencils" Osborne, who was still on his diet.

After dessert came the part of the evening the diplomats had dreaded most. They knew the assembled worthies were required to venerate the massive Chinese arse, but even the most accomplished translator had been unable to ascertain whether the Chinese government's instructions meant the massive Chinese arse was to be licked or to be kissed.

Archbishop Justin Welby officiated, the dignitaries processing towards the massive Chinese arse in a sick pantomime of the Communion. Some – David Cameron, Mark Carney and

246

the Duchess of Cambridge – chose to kiss the massive Chinese arse. Others – Prince William, Prince Andrew and the Queen – elected to lick it.

From where I was sitting I saw the Queen's eyes, as she licked the massive Chinese arse, meeting Jeremy Corbyn's eyes. It seemed to me they shared an intimate moment, as she communicated to him the terrible bondage of duty, perhaps envying the rebellious leader of the opposition, and her own absent firstborn son, their uncompromised freedom, perhaps asking for understanding. And I like to think that it was in solidarity with the quietly dignified Queen that Jeremy Corbyn too then leaned forward to lick the massive Chinese arse himself.

The arse-licking and arse-kissing done, the band struck up the James Bond theme "Nobody Does It Better" and George Osborne took centre stage. Testing the opening with his usual pencil, he rolled up his shirt sleeve, James Herriot-style, and began his diplomatic negotiations, pushing through the half-digested fillet of west-coast turbot with lobster mousse, the semi-dissolved roasted loin of Balmoral venison in a Madeira and truffle sauce, the broken-down braised red cabbage, the condensing cocotte potatoes, the disintegrating timbale of celeriac and the dissipating délice of dark chocolate, mango and lime. And finally the chancellor pulled out a plum! "What a good boy am I!" he cried, holding up the filthy fruit, to the applause of all. "This plum is worth £30 billion."

The week dragged on. Unfortunately, the massive Chinese arse was unable to find time to see Ai Weiwei at the Academy, the capital's most important cultural event. But David Cameron did manage to take it to his local, The Cock and Pig, in Chipping Norton, where it enjoyed fish and beer, and was then forgotten, as the prime minister drove off, leaving it in a toilet.

"This article is so vile. Wonder how *Guardian* could have allowed it to be published. Speaks volumes about today's journalism standards." Bouzoukia

"What to make of Mr Lee's article in the *Guardian*? It can only be that the *Guardian* thinks racism is OK if directed against Chinese people. Would the charming Mr Lee have been allowed to say the same sorts of things about any other nationality, apart from the Americans and the English?" Hellomydears

"It interests me how the progressives are quite happy to criticise China, and make all sorts of stereotypes, but go mad if a Tory or UKIPPER does the same for any place." Treflesg

"The reference to flatulence suggests the author really is not up to the job." Namenottaken

"What a load of smug, right-on self-righteousness. Which countries over the world would you like the UK to have economic relations with? Or would you rather that the whole population join with you in your 'edginess' (must be edgy, because of all the toilet words), let the economy go hang, see the unemployed suffer even more, and condemn Osborne (or possibly Thatcher) for the ills of the world – safe from any need to be constructive or to take responsibility for anything?" Timinsingapore

"What Lee fails to mention is that Xi Jinping has overcome the most extreme adversity to achieve the leadership of the world's second nation. Normally such a feat of human achievement would be both recognised and held out as an example to others. In brief, his father was falsely imprisoned during the Cultural Revolution, Jinping was sent away to work and missed much of his secondary education, he became secretary of the Party branch and then despite everything won a place at Beijing's prestigious Tsinghua University from 1975–79, studying Chemical Engineering. Science and engineering majors spent 80% of their time on learning practical subjects and working in factories, (how unlike the educational experience of our own Prime Minister) 15% of their time studying Marxism–Leninism– Mao Zedong thought and 5% of their time doing farm work and 'learning from the People's Liberation Army'. In the lands of the free he would be considered a national hero – as indeed he is by many in his own country. Not quite rags to riches but certainly a life worthy of recognition by the UK's own heredi- tary elite and those many *Guardian* readers who extol the virtue of manual labour, intellectual achievement and career success." Magnolia Boulevard

My name is Stewart Lee, and I'm an AAlcoholic

Observer, 1 November 2015

An extract from the nasty TV and restaurant critic AA Gill's memoir on his alcoholism appeared in the Sunday Times, *and it was so smug, snobbish, self-pitying and self-aggrandising that it made me laugh out loud. I hacked through the Murdoch pay wall and cut and pasted it into a document and then changed the bits that were about booze so they were about AA Gill and the horrible bullying things he says about people, thus:*

> Stewart Lee's new memoir, *AAlcoholic AAnonymous*, is an honest, searingly brutal saga of a privileged and educated man in the midst of a relatively short-lived and ultimately self-induced torpor, who repays the world for his undeserved second chance at life with nothing but scorn and contempt. In this extract he writes – for the first time – of the descent into his near fatal addiction to the columns of AA Gill.

We're in a room in a private hospital in the west of London. Today the doctor, holding a copy of the *Sunday Times*, said: "Have you stopped reading AA Gill's columns yet? If you don't, you will destroy yourself." I'm forty-five. I have been reading AA Gill columns for twenty years. I think of Welsh lesbian TV presenter baboons, with breasts and vaginas, and vomit into a wastepaper basket. It is the most hopelessly sad and loneliest wastepaper basket I have ever seen.

I met my first wife in a newsagent's near Wapping. A busted sign above a door opened into a thin newspaper-filled space. The place was coated with nicotine and despair. It was the most hopelessly sad and loneliest newsagents I had ever seen. You handed your money to Fanny behind the counter, a hideously ugly woman with breasts and a vagina like all the others, and she would give you a *Sunday Times*. Most of the newspaper went to my dog, Langtree, a lurcherly mongrel who lived on sports sections. I kept only what I needed: pure uncut AA Gill, as early on a Sunday morning, as hot off the press and as near to the source as possible.

Today was special. AA Gill had written a piece calling the Welsh "loquacious dissemblers, immoral liars, stunted, bigoted, dark, ugly, pugnacious little trolls". It hit the windscreen of my mind like a dying pigeon. It was so thrillingly futile I could taste it, cold and metallic in my hot stumpy mouth. I needed to be alone with the column next to me in the dark, on my orphan bed, not moving much, just crapping a little.

But my pocket was empty except for an orphan raw steak, a drawing of an old man holding an orthopaedic shoe, and a pirate's eye-patch. The pocket was coated with nicotine and despair. It was the most hopelessly sad and loneliest pocket I had ever fingered. "Take the paper free," said Fanny, "and when we get married, I'll always make sure there's AA Gill in the magazine rack." Romantically, we peaked too soon.

The flat was in the basement of a terraced house in Wandsworth. A living room, a bedroom, a bathroom, a kitchen, a small garden, a television, hot and cold running water, bedding, carpets, working radiators, cupboards, doors, some storage space, a sink, an oven, a fridge, a table, some windows and an orphan chair. There was a Welsh dresser pushed up against the wall. It was a loquacious, dissembling, immoral, lying, stunted, bigoted, dark, ugly and pugnacious little Welsh dresser. It was coated with nicotine and despair. It was the most hopelessly sad and loneliest Welsh dresser I had ever seen.

I didn't mind the terrible hardship of Wandsworth. I had been to boarding school. We couldn't really afford school fees and St

Crispin's were particularly excessive, but somehow my parents found a few spare tens of thousands down the back of a sofa. A busted sign above a door opened into a thin bed-filled dormitory. A horrible, foul, stinking matron, with breasts and a vagina, showed me my bed. I lay down, not moving much, just crapping a little. The bed was coated with crinoline and despair. It was the most hopelessly sad and loneliest bed I had ever seen. Educationally, I peaked too soon.

One night in our Wandsworth gulag I had been bingeing on pure undiluted Gill, reading for the first time a 2009 column I had missed, about Gill shooting dead a disgusting baboon, with breasts and a vagina, despite knowing full well there was absolutely no excuse for killing her. Gill wrote that he killed the animal to "get a sense of what it might be like to kill someone".

I expect Gill would have ended up in bed with the baboon, not moving much, just crapping a little, coldly traversing the great hairy bosoms of its corpus incognita. But he had already killed it, only to be haunted years later by the orphan memory of its monkey body, the texture of cool brown hessian.

The column was coated with nicotine and despair. It was the most hopelessly sad and loneliest AA Gill column I had ever read. During the night, I rose and carved a cabbage into the shape of AA Gill's head with a large French iron cooking knife, heavy as obligation, workmanlike as desperately contentious prose, to another weekly deadline. And I did this in a complete blackout, too shit-arsed with AA Gillstritis to care.

But all that wasn't the mad thing, the weird thing. The spooky unhinged thing was that I was doing this in my sleep every week, week after week after week, in the cold echoes of absent memories. And it was the next morning that the AAs, as we AAlcoholics call them, finally came.

I woke up. And there, just there, right on the ceiling, were Clare Balding, whom Gill had called "a big lesbian" and "a dyke on a bike", and Mary Beard, whom he had said "should be kept away from cameras altogether". Clever female television presenters hanging onto the ceiling. They were off the netball pitch, out of the roller rink. They weren't the Shades of Night, they were the Daughters of Eve, and they were huge, the size of Sunday supplements, heavy as guilt. They scuttled. No, clever female television presenters don't scuttle, they moved with a horrible purpose, their breasts and vaginas and women's brains coming nearer, nearer and nearer in the orphan night.

And, as I got out of bed in a cold panic of palsied sheets and twisted limbs, the hallucinations took hold and I literally became AA Gill. I was coated in nicotine and despair. I was the most hopelessly sad and loneliest newspaper columnist I had ever seen. The bed became a trampoline and I lay back on it, not moving much, just crapping a little, and waiting to bounce back up again, away from my addictions and my temporary drop in living standards, away away away, to reassume my rightful position of power, wealth and influence in the natural order of things.

"I see what Stuart has done here, very 'cleverly' (in the *Guardian* sense of the word) titted around with AA Gill's extract for comic effect. Sadly for Lee, it reinforces the image of him as bitter, jealous and generally 'self-educated'. AA Gill can bloody write, the guys a modern day Hardy (who I'm sure was also a tad sexist and possibly slept/shot around). Lee, isn't." Daniel Coll

"The strange thing is, unless you have actually read last week's extract from Gill's memoir in the *Sunday Times*, surely most of this won't make any sense? This doesn't really work, perhaps because Gill is a much better writer. There's a reason he wins awards." Superdale

"The fundamental mistake here was for someone who can't write decent prose to attempt to pastiche someone who – for all his shortcomings – writes beautifully. As a consequence, anyone who reads this just finds themselves wishing they were reading a real AA Gill column instead." Triveti

"AA Gill writes wonderfully. If Stewart Lee had 10% of his talent he would produce something much more entertaining and readable than this tedious self absorbed rubbish." Jah777

"The problem is, whether you are trying for parody or pastiche, you should be at least as good a writer as the one you are trying to send up. Lee is a shoddy writer. He also suffers from comedians' disease: 'trying too hard.' That might work or even be necessary on the club circuit but it makes for tiresome columns." Jantar

A pyre of burning hate in a pagan, polluted England

Observer, 8 November 2015

It turned out Volkswagen had cheated on their emissions tests, and like a good Guardian *reader, I'd been driving the kids round in a Passat for years, partly because it was supposed to be eco-friendly. I got in a depressed funk and thought about Arthur Machen, the Welsh horror writer and mystic who, like listening to free-improvisation records, usually offers me a way out of a block. My favourite pastiche of this sort of story was the comedian Roger Mann's Edgar Allan Poo act, which began with the line: "I had been called upon to invent a new kind of pig." Monk's Norton is the fictional hamlet in* Portrait of a Village *(1937) by* Francis Brett Young, *a great lost British author. Many believed the book to be a real description of a real place, and went searching for the settlement. I have many childhood memories of strange weekends observing odd rural rituals. My auntie Elsie was a servant in stately homes. Maybe that is why.*

Have you ever looked into the eyes of a hedgehog and known that it wanted to die? I have. But wait, I am getting ahead of myself.

On Halloween, as we headed west in our Volkswagen Passat, I realised the most horrifying thing in the vicinity was our own family estate. With our car belching toxic death, courtesy of a secret cabal of heartless engineers hell-bent on the end of humanity and the ecosystem as a whole, I joked to my wife, "Next Halloween I'm going dressed as a Volkswagen!" "You should," she replied, stony-faced and expressionless, like a cement yak, "and you certainly wouldn't have any trouble providing the noxious emissions."

(This may seem like amusing marital banter to you, but my wife knows full well that I have had a long history of painful bowel problems, beginning with an unexpected bout of ulcerative colitis as a teenager, and culminating in hospitalisation as a result of diverticulitis in my late thirties, a condition which still requires careful daily management and, admittedly, can lead to occasional and unpleasant flatulence. I include her supposedly amusing comment here only to bolster the legal dossier I am preparing in advance of our divorce.)

When I was a child in the 1970s, my mother would take me out into deepest rural Worcestershire, on the Saturday before 5 November every year, to see the ageless traditional celebrations in the tiny village of Monk's Norton. We stayed each year with the elderly Dr Hemming, for whom she had worked as a medical receptionist in Birmingham, before he retired in the mid-'60s after a scandal involving a missing carton of Drinamyl, some ancient manuscripts, a replacement aortic valve and a dead weasel.

"How nice to see you again, Dr Hemming," I would say politely, as my mother had rehearsed me in the Hillman Imp. "I hope you have had a pleasant year." "Years are meaningless, boy," he would reply, vaguely. "Time is an illusion. Flesh is a gossamer shroud. One day I will take on any body I choose. Would you like some hot eels?" I always enjoyed our visits.

As the flames flickered outside his window, Dr Hemming would stare at them in a thaumaturgic trance through a haze of self-prescribed temazepam and hand-pulled Watney's Party Seven, and my mother and I would head out into the famished night to seek out the ancient pagan England of our collective northern European subconscious, and some sausage. You have not known sausage until you have known it while watching an effigy of Joe Gormley burning on a bonfire in 1975 in a solidly Conservative-voting Worcestershire village.

While I applaud how the American tradition of trick or treat has taken off in my London neighbourhood, I worry it has made Halloween too commercial. This year our neighbours were ritually intimidated by resentful children dressed respectively as Siri, the *Playboy* Bunny logo and an Amazon Fire TV Stick. Another satirically minded youngster appeared inside the severed head of a pig with a Conservative Party rosette pinned to its face, which I thought inappropriate, as we live in an orthodox Jewish area.

But I wanted my own children to enjoy the same festivities that I experienced as a child, and so it was we loaded up the Deathwagon last Saturday morning and headed to Monk's Norton. The hamlet was hemmed in now by the heavy traffic of the M5 and the M50, and smells more of fuel than it did forty years ago, but is still identifiably itself. Dr Hemming was long dead, I expect, but as we drove at dusk down the leafy lane past the vicarage where the obtuse physician had lived, I saw a small white-faced boy staring all-knowingly from the window, as if heavy with the apprehension of eternity, and then withdraw.

I think it was the TV fisherman Robson Green who said, "You cannot step twice into the same river." I had perhaps been foolish to expect the Monk's Norton festivities to have remained unchanged. In the '70s, each year an effigy of a trade unionist burned on the pyre – Jack Jones, Derek Robinson, Len McCluskey, Mick McGahey – but now even in relatively homogenous rural Worcestershire, Britain was clearly divided on who it chose to demonise.

Upon the village green, by torchlight, in the flickering shadows of the tall Tudor houses, rival factions squabbled, dragging different effigies towards the unlit bonfire. Here was Jeremy Clarkson, innocently piling his fist into a selfish minion's face; and here was a selfish minion, stupidly allowing his face to connect with Jeremy Clarkson's fist, denying us future *Top Gear*; and here was David Cameron, in farm girl's frock and bonnet, borne aloft in plywood pigsty, fair Chloris, innocent and pleased; and here, a papier mâché Martin Winterkorn, head of Volkswagen, strangling the green earth with his clean hands. And so on, and so on, a multitude of villains and no clear candidate for the conflagration.

And then a shrill voice cut through the commotion: "Burn them all." It was the little boy from the window, in pantaloons and waistcoat, with a cold authority beyond his years. As the people of Monk's Norton surrounded the bonfire, hurling their hated effigies onto it, I was sure I saw him crawl between their legs and into the pyre. Before the head of the Round Table, dressed amusingly as a sponging Pacific Islander displaced by rising sea levels, could light it, I persuaded him to let me crawl inside. The boy was not there. But a hedgehog was. I recognised the look in its eyes. It knew its time was up.

When I was a child, there were 30 million hedgehogs in the UK. We were cavalier about their abundance, and their tyre-squashed early-morning bodies were so commonplace it seemed they must be in almost endless supply. Now – because of climate change and the collapse of their food chain – there are less than a million. We can't even save the hedgehog. How do we expect to save the world?

Last month, we imagined there was a hedgehog in our garden, by virtue of a telltale track, and we invested in hedgehog food from an online outlet. But it has proved to be a phantom hedgehog, and our nightly replenishment of the illusory hedgehog's saucer was an act of delusional wish fulfilment. I think the cat ate the hedgehog food. That would explain why he has developed bristles and a taste for worms. There should have been a warning on the box. I think so anyway.

"I hardly believe a word of this." R Rogers

"What a miserable and unhappy person this must be, to spend

all this time bitching. But some people see their misery as proof of their superior intellect and virtue. Pity." Jkonrad

"'Inappropriate as youlive in a Jewish area'?? This is the problem with life here right now, this type of PC crap." Yukkejang

"What a weird piece of writing. What was it all about? It's like listening to some old codger in a cosy armchair with a rug over his legs rambling on and on." Nina1414

"'I think it was the TV fisherman Robson Green who said, "You cannot step twice into the same river."' But you think wrong, my dear. Those words are paraphrasing words spoken by Heraclitus, oh, about 2,500 years ago." Superdutch

"What an utter utter load of bizarre, garbled bollocks! !!!What is this guy on? This is a typically pseudo intellectual article written by the introverted academics in their little Ivory Towers somewhere .The sort of article that the 'Guardian 'just loves to publish. The introverted academics on about £100,00 a year plus expenses and totally out of touch with their country or its people. Just nauseating claptrap really. It is a wonder this guy isn't called Toby or Tristan Farquart -Smythe or something! !!!!" Alice38

Sun slams Corbyn's nod and gets a rise out of me

Observer, 15 November 2015

Last week's newspaper attacks on Jeremy Corbyn have moved from the dishonest into the deranged. On page seven of Monday's *Telegraph*, Sir Gerald Howarth MP, who once worried that the same-sex marriage bill would be seen by "the aggressive homosexual community . . . as but a stepping stone to something even further", analysed Corbyn's Remembrance Service bow.

Sir Gerald, who was dismayed when the ban on military homosexuals was lifted because many "ordinary soldiers in Her Majesty's forces joined the services precisely because they wished to turn their backs on some of the values of modern society", explained how Corbyn's "slight tip forward" towards the Cenotaph "should have gone down to around 45 degrees from the waist" proving that he was "not cut from the cloth of a statesman".

Perhaps, mindful of Sir Gerald's anxieties, Corbyn had refrained from bending too far forward in order to avoid encouraging any members of the aggressive homosexual community present at the ceremony to see his action as a stepping stone to something even further.

Meanwhile, on page 23 of the same edition, the *Telegraph*'s former editor Charles Moore, whose decision to live in Tunbridge Wells indicates a man at peace with posterity, took a contrary position to Sir Gerald. He said that Corbyn behaved with decorum at the Cenotaph, but that this was actually worse than if he had behaved appallingly, as it was an attempt to foist far-left values on the public "by outward deference to common norms".

Whatever Corbyn does is wrong, it seems. Punching blindly

out of the paper bag of his own lunacy, Moore concluded: "It is sensible, from [the Labour Party's] point of view, to make well-arranged poppies part of their window dressing."

While I don't doubt that Corbyn is a Marxist sociopath hell-bent on the destruction of British society, and indeed I applaud him for this, the best evidence of well-arranged window-dressing in British politics last week was the Conservatives' hasty grafting of a digital poppy onto an all-purpose online David Cameron maquette, which can be speedily adapted to sport the appropriately sincere symbols of any passing festival of remembrance.

Father Dom Bernardo Vincelli's tonic wine was sentimentally drunk by old soldiers years after they had consumed it under fire in Normandy. It is understood that, for next year's remembrance ceremony, the prime minister's tear ducts are to be surgically altered so that he can cry French Benedictine on demand, lick it off his own face, and then transubstantiate it in his bladder, to wee out the holy tears of the fallen.

Taking contrary arguments to arrive at the same conclusion, Sir Gerald and Charles Moore are like terrible hack comedians on some shit TV panel show who've found the same funny punch-line, and now just need to reverse-engineer opinions to justify it.

The *Telegraph* even included a helpful diagram showing the exact angle of Corbyn's bow, with protractor-style annotation to prove that it did, indeed, clock in at below Sir Gerald's respectful angle of 45 degrees.

What constitutes offence is normally a difficult thing to delineate. The N-word, for example, while unacceptable racist filth in the mouth of your dad, may yet be a delight in the gutter poetry of African American rap singers, like Ice Cube, Ice-T or The Insane Clown Posse.

Defining offence is so complicated. That's why it was thoughtful of the *Telegraph* to publish an actual graph of the angle of Corbyn's bow. The existence of a literal calibration of offence relieves us of the obligation of understanding complicating factors like context, intent or the agenda of the observer. Corbyn's bow was undeniably offensive because it fell outside the mathematical parameters of inoffensive bowing.

Oddly, I have previous experience of a protractor being used to calculate offence. Twenty-one years ago I appeared in a TV sketch show, and in an item written by the comedian Richard Herring, Tom Binns featured naked as a showering footballer. When the rushes arrived, there were legal anxieties that Binns's penis appeared to be erect, and that the footage could not be broadcast.

A BBC ombudsman analysed Binns's penis with a protractor, using the Mull of Kintyre test, and found that Binns's penis, while buoyant, was angled downwards at less than the 45-degree mark that would have made it unfit for transmission. Turning from the *Telegraph* to the *Sun*, this knowledge was to come back to haunt me.

The *Sun*'s front page, Leveson a mere memory, maintained Corbyn had not bowed at all, downgrading his movements to a futile nod, and ran a photo of the nodding "pacifist" next to a picture of an apparently topless woman standing heroically in some snow in just tiny pants and ski boots. Her back was towards the camera, but the subconscious 3D modelling in my mind kicked in involuntarily, and I was very slightly excited, surely the paper's intention in displaying the image.

Later that day, as I walked home past a decorated war memorial, the stirring began again, and I realised to my horror that accidentally viewing the image of the semi-naked woman on the *Sun* cover alongside their story on Corbyn and the Cenotaph had caused me to associate subconsciously Remembrance Day with mild sexual arousal.

Appalled at what had happened to me, through no fault of my own, I might add, and terrified of incurring the wrath of

Sir Gerald for my inappropriate response to the sacred symbols around me, I grabbed my protractor from my satchel and rushed into a toilet cubicle to calibrate the extent of my unintentional disrespect.

Luckily, I realised that, as usual, my penis fell below the required standard to constitute legal tumescence, and quickly mailed off mathematically annotated photographic evidence of this to Sir Gerald, for fear of becoming the subject of a *Daily Telegraph* exposé myself, while praying that he himself would not interpret this desperate gesture as an invitation to a stepping stone to something even further.

We all remember the dead in our own way, and contextualise their sacrifices as we see fit. I stood among a small crowd at the war memorial at the library where I was working at eleven o'clock on Wednesday. Someone's phone went off, of course. Young mums walked past unaware of the significance of the moment. I thought about my grandfather, an RAF crewman, quietly and privately traumatised, I think, by flying over Dresden, days after the firebombing. Though he continued to profess hatred of all foreigners until his death, as was the way of his generation, I suspect that, from that day onwards, his heart wasn't really in it.

"'Corbyn is not a sociopath. He is however a Marxist hellbent on the destruction of British society', yes. And more and more people are realising this every day. That Stewart Lee – whoever he is – applauds Corbyn for this, says everything about Stewart Lee. We can, however, sincerely thank his grandfather for his service, helping to keep Britain democratic. A different generation, less narcissistic, less vain and less prone to numbing rubbish." Abdalsoquodlibet

"Correction needed: the Insane Clown Posse are white guys under the make-up, so it would be racist if they said the n-word." E J Boulton

"What I like about Stewart is that he's not scared to skewer those really tricky targets – The Royal Family, UKIP, Jeremy Clarkson, the right wing press, the Tories. Time and again Stewart shoots those fish in a barrel with aplomb. Fuck, he's dead clever." Normington

Out of the mouths of babes, real religious truth

Observer, 3 January 2016

The following, bar a few details that have been changed to protect the inno-cent, is a sincere and honest depiction of my feelings in the emotional wilder-ness between Christmas 2015 and New Year 2016. To be honest, I don't much care for it, and it's not of a piece with the rest of this sarcastic, self-aware collection.

On 28 December, I performed my annual progress around a Midlands motorway triangle, through sluggish bank holiday traffic, to venerate relatives' graves. My eight-year-old daughter accompanied me, leavening my loneliness, and I made the duti-ful day delightful by insisting we listen to Jeff Wayne's *War of the Worlds* in its entirety. Don't you wish I was your dad?

We enjoyed impersonating the portentous tones of Richard Burton at appropriately banal points in our pilgrimage: "No one would have believed, in the last days of Christmas 2015, the length of toilet queues at Strensham services. And yet, slowly and surely, the desperate motorists drew towards the lavatories." The day was like an episode of *The Trip*, but with two Rob Brydons, both of whom could only do Richard Burton.

Between you and me, I have struggled with what Christmas means this year. I dip into the Christian tradition that is my cul-tural heritage with a yearly Mass. And I enjoy Yule ritual that predates the belief system dominant in these islands this last millennium, recently replaced by television, political correctness gone mad, rampant consumerism and gays.

But inappropriate weather skews the season. Things should bloom in spring. That's why the Church dumped the Resurrection onto the festival of the fertility goddess Ostara, giving converts some rebirth-themed continuity.

Where the Easter Bunny fits remains mysterious, though rabbits' reproductive capacity makes them, like Olive and George Osmond, folkloric symbols of fecundity. Indeed, in Utah the Easter Osmond, clad in flares and enormous teeth, flings a boiled egg, smeared with semen, at childless Mormons.

The festival is in flux. Are the obsolete snowflake decorations of today's un-wintery, wet, warm Christmas now merely a race memory of the days when we had definable seasons, rather than just climatic blandness interrupted by catastrophes?

Approaching the cemetery, I said to my daughter, "I do not believe in an afterlife, so why am I putting flowers on graves?" "It makes you feel nice," she said, "and it is nice to remember people." She was right, and rational, but, crucially, she was also humane and sensitive. I tidied up the headstones and placed pot plants. "My life will be forever autumn, now you're not here," I sang, an atheist at Christmas, enacting ancestor worship, in lieu of a lamb to love.

My children's mother is Catholic. We tolerate each other's views with diligent determination, bending magnanimously in the face of educational or cultural obstacles. The children have friends of all faiths and none. I hope they will learn about religions, and non-religious beliefs, in enough detail to allow us all to reference them confidently. And I'd like stand-up comedy audiences of young people to be well versed enough to appreciate my clever jokes about consubstantiation and Islamic taboos, instead of just staring in fear.

The Christmas assemblies I attended this year were, given that the children of parents professing Christian beliefs were a minority, understandable compromises of utilitarian poesy, recalling the Wookiees' Life Day celebrations, in the suppressed 1978 *Star Wars Holiday Special*. (This remains the most thematically coherent of the original's seven sequels, *The Force Awakens* lacking both Bea Arthur doing a recipe and a miniaturised Jefferson Starship.)

I want my kids to appreciate the stories informing Milton and Blake, and *The Life of Brian* and Lenny Bruce, without being told they must believe them. And I think that a diverse religious education could dilute extremism. A child sees that a multiplicity of faiths must mean none can be absolutely true and that, irrespective of whether a God exists, these supposedly revealed truths, in all their manifestations, evidence our desire to dramatise experience.

And so I welcomed the November High Court judgment, by Mr Justice Warby, that the religious studies GCSE should reflect multiple beliefs and non-beliefs. And, despite being a card-carrying secularist, I have been diligently reading the children *The Pop-up Book of the Nativity* every night over Christmas as part of their liberal education, to the particular irritation of my twenty-eight-year-old son.

War of the Worlds finished. ("Can anybody hear me? Come in. Come in.") Radio 4's *Beyond Belief* began. It was. The panellists discussed the afterlife. Shaunaka Rishi Das, a Hindu, believed, like George Lucas and the Jedi Knights, that the spirit continues to live on as energy after the body has died.

Dr Shuruq Naguib, a Lancaster University Islamic studies lecturer, accepted an afterlife because doing so is one of the pillars of Islam, and she is a Muslim and so therefore she believed in it, a circular position I imagined unlikely to make for enlightening listening.

And the writer and broadcaster Peter Stanford, the thinking person's Catholic content provider, said he embraced the afterlife, but with the considered professional caution that plays well with the target demographic.

All believed in life after death. And so, for a moment, did I, as listening to this show in a traffic jam on the M40 was my idea of hell. "There should be a scientist there," said my eight-year-old, with the wisdom of a child, "to spoil everyone's fun."

I thought, "I am going to front a radio discussion on whether the Loch Ness monster is a dinosaur, an alien or a ghost, without anyone to suggest it probably isn't anything at all," but then at the fifteen-minute mark a doctor was interviewed to provide balance and my prejudice was pricked.

Then the news came on. A small story, secreted suspiciously in the builder's cleft between Christmas and new year, revealed that education secretary Nicky Morgan had announced the High Court findings need have "no impact" on schools' religious teachings. There was no obligation for schools to cover non-religious views, and students should be told Britain is "in the main Christian", even though it demonstrably isn't, and we obviously need to work out what cultural cohesion can replace the binding agent of faith.

A spokesperson, who may have been glossing off-piste, said the minister sought to prevent a "creeping ratchet effect" of human-ist attempts to make the curriculum fairer. Always use the word "creeping" if you want to imply evil. You could put the word "creeping" in front of the words "Dame Vera Lynn" and see her become a pariah overnight.

I thought about Nicky Morgan, and I was overcome with a feeling of profound despair that made a dark day darker, as a generation's chances faded. And I wondered how something so obvious to children could be hidden from the person responsible for their education. "Can anybody hear me? Come in. Come in."

"Your child has clearly not yet grasped the following: from the multiplicity of faiths they cannot logically all be entirely true; however, this does not mean that all faiths are false. It is perfectly possible that one (or more but not all) faiths could be true. Stick to what you know." Cdodsie

"'. . . And gays.' What the hell does that mean???? How could you expect that to not come across as prejudice? You should have added transgendered and women's rights. You prat." George Stothard

"I agree, what homophobic claptrap. At least, when compared to any god, we know that gay people exist!" Andy Lombardi

"I'll give him the benefit of the doubt and just assume this is another example of how badly a stand-up comedian falls off the rails when he tries to pen an essay instead of a comic monologue. One of the worst-written opinion pieces I've ever read in the *Guardian* -- and that's really saying something." Hellskitchenguy

I wouldn't have an OBE unless they gave me one

Observer, 10 January 2016

Lynton Crosby, ridiculed below, recently turned up on Twitter quoting my jokes approvingly to Tim Montgomerie, the Conservative content provider and twat. Life is strange when you reach a level of celebrity, however limited, that means Lynton Crosby knows who you are.

The radio producer John Naismith once told me he lost his child's class toy on its weekend visit and had to swiftly order one on Amazon. And when we were sent home from my son's school with his class teddy, the massive social disparity in the toy's weekend experiences, as documented in his accompanying scrapbook, prompted us to pose it smoking outside a betting shop, since remodelled as a fashionable hipster egg diner.

This whole column is basically a rewrite of the timeless Max Miller routine from the music-hall era that ends with the line "You can keep your bloody plough!"

The new year knighting of David Cameron's election strategist Lynton Crosby was the most obscene misuse of Conservative power since George Osborne, unable to locate his satchel, used a friend's chained gimp as a human pencil sharpener.

If the opposition were not in such disarray, and the press not so cowed, giving an honour to the dog-whistle-waving, dead-cat-blowing, evil mastermind Crosby could have brought down the government and seen Cameron airbrushed from the collective memory, a Bullingdon Trotsky carved from marzipan.

Crosby's iniquitous ennobling has discredited the honours system for ever, and it is henceforth utterly without worth. Presenting Barbara Windsor with a DBE is now as offensive as if David Cameron had personally handed her a lacquered fragment of Ronnie Kray's palaeofaeces.

On a related note, last weekend it was my son's turn to bring home the school vole, and as I went to Fresh & Wild to purchase its lemon couscous, I realised a similar system could save the reputation of honours. Everyone in the country should be allowed to have one, but only for a weekend.

There could be problems. At my daughter's old school, when children took home the class fluke worm, they also brought with them a scrapbook, in which they were required to document the worm's weekend, before handing it on to next week's worm-keeper.

Perusing the book was an object lesson in social inequality. Some weekends the lucky intestinal parasite disported itself in a chairlift, accompanying wealthy hosts on skiing trips. Other weekends were spent entirely on the sofas of social-housing flats, the asexual opportunist pictured eating pizza, inhaling helium gas and playing *Grand Theft Auto*.

I refused to be drawn into this web of contrasts on our fluke-worm weekend, and so we photographed the tiny parasite outside a betting shop, coiled provocatively around a packet of Silk Cut and a can of Special Brew, in order to thwart nosy parents.

Nonetheless, I feel this system would work well for OBEs, giving everyone in the country the opportunity of posing delightedly with the medal in a semicircle of delighted relatives. One must take care, though, not to lose the award. During the brief period of our recent vole guardianship the rodent bolted into a French horn before our son's music lesson and suffocated.

Forced to purchase hastily a similar-looking vole online, at replaceyourdeadclassvole.com, we returned it only after having given it a thorough Martin Guerre-style schooling in the exact details of its supposed former life, should it ever be grilled by my son's suspicious headmistress about its changed shoe size.

While there are, undoubtedly, deserving winners in the New

Year's Honours list, all of them, coincidentally, people I personally admire or am related to, it didn't take the garlanding of Lynton Crosby to cast doubts over the system. Jacqueline Gold, the sex-toy magnate behind such products as the Ann Summers Anal Training Kit, got a CBE, so even George Osborne's humble pencils must surely be in line for something.

Examining the New Year's Honours list in closer detail, I began to wonder, almost in spite of myself, why I had not been mentioned, again. Damon Albarn from The Blur was there. His calculating application of culturally lowbrow vaudevillian techniques to essentially middlebrow art forms, flattering the pretentions of middle-class reviewers while remaining on nodding terms with a broad-brushed populism, mirrors my own. Why he and not me?

And while James Nesbitt is a great actor, in terms of critical acclaim and awards I am probably considered, rightly or wrongly, a more significant artist than he is. Nesbitt's charity work is admirable, but it is also visible, whereas the many charity stand-up benefits I help organise operate below the radar, the bills I tirelessly assemble being so strong as to sell out usually without much advertising.

I'm so good at what I do that those in power do not notice. My modesty is a handicap. It's a problem I've had, I think, all my life. I hide my light under a bushel, and then I camouflage the bushel and hire a reputation-management company to remove all traces of the bushel from websites and social media.

Even Gary Barlow has an OBE, and I am definitely a nicer person and a better artist than him. And, more importantly, unlike the tax-avoiding Barlow, I pay all my tax, and when I was investigated by HM Revenue they actually gave me a rebate for overpaying! It seems very wrong to me that this Barlow character has an OBE and I don't. There doesn't seem to be any definable logic in a system that rewards the arrogant and the guilty and yet punishes and insults the meek and virtuous.

I pay my tax. I organise charity benefits. I am a patron of at least three worthwhile arts organisations and four useful pressure groups. I have a BAFTA and an Olivier award. I give frequent talks on the creative process at schools and universities and refuse all payment, no matter how much they press me. I leave out little trays of water to give the rare newts in my garden somewhere to spawn. I recycle, even food waste.

I am environmentally ashamed to own a Volkswagen and will get rid of it as soon as possible. I am kind. I tolerate people who are different from me. And I have never done a comedy character on national television based on anyone with learning difficulties. And yet once more I am passed over. What is going on?

I would love to use my OBE to draw attention to all sorts of problems in the world, not least of all the continuing neglect of deserving OBE winners, and yet I am repeatedly, and apparently deliberately, denied that chance. And you know what, because of the years of calculated insults, if David Cameron offered me an honour now, I'd tell him where he could stick it. You can keep your bloody OBE!

Stewart Lee is appearing, for free, in a benefit for the homeless, "A Belter for the Shelter 3", at the Hackney Empire, London, on 6 February, with Daniel Kitson, Earl Okin, Lewis Schaffer, Francesca Martinez, Sofie Hagen and James Acaster; and in a fundraiser for South London Cares, "Hilarity for Charity", at the Leicester Square theatre, London, on 3 March with Eleanor Tiernan, Earl Okin, Ginger and Black, John Kearns and Shappi Khorsandi. He personally booked the bills for both of these by email and text message, which took some time, and he expects no thanks.

Why I mourn for Eddie Redmayne's old phone

Observer, 17 January 2016

I hadn't realised what a massively significant figure David Bowie was to so many people until he died. I appreciate this is my fault. Nonetheless, social media and people's instant access to comment platforms quickly made it impossible to process the public reaction to his death properly. In the same week as David Bowie died, the (late, great) Independent *newspaper ran a desperate click-bait news story about the actor Eddie Redmayne's attitude to mobile phones. I cut and pasted a selection of Bowie tributes together and weaved bits of the Redmayne interview into them.*

I'm sure everyone will always remember where they were last Monday when they heard that Eddie Redmayne's analogue handset had died.

I was in a traffic jam on the Seven Sisters Road, with my two daughters, nine and five, as the quizzical tones of the *Today* programme's Nicholas Robinson broke the news. At his wife's insistence, it appeared the actor Eddie Redmayne had finally abandoned his analogue handset in favour of a modern iPhone.

In an instant, I processed my shock into potential content provision, opining internally that Eddie Redmayne's analogue handset represented, to me, almost the last link to a better time: a time before the stress of instant communication, the death of casual contemplation and the inevitable dumbing down caused by an oceanic volume of immediate information – train times, species of woodlouse, the original line-up of BMX Bandits.

I wanted my girls to witness the final flowering of that other age, even as it faded before us. "One day, your own children will ask you where you were when you heard about the death of

Eddie Redmayne's analogue handset," I advised my daughters, "so fucking shut up and listen."

Clearly grief-stricken himself, Nicholas Robinson haltingly sniffled out a brief Twitter statement from Eddie Redmayne's wife, Lili, saying of the analogue handset: "Sad 2 report handset gone. Eddie love analogue handset in theory. In end he too tied 2 laptop ans-ing email. I happy he iPhone now."

Tributes were already flooding in, many rather thoughtlessly delivered in the form of tweets sent from smartphones. David Cameron's tweet, clearly dispatched in hurried woe, said simply: "A huge losp."

The warlock Russell Grant did a tweet that said: "Part of my past has left me today with the death of Eddie Redmayne's analogue handset. Even I, with my third eye, couldn't have seen this coming."

Richard Wilson, star of *One Foot in the Grave*, did a poorly judged tweet, attempting to lighten the mood of national mourning, joking: "In the words of my famous creation Victor Meldrew, I don't believe it!"

And Twitter's David Schneider, the director of BBC3's flatshare sitcom *Josh*, did a tweet that said: "It's only when you hear something like this that you realise how much an actor's analogue handset can feel like part of you. RIP Eddie Redmayne's analogue handset and thank you."

But my Eddie Redmayne's analogue handset is not gone. Nor ever can be. What it gave to me is eternally in my grasp. I know this to be a known known. I need no eulogies from politicians or disc jockeys with their blurred recollections of its "limited analogue functions". I need no ranking of where it rated alongside the Sinclair C5 or *Asteroids*, or other supposedly dated bits of technology.

Less than a decade before Eddie Redmayne's analogue handset's emergence, vast chunky mobiles with briefcase-size chargers were first seen around Soho media meetings, dead heavy symbols of a dead heavy system. And though it only arrived decisively in the '00s, Eddie Redmayne's analogue handset was the individual device that most spectacularly embodied the advances of its age, forcing open drawers that older, more conservative gadgets left locked.

Eddie Redmayne's analogue handset was the shining star that led me to the Bethlehem stable of my own identity: through the decades when I wore the multiple imaginary pierrot hats of the selves, it stored many milliners in its memory, literally and figuratively. The thought of that handset gave me one hell of a buzz. It's pinging alarm was a clarion call. It's 9.30 a.m.! A change is gonna come!!

Horror was a fat slice of how we all reacted to Eddie Redmayne's analogue handset's abandonment, but so was something else: in all the memories of this or that certainty, and too-late-now lamentations for a world in which a handset that fitted into a man's pocket could fracture normality, one idea seems quaintly strange.

It is the fact that we wished to hear that handset, and that handset alone, in real time, in a real place. We imagined its blips as religious communiqués. Eddie Redmayne's analogue handset was our encyclopedia of experience. I was a small man from a small town, an outcast from what my choirmaster called "a barrel of broken biscuits". Eddie Redmayne's analogue handset split my world open like a melon.

My hands never got too big for Eddie Redmayne's analogue handset. It was never back there. Always right here. It has merely slipped into another room. That drawer once more. It rendered up the key. For me, for you. For him, for her. For it. For us.

But not for *them*. It gave us ambitions. Ambitions above our airspace. All the ambitions and a lone enormous ringtone. Meep meep! The cosmic concept that we can contact ourselves directly and instantly, whoever we are. ET, phone home! It let us be more than we ever dreamed. Peter Pan. Pan. Peter Panpan. There was something more significant. Something.

Smartphones serve a different function. They are omnipresent in presence and purpose, offering a sofa-soft fuzz of reassurance or standing for nothing but themselves. But this weird boy, who experimented with feminine clothes and falling down in a quadrangle, with his analogue handset gave me and a whole generation of kids permission to ring at random and raspberry. The sheer danger of it made it extraordinary. I would call it social spelunking. Dark but also wet.

As our characters coalesce, we look for something in the culture that reflects our subconscious desires. Eddie Redmayne's analogue handset certainly did that for me. Sure, the handset wasn't perfect, but the time it sent all those swastikas to everyone in its address book can be explained by Mrs Redmayne having "accidentally" dropped it into a bucket of glühwein.

Most importantly, Eddie Redmayne's analogue handset arrived in an age where the idea of post-war individuality was being replaced by taking one's place in the cosseted, opiated mass. When Eddie Redmayne's analogue handset declaimed, "Bleep bleep bleep bleep bleep bleep bleep bleeeeeep," it seemed somehow to survey certainties, invert its surroundings and loudly proclaim, "It's time to get up."

I dispatched the daughters, drove home, broke the news to my wife and went to do my business. "Are you in mourning?" my wife taunted as she left for work. "No, I'm in the lavatory," I laughed, through gritted teeth. I stood, a forty-seven-year-old man, my crying mixing with my micturition, as I wept into the toilet.

"For years I gave you the benefit of the doubt, but this isn't satire. You're just a vile, sneering, cowardly little bully."
Doyoureallyreally

"What a mean-spirited and ham-fisted rehash of some of the various articles on the death of David Bowie. Yes slebs in search of copy for their next guest column are always going to choose to tell everyone how they, personally, were bereaved by someone they likely never met. We get it. Choose a harder target." Snelix

"Apart from being a very dull article, it is based on an untruth. Redmayne's mobile was not an analogue model. The analogue signal was shut down in 2008 so he was simply still using a digital non-smart phone. Just as many other people still do." Saintpierre

"A dull unfunny piece of nastiness by a dull unfunny nasty comedian." Jorong

"To daughters aged 9 and 5 'fucking shut up and listen!' Do I really need to add anything?" Janevski

In need of an affordable home? Turn left at Pluto

Observer, 24 January 2016

A new Neptune-sized planet has been discovered, lurking beyond Pluto, after a prolonged study of unexplained orbital patterns. This method of detection has a precedent. As long ago as 1846, the French mathematician Urbain Le Verrier wrote to the physicist François Arago, saying, "Sir! Surely you can see there must be a ninth planet, if only because of terrible irregularities in the behaviour of Uranus."

Sadly, the letter, which had inexplicably been written by Le Verrier in English, even though both boffins were French, was read aloud to Arago by his housekeeper, and the incensed physicist, who suffered terribly with haemorrhoids and so assumed Le Verrier was attempting to satirise him, was never to speak to his mathematician friend again.

(To clarify, Arago had thought that when Le Verrier wrote "Uranus" he was actually talking about Arago's anus. But this was a misunderstanding caused by the letter's being in English, and then having been read aloud by Arago's housekeeper. Had this letter, which did exist, been read off the page by Arago himself, Le Verrier's intentions would have been obvious. But Arago wouldn't touch it, see, because he had some cassoulet or something on his finger that day and didn't want to get it on the letter in case it made a duck-flavoured mess.)

Meanwhile, here on planet Earth, the prime minister, David Cameron, revealed last week that sink estates are to be demolished. He is, however, unable to reveal the future location of their former residents. These feckless humans are an inconvenient and minor element of the regeneration process, like those tedious newts that have to be seen to be transported to other waterlogged areas when begrudging builders tarmac over an ancient wetland.

It doesn't matter. Prime inner-city real estate, clogged with a profligate underclass, can now be freed for redevelopment by interested parties. Old street names will haunt the rechristened work–live landscape in a precisely ordered pantomime of provenance.

And the definitions of "affordable housing" will doubtless be redrawn once more, to maximise the investors' return. Perhaps the Conservatives can look to the French, as they investigate ways of storing their own troublesome tenants.

In Calais this week, the migrants' camp was bulldozed, and the desperate people who lived there were rehoused in shipping containers, as if they were a cargo, ready to be transported. But to where? To anywhere, as long as it's not anywhere we have to look at them. If the French had known how things were going to work out, I expect they would have let Queen Mary keep Calais after the siege of 1558, instead of securing victory from a decisive move by their artillery into Fort Nieulay on 3 January of that year. But, hey, hindsight is 20:20.

On her deathbed, Mary said, "When I am dead and cut open, they will find Calais inscribed on my heart." When David Cameron is dead and cut open, they will find no heart, but, if they check his pockets, they will find Calais written at the bottom of a very long "to do" list, just underneath "fix cat flap" and "try to make space for more me time".

In a related development on Wednesday, the British astronaut Tim Peake uploaded to the Internet a film of himself explaining how he goes to the toilet. If I did that, I would either be questioned by the police or be given my own breakfast show on Xfm. But apparently, because Tim is "in space", his toilet procedures are a matter of public interest.

Once upon a time, journalists would have had to hack a phone to know as much about a public figure's private doings as Peake has disclosed voluntarily. Seeing the exhibitionist space traveller's toilet talk in the same week as the newspapers carried blurred photos of Chris Evans vomiting into a lay-by, I longed for the old days when celebrities were still glamorous and mysterious.

One doesn't have to reveal everything. Keep them guessing. Maggie Moone was never photographed being sick next to an Audi R8 V10, and the exact nature of Arthur Negus's toilet routine remains something to be fondly imagined, rather than detailed intimately on the World Wide Web.

Despite his lavatorial indiscretions, Tim Peake remains a persuasive brand ambassador for space travel, declaring on his departure from Kazakhstan's Baikonur Cosmodrome in December, "This isn't a one-off mission. We have a serious project in the European Space Station to land on the moon, install full sit-down and wall-mounted urinal-trough facilities, and use the satellite as a stepping stone to the solar system, going to the toilet along the way whenever needed, in whatever tubes and cavities are available."

I wondered why we had suddenly invested in this crazy dream of long-distance solar human conveyance? And then the news stories aligned, like planets in a perfect orbit, as if guided by unseen hands.

Planet X, as astronomers are imaginatively calling the new world, is at present a stale and unprofitable wasteland. The question is, who owns it, and how can it be monetised? What environmental restrictions, if any, have interfering Brussels bureaucrats put on its exploitation? Would Planet X be governed by idiotic EU human rights regulations? How soon will the sort of extended solar journeys Toilet Tim has posited be a genuine possibility? Is there any legislation in place preventing the former inner-city sink-estate dwellers from being temporarily rehoused in the same shipping containers currently used in Calais? And would there be some way of yoking these shipping containers, and their French counterparts, together in some kind of loose wagon-train arrangement, behind a long-distance spacecraft of some kind?

The idea of sending the unwanted and irredeemable dregs of human society to a supposedly barren, largely unknown, probably inhospitable and impossibly faraway place seems cruel. But today Australia, for example, has transcended its degrading origins to become if not a fully fledged civilisation, then at least a place that gave us the Up & Go Australian breakfast drink and eventually became mildly embarrassed by Tony Abbott.

Would it be so very wrong to give those whose poverty both shames and inconveniences us a chance of a life which, if not necessarily better than their current one, would at least be markedly different to it, involving, as it would, an impossible struggle for survival on a hostile and remote world of ice, tilted at a chaotic angle, revolving slowly in a vast elliptical orbit, far, far away from our embarrassed gaze?

"Great anecdote at the beginning, but the effect was rather destroyed by the childish clarification that follows. I hate it when people follow up a joke with 'do you get it' and a detailed analysis of the punchline. I reeks of a patronising assumption that the listener is stupid." Richesrant

"What I got out of this article: 'We must secure the existence of our people and a future for white children.' Stewart Lee, 2016." Vladdaman

Osborne's tax deals are the stuff of spaghetti westerns

Observer, 31 January 2016

Challenged, quite effectively, by Jeremy Corbyn in that week's PMQs over his government's cosy deal with tax-dodging Google, David Cameron, desperate to land a blow, said, irrelevantly, of Labour: "They met with the unions, they gave them flying pickets, they met with the Argentinians, they gave them the Falklands, they met with a bunch of migrants in Calais and said they could all come to Britain."

My usual methods of decoding experience – art, literature and old punk-rock records – have been rendered irrelevant by the sheer unscrupulousness of our public figures. We are in a post-*Thick of It* world, where the fictional PR attack dog Malcolm Tucker seems, compared with those schooled by Lynton Crosby OBE, dancing in Dionysiac reverie on the ruins of democracy in a downpour of dead cats, to have been charmingly hampered by principle.

But help is at hand. Pretty much all I have watched since Christmas 2014 is Italian westerns of the '60s and '70s. I have seen 108 now. And I started pursuing this monomaniacal psychological experiment long before Mark Zuckerberg of Facebook told us this week that we should all live "post-choice", demonstrating his commitment to his aesthetic by displaying a wardrobe full of dozens of expensively identical shirts, all presumably tax deductible and purchased online via an account in Luxembourg.

I've given up on twenty-first-century films, which are all about either outer space or a man being sad. But the so-called spaghetti westerns espouse a bleak, fatalistic view of humanity where no one is motivated by anything other than naked self-interest and everyone has a price, and none of them feature Eddie Redmayne giving a heart-rending performance as someone with some kind of issue.

In fact, I'd go so far as to say that Gianfranco Parolini's *If You Meet Sartana Pray for Your Death* (1968), in which the eponymous anti-hero slaughters all who stand between him and a coffin full of stolen gold, tells us more about twenty-first-century business and politics than David Fincher's *The Social Network* (2010), even though I have seen neither.

Since Lynton Crosby OBE started showing off about his "dead cat" news-management methods, we can now see dead cats coming a mile off, like smallpox-infected pigs catapulted over the walls of a besieged medieval citadel, and a political gaffe one might once have forgiven as a thoughtless slip of the tongue we now realise is, in fact, a cynically scripted media-misdirection strategy.

In short, if Cameron said "bunch of migrants" by accident, he is a dick, but if he said it on purpose, in order to draw the eye, dead-cat style, away from the Google atrocity, which he did, then he is a bastard, which is worse.

Increasingly, the once-proud visionary dreamer of the "big society" is like those sleazy guys they warn you about on posters at railway stations, who call your attention to an imaginary problem while pick-pocketing your wallet and grabbing your genitals. David Cameron is the Cologne New Year's Eve of British politics.

Contemplating my tax returns, in the light of George Osborne's pitifully cautious pencil probe into the rectum of Google's financial affairs, I struggle to make sense of my obligation to contribute vast swathes of my income to the maintenance of a society whose leaders seem to hold its citizens, its flora and fauna, and those stranded in limbo at its borders, in haughty contempt.

I have considered my options. Presumably, as a stand-up comedian, I am paid to generate laughter, which I do, almost nightly, in rooms all around the country, and simply putting the word "comedian" in inverted commas in your below-the-line comments about me will do nothing to alter that demonstrable fact.

If there were some way I could move the point at which the laughter I produce was released from, say, William Aston Hall, Wrexham, to Luxembourg, could I then say that the end point of the financial transaction I had entered into with my paying audience was in a region where UK tax did not apply?

The initial outlay of developing a system where the audience laughed into airtight, sound-proofed bags, which were then driven to Luxembourg in a van and opened noisily but harmlessly on an alpine meadow, to the bewilderment of billy goats and trolls, would be costly, but in the end I would be able to avoid paying tax on the vast majority of my income.

It's a system that Google's creative accountants, Ernst & Young, could doubtless find a way of making legal, laughter being as invisible and slippery a commodity as the online transactions whose virtual existence they magically transport from one theoretical taxation zone to another, but would that make it moral, a distinction that seems to have been deliberately obscured this week? Perhaps the oracle of spaghetti westerns could tell me.

On a midnight train out of Brighton on Wednesday, I watched most of a 1971 film called *Black Killer* on my laptop. It's an incoherent effort, but its low opinion of officialdom and its nihilistic world view meant its barely competent director, Carlo Croccolo, reached across the decades directly into my current anxieties in a way that *Star Wars: The Force Awakens* did not.

Black Killer concerned a corrupt and unaccountable judge who makes farmers sign over their lands and then has an outlaw band, the O'Haras, kill them. The O'Haras, despite having an Irish name, look totally Mexican. Perhaps they are a multinational outlaw band, advised by Ernst & Young to stash the judge's blood money in an iron safe in Luxembourg via a complex network of carrier pigeons.

A lawyer, played by a misspelt Klaus Kinsky, arrives and spends the whole film arguing with the judge in an office, trying to get him on legal technicalities. I thought he was supposed to represent powerless justice, to '70s Italian audiences as familiar with Mafia corruption as we are with Google and Osborne today.

Meanwhile, contrasting the apparent impotence of proper procedure, an arrow-slinging Native American woman (Marina Malfatti), who keeps getting injured and having to undress to receive treatment, usually to her bottom, takes matters into her own hands, picking off the officially sanctioned O'Hara Gang plc one by one.

It is here that Croccolo's clumsy fable parts company with our experience. There is no intermittently naked Native American woman to come to our aid against Google and Osborne and all the tax-dodging multinationals. There is only Eva Joly, vice-chair of the special European parliamentary committee on tax rulings, who has defied death threats in the past to investigate big-business corruption. And who, one hopes, can dodge any of the dead cats David Cameron's own hired thugs can throw at her. I don't know what will happen. I fell asleep before the end of *Black Killer*, and woke up at 3 a.m. in Bedford, itself a vast filmic metaphor for the unknowable.

"You could easily set up a company in the Isle of Man or Monaco and get that company to employ you. Then you get a promoter to hire you through a contract with that company (rather than directly with yourself) and remit cash to it. No corporation tax and you collect all your cash gross. Then when you need cash to pay for renting those movies or buying black t-shirts or hair gel you get the company to pay you your salary (on which you pay tax). You could i suppose get the company to make you a loan to defer that income tax such that you repay the loans when the company finally gets around to pay or distribute through dividends the funds it now holds. There's probably a marginal National Insurance advantage to doing so for your good self too. Of course I understand that your social conscience would preclude you from doing so, and your net tour revenues currently don't quite make sense to go through the expense of opening up a corporate entity in a different country, but legally you could do. In fact from an entertainment perspective it would be a rich seam, a gold mine for next seasons material to go through the experience, a bit like that stupid Welsh town – if you're struggling for a theme?" Sebastianbates

Who will write the front page this nation needs?

Observer, 7 February 2016

Peak Daily Mail *was achieved on Thursday 4 February 2016, with a front-page editorial about Europe so insane the paper risked leaving itself no way of ever topping it. "Who Will Speak for England?" it thundered. The following is merely the same piece reproduced with a few words changed, and completed under the influence of Chaucer, Bede, Wyndham Lewis's* Blast *magazine, Mark E. Smith and Simon Munnery's League Against Tedium.*

On Wednesday night the infinite number of monkeys that usually write the editorial for the *Daily Mail* had fallen victim en masse to the zika virus. And so, having made something of a name for myself in Fleet Street, after filling in for David Mitchell here these past few months, I was called in at short notice to articulate a *Daily Mail* front-page question of profound significance to our destiny as a sovereign nation.

A nation, let us not forget, with justifiable and fair provision for successful businesses to establish their principal trading bases in Bermuda and Jersey.

Yea, I was to ask indeed a question significant profoundly also unto the fate of our children, grandchildren, great-grandchildren, great-great-grandchildren, great-great-great-grandchildren, great-great-great-great-grandchildren, great-great-great-great-great-grandchildren and Michael Caine.

Whom wilst spakey for England?

And, of course, by "England", like Leo Amery MP in 1939, I meant the whole of the United Kingdom, although I did suggest to the paper's proprietor, Viscount Biscuit, that the Scottish *Daily Mail*'s cover should not perhaps, in the current climate, feature the words "Whom Wilst Spakey for England" in massive letters.

So instead, Biscuit raided the padlocked underground safe where the imaginary photos of the magician's excited dog are kept to provide a picture of Simon Cowell staring woefully into Cheryl Fernandez-Versini's ear.

Nonetheless. I was to ask again. Whom wilst spakey for England?

And again askest I. Whom wilst spakey for England?

It was a question inspired by one of the most dramatic moments in the history of journalism.

The date was 2 February 2016, the day after David Cameron returned from Europe, having just made an ambivalent statement regarding spurious migrants' benefits and waving a draft agreement from Brussels, saying to anyone who would listen, "I have in my hand a piece of paper."

Next door to Harrods, the *Daily Mail*'s editor Paul Dacre was incensed and bellowed across the Tardis-like dimension-defying pen wherein his infinite and comatose monkeys slept: "Whom Wilst Spakey for England?"

And so, with my help, he hoped the entire front page of Thursday's *Daily Mail* would do just that, voicing anger over the premier's reluctance to enforce new obligations to Brussels, as surely as Neville Chamberlain had failed to constrain the paper's old friend Adolf Hitler, chancellor of Nazi Germany, in 1939.

I was not, of course, to suggest there were any parallels whatsoever between the Nazis and the EU. Indeed, the *Daily Mail* would argue that one of the Union's great achievements, along with NATO, has been to foster peace in Europe.

But I did realise it would play well with my temporary *Daily Mail* paymasters if I could somehow create the association of the EU and the Nazis in the subconscious minds of my readers, without appearing to endorse the idea officially.

But, I was prepared to suggest for money, just as in 1939, we were once more at a crossroads in our island history, and hopefully not at a roundabout where all the exits have been blocked off, except the one where you have to go into a Euro-style cafe and be force-fed accurately measured Toulouse sausages by women in French maid's outfits and Islamic veils.

Whom wilst spakey for England?

In the small hours of Wednesday night I sat high above Kensington High Street and looked at the sleeping, sweating monkeys. And I knew that if I could pull off this front page, I could have their jobs. And if Viscount Biscuit paid me only a fraction of their daily monkey banana bill, I would still be rich beyond my wildest dreams.

Now was the time to write the most brilliantly incendiary front page ever, driving billions through the *Daily Mail*'s website, both those in furious, bewildered agreement and those who would be clicking through only to check if my insane opinion was for real.

Now was the moment and the moment was now. For in perhaps as little as twenty weeks' time, ill-informed voters, stuffed with incoherent arguments, like hissing geese force-fed nostalgia and hate to produce an inedible pâté of groundless opinion, would be asked to decide nothing less than what sort of country we want to live in and bequeath to those who come after us.

Our children, grandchildren, great-grandchildren, great-great-grandchildren, great-great-great-grandchildren, great-great-great-great-grandchildren, great-great-great-great-great-grandchildren and Michael Caine.

Whom wilst spakey for England? I would ask again. And again. Whom wilst spakey for England?

But could I write the inflammatory piece that would secure my financial future? Could I live with myself if I consolidated the *Daily Mail*'s case? Could I sleep soundly if my ambition tossed those infinite monkeys onto an infinite heap of banana skins?

Would our liberty, security and prosperity be better assured by submitting to a statist, unelected bureaucracy in Brussels, accepting the will of unaccountable judges and linking our destiny with that of a sclerotic Europe that tries to achieve the impossible by uniting countries as diverse as Germany and Greece?

Or would our liberty, security and prosperity be better assured by submitting to an elected Bullingdon bureaucracy here at home, accepting the will of demonstrably unaccountable politicians and linking our destiny with that of a sclerotic Eurosceptic camp that tries to achieve the impossible by uniting personalities as diverse as Theresa May, former UKIP hat-wearer Winston McKenzie and Michael Caine?

Whom wilst spakey for England? Who for England wilst spakey?

Were we to be a self-governing nation, free in this age of mass migration to opt out of the attempts of the wider European community to co-operate to solve the greatest refugee crisis since the Second World War, strike trade agreements with tyrannical dictatorships whenever we choose and dismiss codes of practice regarding environmental safeguards, pollution and human rights if they displease us, like some pusillanimous ostrich, sticking its stupid head into the rapidly dissipating sands of time?

Whom? Whom wilst spakey for England? For England whom wilst spake?

For years we have been bombarded with propaganda from one side, principally the *Daily Mail*, and from the *Daily Express*, whose tangential relationship with the very notion of a newspaper hinges only on the slim fact that it contains words.

Should I be part of the problem? Or part of the solution?

Whom wilst spakey for England? For England whom wilst spake?

I nailed my courage to the sticking plate. I banished the monkeys from my mind and wrote the editorial. The rest is already history.

"What complete drivel." Andy

Jeremy Hunt is an ethical columnist's nightmare

Observer, 14 February 2016

I was on tour in a hotel room, trying to file my copy to a deadline, while the news was unravelling around me, making everything I wrote instantly irrelevant. I decided to embrace the problem and make it part of the piece.

It is not always easy to do the right thing. In the '80s, for example, I remember when we all tried to avoid buying apartheid-era South African fruit. "Are these apples from South Africa?" a photographer friend asked a cockney grocer. "Because if they are, I can't buy them." "I don't blame you, mate," replied the cheery shopkeeper, "what if them Africans have touched them?" It would be an understatement to say they had been talking at cross purposes.

As an ethical consumer in today's choice-crowded marketplace, I buy tax-avoiding Starbucks coffee only as a last resort, when no other chain coffee stores are available, perhaps at a motorway service station. But, like an anarchist Fagin, I have trained my children, aged two and four, to wait until the barista has turned round and then knock as many of the chocolate coins off the front of the display as they can. These I then pocket while pretending to tie my lace, thus costing Starbucks more on each transaction than they make.

I have explained to the children that though this act is not legal, it is nonetheless moral, in a neat reversal of Starbucks' historical tax avoidance, which though legal, was not moral. Teaching children to steal from Starbucks is a way of making ethics fun for kids and bringing philosophy alive. And they get to eat chocolate which, under normal circumstances, I would forbid them. It's a win–win situation for all of us. Don't you wish I was your dad?

Since privatisation, travelling on trains is also clearly morally wrong. How can it be right that privatised rail providers are still in receipt of public subsidies while paying shareholders dividends? But if I'm not on the train, I'm on the motorway, clogging up the environment with evil emissions from my doctored Volkswagen Passat, although this does at least mean I can visit service-station Starbucks branches and steal their chocolate coins. Swings and roundabouts.

Due to their unethical milk-powder marketing strategies in the developing world, I have a blanket ban on Nestlé products, meaning when my four-year-old was offered Shreddies for breakfast after a sleepover, she told her friend's perfectly pleasant parents that they were murdering babies. I worry I have been overzealous in my indoctrination and that when the kids enter their rebellious teenage years, they will turn into a pair of Jeremy Hunts.

But who would have thought the latest challenge to the ethical consumer would come from the NHS? On Monday, it was revealed that health service rules preventing NHS managers offering contracts to companies with Google-style tax arrangements are to be scrapped. If a company subcontracted to provide NHS care is technically legal, then it is unfair, under the free-market ethic of competition, to discriminate against them. Soon it won't even be possible to die ethically, let alone buy breakfast cereal.

Clinical commissioning groups in Bristol and Hackney, where I live, are to suspend their objections to using care services provided by companies registered in tax havens. But I haven't spent my whole life not eating Shreddies and stealing Starbucks chocolate only to be taken fatally ill and see public money paid to a care provider overseeing my expiry while not contributing any of its profits back into the public purse.

Twelve years ago, I collapsed backstage at the Soho theatre after a long-standing stomach disorder finally turned critical, vomiting and discharging blood from my bottom. Had I been obliged to make my own way to a hospital whose ethics I agreed with, I could have wriggled like a filth-trailing snail along Dean Street without any trouble. Indeed, I have seen the wealthy night-revellers of Boris's brave new London step gingerly over expiring homeless folk in worse states, so there would be little risk of a kindly Samaritan forcing me to seek succour from a politically inappropriate service provider.

I lined up black coffees in a Leeds hotel room and started this column on Thursday morning, having seen the story about the tax-avoiding care providers on Monday, and thought it might be funny to write a piece playing up to the image of myself as a left-wing zealot, someone who would rather die in the street like a sick dog than be nursed in a hospital by Virgin Care or GE Healthcare. Ha ha ha.

Then around lunchtime, while writing this sentence, I saw junior doctors on the Internet complaining about Jeremy Hunt lying about their pay offer. My deadline was looming and suddenly the intricacies of NHS service providers' tax arrangements seemed irrelevant compared to the problems facing its very survival. At 1 p.m. Jeremy Hunt appeared on Sky News, saying he had the support of twenty NHS CEOs. But twenty minutes later Twitter showed four had already jumped ship. A news surge had put my funny column into free fall.

On my desktop I still had a website open where I was trying to see if there was a scientific word for the mixture of blood and excrement a sickly snail would leave behind, so I could use it as an over-the-top adjective in the bit about crawling along the road earlier. But the story had moved on. I had no column. I know this dispute isn't all about me, but I wish people like Jeremy Hunt and these junior doctors would think about the hidden costs of their actions to freelance writers trying to file barely amusing copy on a deadline. How selfish!

The hours passed. Public anger boiled. I wondered why Hunt

was imposing on junior doctors a non-negotiable contract which any sensible person could see will decimate the profession and ultimately make the NHS in England untenable. But perhaps, I started to wonder in my caffeinated paranoia, perhaps this was the idea all along.

I don't want to sound like the *Daily Telegraph*'s idea of an out-of-his-depth alternative-comedian columnist, citing barely understood quotes from books I have never read before going off to talk about farts and cocks on stage for two hours, but Noam Chomsky described the standard technique of privatisation thus: "Defund, make sure things don't work, people get angry, you hand it over to private capital."

Suddenly, the removal of moral objections to NHS managers offering contracts to the world's worst companies seems like part of a bigger picture. Those doctors will defect. And who can blame them? But the way will be cleared to plug the gap with privately supplied, unregulated labour. And the free-market fundamentalists will maintain that their hands were forced.

"'Teaching children to steal from Starbucks is a way of making ethics fun for kids and bringing philosophy alive.' No, it isn't. It's a way of teaching children that it is 'progressive' to commit crime and 'justify' it by your ill-placed moral superiority. The fact that you have decided that a particular company (and it always has to be a large multinational for political reasons) hasn't paid enough tax does not justify you stealing the money which you believe they stole. Tax is to pay for public services not to feed the gluttony of smug and over-privileged socialists." Inspai

"'But, like an anarchist Fagin, I have trained my children, aged two and four, to wait until the barista has turned round and then knock as many of the chocolate coins off the front of the display as they can. These I then pocket while pretending to tie my lace, thus costing Starbucks more on each transaction than they make.' I presume this is a joke otherwise I think it pretty poor parenting to teach your children to steal/take the law into your own hands." BJz001

"Stopped reading after this. Nothing else you may say has any value. I am glad my father was not like you." Amwink

"You openly admit to theft in a newspaper article. Regardless of how justified you think you are, the law applies equally to everyone." The Witchfinder General

"Why is the *Guardian* employing a thief as a columnist? Is it child abuse these days to steal in front of one's children? Should anyone take the slightest notice of this 'journalist'?" AJBTemple

Wolf People – *Fain*

Press release, March 2013

For two decades I wrote two record reviews a week for the Sunday Times *for money. The work kept me afloat during the opera years, when I was broke and not doing stand-up, but in the end it became a chore, and the wordage didn't pay as much as the childcare I needed to buy the time to produce it. But I learnt a lot and I emerged from the experience still in love with music. And sometimes it's still fun to write about it, enthusiastically, and without looking for a way of making an increasingly bleak world funny in some way. Here is a press release I wrote for the third album by Wolf People.*

Last night I had dinner with the molecular microbiologist Professor Keith Gull. He discussed the information overload that has taken shape in academia during his lifetime, and how it has affected the working methods of his students. Over spinach and egg, Professor Gull identified the ability to extract the relevant points from the unprecedentedly vast mass of material now available as a key skill in the contemporary data-dense environment. Tangentially, it seems to me that all twenty-first-century musicians are likewise potentially swamped by a vast range of influences largely unavailable to their recent predecessors.

This World Wide Web that you all have now has made pretty much everything that ever was available, by legal or illegal means. But Wolf People are one of the few groups to funnel this oceanic torrent of endless sonic information into a fine and purposeful point. And that fine and purposeful point is their second album proper, *Fain*.

The peripheral early-'70s British underground influences that Wolf People acknowledge on their website playlists – Linda Hoyle and Affinity, Arzachel, Tractor, Beau, Thundermother, High Tide, May Blitz, Arcadium and The Way We Live – were all familiar to me as a post-punk fundamentalist teenager in the early '80s, but in name only. Theirs were the already culturally obsolete gatefold albums with gloomily meaningful sleeves spilling out of the racks in the second-hand shop in the underpass by Moor Street Station at low, low prices that our generation thrust aside in search of twelve-inch singles by angry ironists on the Rough Trade and Vindaloo labels. This dopey beardo wizard shit was kulturally *verboten*. It was never coming back, granddad, and without the open-access information experiment of the newfangled Internet, could a band like Wolf People ever have sounded quite the way it does?

"I don't think it could have, or at least not in the form it's taken now," concedes Wolf People's founder, vocalist and co-guitarist (with Joe Hollick) Jack Sharp. "We were very much involved in collecting records and sampling, and interested in '60s and '70s subculture (as well as hip hop), in the 'pre-Internet age', but things were a lot harder to come by when you didn't have the almost brain-numbing instant access to pretty-much-everything-ever that you have now. Getting involved in online record-collecting communities around 2002/3, when we were in our early twenties, had a massive impact on Tom and myself, and it still provides a lot of inspiration and ways of finding music that is still off the radar even now."

Having burrowed out of Bedford in the mid-'00s, Wolf People are a formidable hybrid. Yes, they're crate-digging, record-collector completists with time on their hands and the sort of international file-trader connections that means they can legitimately say, "There has always been a 1970s Finnish progressive-rock influence on our music." But, crucially, they're also dedicated musicians demonstrating, with their zen mastery of Tom Verlaine-type twin-guitar starbursts and Pythagorean progressive-rock timekeeping, the lost art of what long-dead rock scribes used to call "chops".

"We'll probably look back and realise what idiots we were being!" volunteers Sharp. "I suppose it's strange that we're using the Internet as a tool to reference a craft of music-making that would otherwise be extinct or buried." If only Wolf People had been able to enjoy the housing-benefit scams, generous student grants, aristocratic major-label patronage and communal-squat culture that bought their spiritual '70s forebears endless practice time. Had they been relieved of the obligation to sustain themselves, we'd have seen Wolf People's debut mini-masterpiece, 2010's *Steeple*, some years ahead of schedule.

I'm worried I've made Wolf People sound like mere historical revivalists, the prog-blues-folk-rock equivalent of those people who dress up as cavaliers at weekends and lose once more battles already lost long ago. Crucially, there's something else entirely going on in their rehearsal room. We know the technology now exists to clone and revive an extinct woolly mammoth from DNA found in frozen specimens perfectly preserved in Arctic ice fields, which is arguably partly what Wolf People have done, referencing artists on the missing-presumed-extinct Holyground label, for example. But what if we were to take that mammoth and cross-breed it with a similarly re-vivified sabre-tooth tiger?

It was on the closing pair of tracks on Wolf People's last album *Steeple*, namely "Banks of Sweet Dundee Parts 1 and 2", that their unique selling point became clear. Wolf People are positing an alternate early-'70s musical reality that nearly, but never quite actually happened. Yes, Fairport Convention's *A Sailor's Life*, the extended epics of Trees' unbeatable 1970 album *On the Shore* and bits of Carolanne Pegg's '73 solo album posit a British folk music informed by then contemporary rock practice, with extended modal soloing and driving rhythm sections.

And yes, the title track alone of Traffic's *John Barleycorn Must Die* album and "The Battle of Evermore" from *Led Zeppellin IV* and bits of the inexplicably English-sounding German band Carol of Harvest's eponymous 1978 release suggest a more densely entwined, more fertile future for this unlikely cross-breed. But it was a future that was never quite fulfilled, Traffic wandering off into a flutey jazz fog and Led Zeppellin climbing the Giant's Causeway to an immortality not tainted by folksy flavours.

"I think subconsciously we're trying to make the type of records we would like to find," says Jack. "I love Trees and Fairport and Mr Fox, but I find myself thinking that there aren't enough groups like that, and sometimes I want it to be heavier. So we've tried to stretch both the folk and the heavy element as far as it will go in either direction and see what happens." I think the modest Wolf Person is selling the band short. *Fain* doesn't sound stretched. Its eight substantial songs sound, given the incompatible diversity of its sources, implausibly integrated.

"Empty Vessels" skewers California '60s folk-rock rhythm guitar with Hollick's insurgent soloing; "All Returns"' truncated hairy-funk licks, from bassist Dan Davis and drummer Tom Watt, suddenly bristle into the red, finally unable to contain themselves, bursting free of a psalmodic structure, like The Stooges' "We Will Fall" retooled by jazz monks; "When the Fire Is Dead in the Grate" is the album's first stone classic, a funky folk-metal work-out that trails off into a compellingly extended coda, both guitarists circling and dovetailing and spiralling; "Athol" is a downbeat minor-key boogie, like an uncommonly reflective Canned Heat gone native somewhere in the Suffolk fens.

Massed witches' sabbath backing vocals swell and rise under the arching leads of the painfully disciplined "Hesperus", the song dissolving into a peat-bog super-fuzz sphagnum-moss sludge; "Answer" drapes hop-harvest harmonies over pointillist pinpricks of lead guitar; "Thief"'s Can-style atomic-bomb-blast opening spills over analogue synth noise into an all but unaccompanied

300

plaintive folk-ballad vocal, which breaks down into collapsing arpeggios of twin guitars; and "NRR" sounds like it was written to make Hell's Angels, and their molls, attending an outdoor blues-rock/rock-blues festival in a disused WWII airfield in 1973 do that dance where they bend sideways and bump their butts together, the rather self-conscious set-closer that would once have provoked mass applause and the ritualised discarding of bras.

Music fans like to speculate on what-ifs. What if The Fall had followed *Hex Enduction Hour* with more of the same, instead of switching track to escape expectation? What if The Buzzcocks had held onto and harnessed the high-art aspirations of Howard Devoto alongside the pop-art punch of Pete Shelley? What if Jimi Hendrix had made that album with Miles Davis? What if Television had run in the songs for their belated third album live, and found all the jumping-off points they discovered in the years spent woodshedding *Marquee Moon*? What if all the great songs the final line-up of The Byrds squandered in half-realised solo projects had made one last brilliant band album? And so on.

If you've ever listened to those furtive early-'70s fusions of folk and rock and wondered if there was another way those superficially incompatible genres might have intertwined, then Wolf People offer an answer, with *Fain*'s patchouli-scented stews of perfumed-garden pre-punk, each shadowed by a creeping deep-country darkness of backwater occult imagery, utilitarian King James Bible lyricism and knowing nods to primordial melodies that already lurk deep in the collective subconscious. Reorganising the re-available past, Wolf People cast a cup of bones against the back wall, and play the patterns of the runes where they fall.

Acknowledgements

I would like to thank: Ursula Kenny, my editor at the *Observer*, who treads a careful path between my deliberate misspellings and my accidental ones; Hannah Griffiths, who originally encouraged and advised me at Faber and Faber nearly a decade ago, and Dave Watkins, her successor; and the mod *flâneur* Andy Miller, who edited this, and all my other books, with skill and judgement. Peace! I'm outta here. You shoulda killed me last year.